Just What the Doctor Ordered!

A Collection Of Recipes Compiled By The
Peoria Medical Society Auxiliary, Inc.

For the Benefit of
The Peoria Medical Society Charitable and
Educational Foundation, Inc.
Peoria, Illinois

ISBN: 0-9615434-1-8

First Printing: 3,000 copies
Second Printing: 5,000 copies

Printed in the United States of America

Wimmer Brothers Books
P.O. Box 18408
Memphis, Tennessee 38118
"Cookbooks of Distinction"™

Introduction

This cookbook is a project of the Peoria Medical Society Auxiliary, Inc. All funds from the sale of this book go directly to the Peoria Medical Society Charitable and Educational Foundation. The Foundation, a cooperative venture between the Auxiliary and the Society, provides scholarships to the leading health care professionals of tomorrow from Peoria, Tazewell and Woodford counties.

The Auxiliary is composed of the spouses of physicians who are members of the Peoria Medical Society. Founded in 1940, the Auxiliary was incorporated in 1979 as a not-for-profit corporation in the State of Illinois.

Auxiliary members are pleased to share with you the recipes they enjoy preparing for their families and friends. We hope you'll find them **"Just What The Doctor Ordered"**.

Cookbook Committee

Co-Chairman and Editors

Marilyn Bauer
Marianne Wright

Chapter Coordinators
and Test Kitchens Editors

Dottie Flores
Kacky Heinzen
Carolyn Jakopin
Joan Leu
JoAnne Richardson
Delores Sheen
Bernadette Shekleton
Viv Solomon
Clara Remolina

Cover and Section Illustrations

Ben C. Berg, M.D.

Other Illustrations

Clara Remolina

About the Artist:

Ben C. Berg, Jr., M.D., FACR, FACNM, practices the art and science of medicine and dabbles in the art and whimsy of doodling. Doodling was a love before medicine. The three of them, medicine, the doctor and the doodling have been humoring each other along for many years, lest one of them might take himself too seriously. Each of them hopes to have made a contribution to others during their journey together in this life.

VI.

Table of Contents

VIII.

Appetizers and Beverages

CARLA'S MEXICAN CHEESE DIP

1 2-pound box Velveeta cheese, cubed
1 to 2 medium onions, chopped
2 16-ounce cans stewed tomatoes, drained and chopped
1 3-ounce can green chili peppers, drained and chopped

Melt and mix together in a fondue pot. Serve warm with taco chips.

Pat Russo (Mrs. Frank)

ARTICHOKE DIP
Tastes like crabmeat.

2 8 ½-ounce cans artichoke hearts, drained and chopped
1 cup mayonnaise
½ cup Parmesan cheese, grated
1/16 teaspoon red pepper or Tabasco sauce
garlic salt to taste
Slivered almonds or paprika

Mix all ingredients together and bake uncovered in 350° oven for 20 minutes. Sprinkle with slivered almonds or paprika. Serve with crackers or vegetables as a dip. Recipe may be halved easily.

Ann Miller (Mrs. William)

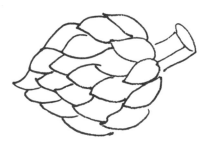

CLAM DIP

1 3-ounce and 1 8-ounce
  package cream cheese
Juice of ½ lemon
⅓ cup mayonnaise
⅓ cup half and half
Dash Worcestershire sauce
1 6½-ounce can minced clams,
  drained (reserve juice)
Almonds (slivered) to taste

In mixer bowl, mix cheese, lemon juice, mayonnaise, half and half, Worcestershire sauce, and ⅓ cup clam juice. Mix well. Add clams by hand. Place in small casserole or Pyrex serving dish. Sprinkle on almonds. Bake at 325° for 20 to 30 minutes. Serve with corn chips.

Mary Ward (Mrs. Clarence V., Jr.)

SPINACH DIP
Everyone's favorite dip!

1 cup mayonnaise
1 cup sour cream
1 10-ounce box chopped
  spinach, thawed and drained
1 package Knorr's vegetable
  soup mix
1 8-ounce can water chestnuts, drained, chopped fine
3 green onions, chopped
  fine

Mix well. **Food processor method:** Put water chestnuts and green onions in food processor and process until finely chopped. Add mayonnaise, sour cream, and spinach. Process several seconds. Add soup mix and process to blend.

Dolores Sheen (Mrs. John)

MOLDED CRAB DIP

1 10 ½-ounce can cream
   of mushroom soup
6 ounces cream cheese
1 cup celery, chopped
2 green onions, chopped
1 envelope unflavored gelatin
1 6-ounce can crab meat,
   drained

Heat soup and cream cheese in sauce-pan until melted and blended. Remove from heat. Stir in celery and onions. Dissolve gelatin in 3 tablespoons warm water. Add to soup mixture. Stir in crab meat. Pour into oiled mold. Chill 3 hours. Unmold and serve with crackers. A fish mold is nice. Looks pretty on a silver tray with a parsley garnish. Easy!

Carol Nelson (Mrs. John)

ARTICHOKE AND SHRIMP DIP
Tired of the same old dips — try this

1 pint sour cream
1 0.6-ounce package Good
   Seasons Italian or garlic
   salad dressing mix
dash Worcestershire sauce
dash Tabasco
dash garlic powder
1 4 ½-ounce can shrimp,
   drained
1 8 ½-ounce can artichoke
   hearts, drained and chopped
2 tablespoons chopped chives
1 tablespoon chopped parsley
paprika

Combine sour cream and salad dressing mix. Season to taste with Worcestershire sauce, Tabasco, and garlic powder. Add shrimp and artichoke hearts. Mix and add parsley and chives. Mix well. Place in a small casserole dish and sprinkle top with paprika. Refrigerate at least 2 hours. Better if made the day before. Serve with thick potato chips.

Marianne Wright (Mrs. Robert)

CHESTNUT DIP

1 8-ounce can water chestnuts, diced
1 cup sour cream
1 cup mayonnaise
¼ cup freeze-dried chives,
  chopped
¼ cup instant minced onions
1 tablespoon soy sauce
¼ teaspoon ginger
¾ teaspoon garlic salt

Combine ingredients. Chill. Serve with chips, crackers, or vegetables.

Rita Hertenstein (Mrs. Robert)

VEGETABLE DIP
A tangy dip that is good with raw vegetables, pretzels, or chips.

8 ounces cream cheese,
  softened
8 ounces sour cream
½ cup mayonnaise
1 (0.7 ounce) package Good
  Seasons Cheese Garlic
  Salad Dressing Mix
⅛ teaspoon Tabasco

Mix all ingredients until smooth and creamy. Serve with any variety of raw vegetables as dippers.

Marianne Wright (Mrs. Robert)

SHIRLEY'S SHRIMP DIP

2 8-ounce packages cream
  cheese, softened
1 can Campbell's Cream of
  Shrimp Soup
1 tablespoon onion juice
1 clove garlic, crushed
1 teaspoon parsley flakes
1 4-6 ounce package frozen
  baby shrimp, thawed

Mix all ingredients except shrimp with mixer. Add shrimp by hand. Serve with crackers or fresh vegetables.

Pat Russo (Mrs. Frank)

SHRIMP DIP FONDUE

**1 10 ½-ounce can cream of
shrimp soup
1 teaspoon sherry
1 8-ounce package cream
cheese
½ cup sour cream
1 teaspoon Worcestershire
sauce
½ teaspoon horseradish
1 large loaf French bread,
cubed**

Mix and heat ingredients. Dip bread in
fondue.

Judy Zimdars (Mrs. John)

BLUE CHEESE DIP
A real compliment getter!

**1 cup sour cream
1 tablespoon dry minced
onion
1 teaspoon lemon juice
⅛ teaspoon Worcestershire
sauce
½ cup blue cheese
½ teaspoon salt
1 teaspoon horseradish
1 teaspoon dry parsley
Paprika**

Combine all ingredients. Sprinkle paprika
over to garnish. Serve chilled with fresh
vegetables.

Pat Russo (Mrs. Frank)

TEX-MEX DIP
A real tastemaker!

2 10-ounce cans Frito Lay
  bean dip
2 to 3 ripe avocados
2 tablespoons lemon juice
1 cup sour cream
½ cup mayonnaise
1 package dry taco seasoning
3 tomatoes, unpeeled,
  seeded and chopped
½ cup chopped ripe olives
1 cup green onions, chopped
8 ounces cheddar cheese,
  shredded

Spread bean dip on a large round tray. Mash the avocados and mix with the lemon juice. Spread avocado mixture over bean dip. Mix sour cream, mayonnaise, and taco seasoning together. Spread over avocado layer, sealing to edge. Add remaining ingredients in order given. Serve with taco chips or corn chips.

Bertha Dean (Mrs. Robert)

TACO BEAN DIP

8 ounces sour cream
1 package taco seasoning mix
1 16-ounce can refried beans
1 4-ounce package sharp
  cheddar, shredded

Mix well the sour cream, taco seasoning and refried beans. Place in baking dish and top with cheese. Bake at 350° for 30 minutes. Serve hot with corn chips or tortilla chips.

Rita Hertenstein (Mrs. Robert)

TACO DIP

1 package taco seasoning
  mix
16 ounces sour cream
8 ounces cream cheese,
  softened
1 large onion, diced
1 4-ounce package cheddar
  cheese, shredded
1 large tomato, diced

Mix well the taco seasoning mix, cream cheese, and sour cream. Spread in a serving dish and top with onion, cheddar cheese, and tomato. Serve with corn chips as dippers.

Rita Hertenstein (Mrs. Robert)

BLACK OLIVE DIP
May be used as a sandwich filling.

1 soft ripe avocado,
  peeled and halved
1 tablespoon onion, minced
2 tablespoons mayonnaise
2 tablespoons lemon juice
½ teaspoon salt
¼ teaspoon Tabasco
1 8-ounce package cream
  cheese, softened
½ cup ripe olives, chopped

Process in order given in food processor, omitting black olives. Stir in olives and chill. Serve with crackers.

Susie Best (Mrs. David)

CRAB DIP

1 8-ounce package cream
  cheese, softened
1 tablespoon lemon juice
⅛ teaspoon onion flakes
⅛ teaspoon garlic powder
1 7 ½-ounce can crab meat,
  drained

Stir first four ingredients together. Add drained crab meat and mix thoroughly. Put in oven-proof serving dish and sprinkle with paprika. Bake at 350° for 30 minutes. Serve with crackers.

Ella Thompson (Mrs. Robert)

SAVORY EDAM CHEESE

1 ¾ pounds edam cheese
1 cup beer
¼ cup soft butter
1 teaspoon caraway seeds
1 teaspoon dry mustard
½ teaspoon celery salt

Let cheese stand at room temperature for one hour. Remove one-inch shell from top and scoop out the cheese, keeping the red shell intact. Refrigerate shell; discard top. Grate cheese fine. Let soften. Add beer, butter and spices. Blend well. Fill shell with cheese mixture, mounding high. Wrap in plastic wrap, then in foil. **Store several weeks.** Serve at room temperature. Makes 3 cups.

Berenice Consigny (Mrs. Paul)

MY FAVORITE CHEESE BALL

2 8-ounce packages cream cheese, softened
6 ounces blue cheese, softened, crumbled
¼ teaspoon garlic powder
1 4½-ounce can ripe olives, chopped
chopped nuts

Blend cheeses well. Add garlic powder and chopped ripe olives. Shape into two balls and roll each in chopped nuts. Use one and freeze one.

Berenice Consigny (Mrs. Paul)

TRILBY

1 pound sharp cheddar cheese, grated
6 hard-boiled eggs, chopped
3 or 4 green onions, chopped
2 tablespoons parsley, chopped
¼ teaspoon seasoned salt
dash salt
dash paprika
dash garlic powder
3/4-1 cup mayonnaise

Mix all ingredients well. Mold to serve. Make at least a day in advance. May halve recipe. Serves 25-30.

Goldijean Turow (Mrs. E. Alan)

BLUE CHEESE BALL
Great for a large party.

4 3-ounce packages cream cheese, softened
6 ounces blue cheese, softened
6 ounces processed cheddar cheese spread
2 tablespoons grated onion
1 teaspoon Worcestershire sauce
⅛ teaspoon MSG (optional)
1 cup pecans, ground
½ cup parsley, finely chopped

Reserving ½ cup pecans and ¼ cup parsley, blend all ingredients. Shape into a ball. Wrap in plastic wrap. Refrigerate overnight. About one hour before serving, roll cheese ball in remaining pecans and parsley. Place on serving plate and surround with crackers.

Carol Nelson (Mrs. John)

CHILI CHEESE LOG

⅓ pound cheddar cheese, grated
1 8-ounce package cream cheese
¾ cup pecans, chopped
¼ cup chili powder

Have cheeses at room temperature. Blend. Mix in pecans. Shape into a log and roll in chili powder.

Berenice Consigny (Mrs. Paul)

CRAB MEAT PIZZA
This is outstanding!

12 ounces cream cheese, softened
2 tablespoons Worcestershire sauce
2 tablespoons mayonnaise
1 tablespoon lemon juice
1 small onion, grated
dash of garlic salt
1 6-ounce package frozen crabmeat, thawed and drained
½ bottle (6 ounces) chili sauce
parsley for garnish

Mix the first 6 ingredients together and spread on a round tray or pizza pan, leaving edges a little higher for pizza dough effect. Then pour ½ of a 12-ounce bottle of chili sauce on top of cream cheese mixture. Then crumble crab meat on top of the mixture. Sprinkle with parsley. Refrigerate several hours before serving. Serve with crackers. May use canned crab in place of frozen crab.

Marianne Wright (Mrs. Robert)

CHEESE CRAB SPREAD

1 8-ounce package cream cheese
1 6-ounce package frozen crab meat
2 tablespoons chopped onion
1 tablespoon milk
½ teaspoon horseradish
¼ teaspoon salt
⅛ teaspoon pepper
⅓ cup sliced almonds, toasted

Mix all ingredients together and bake 20 minutes at 375°. Serve on crackers.

Kristy Gorenz (Mrs. David)

CRAB MEAT BACON ROUNDS

½ cup sharp cheddar cheese, shredded
1 6-ounce can crab meat, drained and flaked
2 egg whites, stiffly beaten
20 2-inch buttered bread rounds, toasted*
3 strips bacon, uncooked, finely diced
stuffed green olives, sliced

Fold cheese and crab meat into beaten egg whites. Pile mixture on toasted rounds. Sprinkle diced bacon on top; broil until cheese starts to melt and bacon is crisp. Top each with a stuffed olive slice. These can be made ahead of time and popped under the broiler just before serving. Add olive after cooking.
*Bread rounds—Use a 2-inch cookie cutter to cut rounds from sliced white bread; butter both sides; brown in oven, watching carefully.

Vivian Solomon (Mrs. Ted)

PATTI'S PIGMY PIZZAS
A big hit, especially with men!

1 loaf party rye bread
1 8-ounce can pizza sauce (1 teaspoon on each slice)
½ pound mozzarella cheese, grated
1 pound seasoned sausage, browned and drained
1 8-ounce jar Cheese Whiz, (¼ teaspoon on each slice)
Parmesan cheese

Place bread on cookie sheets. Place the ingredients in the order listed on each bread slice. Sprinkle with Parmesan cheese. Bake at 300° for 20 minutes or until browned. Can be made ahead and frozen. Makes about 36.

Pat Russo (Mrs. Frank)

HAM BALLS

1 pound ground ham
1 ½ pounds lean ground pork
2 cups soft bread crumbs
2 eggs, slightly beaten
1 cup milk
½ cup pineapple juice
1 cup firmly packed brown sugar
½ cup vinegar
1 teaspoon dry mustard

Mix meat, bread crumbs, eggs and milk. Shape into about 50 small balls. Arrange in a single layer on a greased large baking pan. Bake in a 350° oven uncovered for 30 minutes. While meat is baking, prepare sauce: place juice, brown sugar, vinegar, and dry mustard in a saucepan. Heat to boiling. Remove ham balls to a 3-quart casserole, discarding fat. Pour pineapple juice mixture over balls. Bake uncovered 30 minutes, stirring occasionally. Serve warm in a chafing dish for an appetizer or over rice for a main dish. Freezes well. May add one 20-ounce can pineapple chunks, drained, if desired.

Marilyn Bauer (Mrs. James)

TACO TARTLETS

Tortilla Chip Filling:
  ½ pint dairy sour cream
  2 tablespoons taco sauce
  2 ounces ripe olives, chopped
  ¾ cup tortilla chips, coarsely crushed
1 pound lean ground beef
2 tablespoons taco seasoning mix
2 tablespoons ice water
1 cup (4 ounces) cheddar cheese, shredded

Preheat oven to 425°. Prepare tortilla chip filling; set aside. (Mix all ingredients together in a small bowl). In a medium bowl, mix beef, taco seasoning mix, and ice water with hands. Press into bottom and sides of 1 ½-inch miniature muffin cups, forming a shell. Place a spoonful of filling into each shell, mounding slightly. Sprinkle cheddar cheese over tops. Bake 7 to 8 minutes. With tip of a knife, remove tartlets from pan. Serve immediately or cool and freeze. To serve tartlets, reheat in a 375° oven 10 to 15 minutes or until hot.

Marie Adland (Mrs. Moris)

MICROWAVE STUFFED MUSHROOMS

12 large, fresh mushrooms
½ cup onions, chopped
3-ounce package cream cheese
¼ cup bread crumbs
½ cup bacon or ham, cooked and chopped

Hollow out mushrooms. Chop stems and add chopped onions. Cook this mixture in microwave for 4 minutes on high. Add cream cheese to this mixture and stir in crumbs and bacon or ham. Spoon into mushroom caps and cook on high for about 3 ½ to 4 ¼ minutes. Rotate after 2 minutes.

Ruth Easton (Mrs. Robert)

ZESTY MUSHROOMS AND MINIATURE MEATBALLS

½ pound ground beef
1 4-ounce can mushrooms, stems and pieces, drained and chopped
1 medium onion, finely chopped
1 egg, slightly beaten
¼ cup fine dry bread crumbs
½ teaspoon salt
⅛ teaspoon pepper
8 ounces button mushrooms, drained
½ cup Italian salad dressing

Mix together first seven ingredients. To make about 3 dozen miniature meatballs, shape meat mixture into small "footballs." Place meatballs and button mushrooms in a shallow 2-quart baking dish or a 16 x 10 broil-bake tray. Pour salad dressing over all. Bake in a 400° oven for 30 minutes, turning after 15 minutes. Serve hot in a chafing dish or broil-bake tray on a warmer base.

Pat Callaway (Mrs. James)

PU PU TERIYAKI MEATBALLS

2 pounds ground beef
½ cup onion, chopped
½ cup bread crumbs
2 eggs
2 teaspoons salt
½ teaspoon pepper
½ cup soy sauce
2 tablespoons salad oil
4 teaspoons sherry
1 cup water
4 tablespoons brown sugar
¼ teaspoon powdered
  ginger
2 teaspoons garlic, minced
4 teaspoons cornstarch
¼ teaspoon MSG (optional)

Combine ground beef, onion, bread crumbs, egg, salt, pepper and 2 tablespoons soy sauce. Shape into meatballs about 1 inch in diameter. Heat oil in skillet. Fry meatballs until lightly browned; remove from skillet. Combine remaining soy sauce, sherry, water, brown sugar, ginger, garlic, cornstarch and MSG. Cook in skillet over low heat until thickened, stirring constantly. Return meatballs to skillet and simmer, covered. Serve in casserole or chafing dish. Makes 8 dozen. Freezes well.

Hint: I usually put meatballs on a cookie sheet and brown in oven. It is much faster. I then make the sauce in a saucepan while the meatballs are browning.

Marianne Wright (Mrs. Robert)

BEEF YAKITORI
A Japanese appetizer

½ cup soy sauce
2 tablespoons lemon juice
2 tablespoons sugar
1 garlic clove, crushed
½ teaspoon ground ginger
2 tablespoons vegetable oil
1 teaspoon sesame seeds
2 green onions,
  finely chopped
1 pound beef sirloin,
  thinly sliced

In a 9 x 5-inch loaf pan, combine soy sauce, lemon juice, sugar, garlic, ginger, oil, sesame seeds and onions. Thread meat on 18 to 20 6-inch bamboo skewers by pushing a skewer in and out of each meat slice as though sewing. Place skewered meat in marinade, turning to coat all sides. Cover and refrigerate 3 to 4 hours. Drain. Arrange marinated, skewered meat on broiler pan or ungreased baking sheet. Preheat broiler if necessary. Place oven rack 5 to 8 inches from heating element. Broil meat 1 ½ to 2 minutes; turn and broil about 1 minute longer. Serve hot. Makes 18 to 20 appetizer servings.

Barbara Adams (Mrs. Philip)

SPINACH FETA STRUDEL SLICES
Also good as an entree for luncheons or light suppers.

2 pounds fresh spinach, including stems
¼ cup butter
12 green onions, white part only, minced (½ cup)
6 ounces feta cheese, coarsely chopped (1 ½ cups)
½ cup fresh bread crumbs
½ cup parsley leaves, minced
4 egg whites
2 tablespoons dried dillweed
Salt and pepper
¾ pound phyllo leaves
1 cup unsalted butter, melted

Wash spinach; cut off root ends. Cook quickly in uncovered pot only in water clinging to leaves, turning to promote even cooking. As soon as spinach wilts, transfer to collander and run under cold water until cool. Drain well. Place in a kitchen towel and wring out all moisture. Transfer to a food processor or blender and puree. Melt ¼ cup butter in small skillet. Add onion and saute 5 minutes. Using food processor or electric mixer, combine spinach puree, onion, feta cheese, 2 tablespoons bread crumbs, parsley, egg whites, dill, salt and pepper, and blend well. Taste for seasoning (should be highly seasoned). Preheat oven to 375°. Generously butter baking sheet. Place one phyllo leaf lengthwise in front of you on waxed paper set on a damp towel. Cover remaining leaves with waxed paper and wrap in another damp towel. Brush leaf with melted butter and sprinkle with one teaspoon bread crumbs. Repeat buttering and crumbing process using 3 additional phyllo leaves (you will have a stack of 4 leaves, one on top of the other). Spread ⅓ of the spinach mixture on the lower third of the phyllo ¼ inch from the edge closest to you, leaving about one inch uncovered on each side. Fold the unfilled left and right ends toward the center. Roll the strudel tightly and firmly in jelly roll-fashion, using waxed paper to assist. Transfer to baking sheet. Brush top with melted butter. (At this point, strudel may be refrigerated, wrapped in plastic wrap or frozen. If frozen, defrost 30 minutes before baking and increase baking time slightly.) Repeat twice for a total of 3 strudel rolls. Bake until golden brown, about 30 to 35 minutes. Cut into one-inch slices, using electric or serrated knife. Makes 42 appetizer slices.

Marilyn Bauer (Mrs. James)

RUMAKI

Oriental sauce:
 ¼ cup soy sauce
 ¼ cup salad oil
 2 tablespoons catsup
 1 tablespoon vinegar
 ¼ teaspoon pepper
 2 cloves garlic, crushed
6 chicken livers, halved
1 5-ounce can water
 chestnuts, cut into 12 slices
6 slices bacon, cut in half
¼ cup brown sugar

Prepare oriental sauce by mixing all ingredients together. Pour sauce over chicken livers and water chestnuts; cover and refrigerate for four hours or longer. Remove from marinade. Wrap one liver and one slice chestnut in each piece of bacon; secure with wooden pick. Roll in brown sugar. Broil three inches from heat 10 minutes, turning occasionally, until bacon is crisp and liver is done. Makes 12.

Vivian Solomon (Mrs. Ted)

ROSY'S CHEESY BROILED APPETIZERS
Try using as a stuffing for mushrooms for a change of pace.

1 cup (4 ounces) Swiss
 cheese, shredded
⅓ cup bacon, chopped and
 cooked
¼ cup mayonnaise
¼ cup pitted ripe olives,
 chopped
2 tablespoons green onions,
 chopped
Party rye bread

Mix first five ingredients and spread on party rye bread. Broil two minutes.

Alice Sullivan (Mrs. E.A.)

CHICKEN PILLOWS
Crisp and garlicky chicken pastries that are ideal for cocktail parties. Can be made weeks ahead of time and frozen, unbaked.

2 whole chicken breasts,
   skinned and boned (1 pound)
3 tablespoons lemon juice
2 tablespoons olive or
   vegetable oil
1 teaspoon garlic, finely
   chopped
1 teaspoon leaf oregano,
   crumbled
½ teaspoon salt
½ cup butter
½ pound phyllo leaves

Cut chicken into 1-inch cubes; combine lemon juice, oil, garlic, oregano and salt in a small bowl. Mix well. Add the chicken pieces and coat with marinade. Cover and refrigerate overnight. Thaw phyllo according to directions on the package. Melt butter over low heat. Unwrap phyllo and place on a piece of waxed paper. Keep phyllo covered with another piece of waxed paper at all times to prevent drying. Halve phyllo **lengthwise** with scissors, forming two long strips, each about 6 inches wide. Take one strip of phyllo, fold in half crosswise and brush with melted butter. Place two pieces of chicken at one short end and roll up in pastry to midpoint. Fold left and right edges toward the center over filling and continue rolling, forming a neat package. Brush all over with butter and place seam side down on a jelly roll pan. Repeat with remaining chicken and phyllo. Bake in a 400° oven for 15 minutes or until golden brown. Makes about 24 pastries. Serve warm. **To freeze ahead:** Place filled and buttered phyllo rolls on a large baking sheet and freeze. When frozen, transfer to large plastic bags and seal. To bake, place rolls in a single layer in two jelly roll pans. Brush with additional butter. Bake in a 400° oven for 20 minutes.

Marilyn Bauer (Mrs. James)
Joyce Cashman (Mrs. Michael)

SHRIMP AND SCALLOP QUENELLES
Serve this as an elegant first course for a very special dinner party. Can be made in large batches and frozen until ready to use.

½ **pound scallops**
½ **pound fresh shrimp, shelled and deveined**
1 **cup whipping cream**
1 **egg white**
1/16 **teaspoon cayenne pepper**
⅛ **teaspoon salt**
⅛ **teaspoon white pepper**

Process the shrimps and scallops in a food processor, using the steel blade, until very smooth, using quick on-off turns. Add other ingredients and process until smooth. Chill at least two hours. **To shape**, wet a soup spoon and scoop out a rounded mound of the chilled mixture. Smooth the top with another spoon that has been dipped in hot water. Using both spoons, loosen the quenelle and slide it into simmering broth or water. Wet spoons each time before repeating process. **To poach**, simmer gently in broth, fish stock, or plain salted water for twelve minutes. Serve immediately with tarragon sauce or freeze for future use. **To freeze**, after quenelles are poached, cool them on a paper towel, place on a cookie sheet and freeze. After they are firmly frozen, place in plastic bags and return to the freezer. When ready to serve, cover and bake at 350° for 25 to 30 minutes. Makes 20 to 24 quenelles.

Tarragon Sauce

2 **tablespoons butter**
2 **tablespoons flour**
1 **cup milk**
2 **egg yolks**
¼ **cup whipping cream**
½ **teaspoon dried tarragon**
2 **tablespoons sherry**
¾ **teaspoon salt**
⅛ **teaspoon white pepper**

Melt butter in small saucepan. Stir in flour and cook over low heat three or four minutes. Blend in milk and cook, stirring constantly, until sauce is smooth and bubbly. Mix yolks with cream in a small bowl; gradually beat in a little of the hot sauce. Add egg yolk mixture to the sauce and cook over very low heat until well blended and thick. Stir in tarragon, sherry, salt, and white pepper. Continue cooking over very low heat another five minutes to allow flavors to blend. If sauce is too thick, thin with milk.

Marilyn Bauer (Mrs. James)

CHEESE PENNIES
Cheesie flavored cocktail cookie

1 5-ounce jar Old English sharp cheese spread
¼ cup shortening or 1 stick butter, room temperature
⅔ cup all-purpose flour
walnut or pecan pieces for decorative topping, optional

Beat and combine cheese spread and butter briefly. Add the flour. Make into a creamy paste. Divide dough into 4 sections. Lightly roll sections of the dough in flour and shape into rolls about 1 inch in diameter. Roll in waxed paper and chill at least 30 minutes. Cut into ¼-inch slices and place on ungreased cookie sheets 1/2-1 inch apart and bake in a 375° oven 10 minutes or until light brown. A walnut or pecan piece may be placed on top before baking for decoration. Makes 5 dozen.

Jennie Shah (Mrs. K. G.)

ARTICHOKE SQUARES

3 green onions, chopped
1 clove garlic, crushed
Butter
2 6-ounce jars artichokes, drained and chopped
4 eggs, beaten
Salt and pepper to taste
8 Saltine crackers, crushed
½ pound cheddar cheese, grated
Parsley, oregano, Tabasco, and jalapeno peppers to taste

Saute onions and garlic in butter. Mix with remaining ingredients. Pour into an 8 x 8-inch pan and bake 40 minutes at 325°. Cool slightly. Cut into small squares and serve. May be baked ahead. To reheat in oven, bake at 325° for 15 minutes; microwave 1½ to 2 minutes. Serves 10.

Laura Rager (Mrs. Donald)

COCKTAIL SPINACH BALLS

2 10-ounce packages frozen chopped spinach
2 cups garlic or herb seasoned croutons or dry stuffing mix
1 cup Parmesan cheese, grated
6 eggs, lightly beaten
¾ cup butter, room temperature
½ teaspoon white pepper
¼ teaspoon nutmeg

Cook spinach according to package directions. Drain thoroughly. Grind croutons into fine crumbs. Combine all ingredients. Shape into balls approximately 1-inch in diameter. (May be frozen in a single layer and transferred to airtight containers at this point.) Heat oven to 350°. Bake 10 to 15 minutes or until bottoms are lightly brown. Makes about 50. **Variation:** Pat Russo adds salt and garlic powder to taste, one medium onion finely chopped, and 6 tablespoons bacon, crumbled.

Joan Leu (Mrs. Richard)

FAST SAUSAGE APPETIZERS
Make ahead and freeze.

1 package Pillsbury Crescent Rolls
1 pound bulk spiced or seasoned sausage

Divide rolls in 4 rectangles. Roll out each with a rolling pin and pat ¼ pound sausage over each. Roll up jelly roll style. Wrap in foil and freeze. When ready to cook, remove from freezer and slice ¼-inch thick and bake at 400° for 10 to 15 minutes. Makes 190 appetizers.

Joan Berney (Mrs. John)

GUACAMOLE PIE

3 ripe avocados
1 tablespoon lemon juice
8 ounces sour cream
2 green onions, finely
  chopped
1 8-ounce jar taco sauce
1 cup (4 ounces) jack cheese,
  shredded
Tortilla chips

Mash avocados and lemon juice together. Spread mixture in bottom of 9-inch pie plate. Stir sour cream until creamy; then spread over avocado mix, covering completely. Sprinkle with green onions. Spoon taco sauce over sour cream to within one inch of edge. Sprinkle with cheese. Cover and refrigerate. Serve with tortilla chips.

Bonnie Fenton (Mrs. Craig)

BEEF SAUSAGE APPETIZER MAKE-AHEAD

1 pound ground round
1 pound Italian sausage
  (bulk or links)
1 pound Velveeta cheese
1 teaspoon oregano
½ teaspoon garlic powder
⅛ teaspoon salt
⅛ teaspoon pepper

Brown meat and drain well. Add cheese and seasonings. Mix until cheese is melted. Cool slightly. Spread on party rye bread. Place on cookie sheet lined with waxed paper. Freeze until firm. Place in plastic containers and store in freezer. To serve, bake at 450° for about 10 minutes or until warm.

Alice Sullivan (Mrs. E. A.)

PARMESAN CHEESE BREAD

1 loaf French bread, cut into
  2-inch cubes
½ pound butter, softened
½ cup mayonnaise
⅔ cup Parmesan cheese
½ cup onion, coarsely chopped
1 teaspoon Worcestershire
  sauce

Mix and spread on bread cubes. Heat oven to 350 degrees and bake bread for 30 minutes.

Chris Palagallo (Mrs. Gerald)

CHICKEN NUGGETS
This is exceptional! Can be made ahead and frozen and reheated when partially defrosted. Better than McNuggets!

2 cups Bisquick
2 eggs
1 cup milk
1 tablespoon garlic salt
⅛ teaspoon pepper
4 large whole chicken breasts, skinned, boned, and cut into bite-sized pieces, approximately 1-inch square
Dip:
4 tablespoons very hot Dijon-style mustard
1 ½ cups orange marmalade

Combine Bisquick, eggs, milk, garlic salt, and pepper, blending well. Heat oil to 365° in a deep fryer or electric fry pan. Dip chicken into batter and fry until golden brown. Remove with a slotted spoon. (Do not use deep fry basket, as the batter sticks making it hard to remove chicken.) Drain on paper towels. When cool, freeze in a single layer on a cookie sheet; then place in a container. Defrost on a cookie sheet in a single layer. Bake for 8 minutes in a 350° oven, or until heated through. Combine mustard and marmalade and heat slightly. Serve nuggets with dip and toothpicks. Approximately 120 nuggets.

Marianne Wright (Mrs. Robert)

BRUSSEL SPROUT APPETIZERS

1 10 ½-ounce package frozen brussel sprouts
1 6½-ounce can clams, drained
1 3-ounce package cream cheese
2 tablespoons mayonnaise
2 teaspoons chopped onion
2 teaspoons chopped parsley
1 teaspoon Worcestershire sauce
Dash hot pepper sauce

Cook brussel sprouts and cool. Slice in half lengthwise. Core. Fill with chilled clam dip made from mixing remaining ingredients together. Chill until time to serve.

Janet Shipley (Mrs. William A.)

FRENCH BOURSIN CHEESE

For an extra treat, spread over broiled steak. Return to broiler until bubbly.

1 8-ounce package cream cheese, softened
¼ cup butter (no substitutes)
½ teaspoon beau monde seasoning
1 medium clove garlic, minced
1 teaspoon water
1 teaspoon parsley, minced
¼ teaspoon red wine vinegar
¼ teaspoon Worcestershire sauce
⅛ teaspoon each:
  sage
  savory
  rosemary
  thyme
  cracked black pepper

With an electric mixer, beat cream cheese and butter together until light and fluffy. Scrape down sides of bowl frequently. Add remaining ingredients and beat well. Refrigerate for several hours to mellow. To serve, shape into a ball and roll in pepper. Allow to reach room temperature before serving. Serve with crackers. Serves 10.

Chris Palagallo (Mrs. Gerald)

FROSTED LIVERWURST PATÉ

1 pound liverwurst or braunschweiger
1 clove garlic, minced
½ teaspoon basil
¼ cup onion, minced
1 8-ounce package cream cheese, softened
1 clove garlic, minced
⅛ teaspoon Tabasco
1 teaspoon mayonnaise or salad dressing
parsley to garnish

Mash liverwurst with fork; thoroughly mix in 1 clove garlic, basil, and onion. Mold into a ball, cover and chill. Blend cream cheese, 1 clove garlic, Tabasco, and mayonnaise and frost chilled liverball. Refrigerate at least 8 hours. Just before serving, garnish with parsley. Serve with crackers or party rye.

Marianne Wright (Mrs. Robert)

GRAB BAG APPETIZER
You are limited only by your imagination or what you can find at the grocery store!

½ cup sour cream
½ cup prepared horseradish
2 cups mayonnaise
2 tablespoons dry mustard
2 teaspoons lemon juice
1 ½ teaspoons salt
½ teaspoon MSG (optional)
1 cucumber, pared, cut in bite-size pieces
½ pound shrimp, cooked
8 ounces whole mushrooms
½ head cauliflower, broken into flowerettes
1 8½-ounce can water chestnuts, drained
1 green pepper, seeded, cut in squares
1 8½-ounce can artichoke hearts, quartered
1 5 ¾-ounce can ripe olives, pitted

Mix first seven ingredients. Fold remaining ingredients into sour cream mixture and let guests grab with toothpicks.

Ann Nace (Mrs. William)

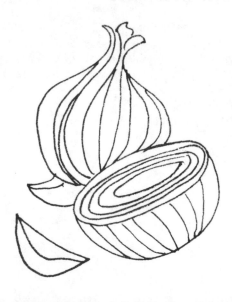

ANTIPASTO

2 10-ounce packages frozen
  artichoke hearts
2 6-ounce cans black olives,
  pitted
1 12-ounce bottle stuffed
  green olives
1 container cherry tomatoes
4 sweet onions, cut in
  thin rings
2 15-ounce cans garbanzo
  beans
1 or 2 cloves garlic, minced
2 4-ounce jars button
  mushrooms
Dressing:
  2 cups oil
  1 ¼ cups wine vinegar
  ¾ cup brown sugar
  ¼ cup white Karo syrup
  salt and pepper to taste

Combine first eight ingredients in a large bowl. Mix ingredients for dressing and pour over vegetables. Marinate 6 to 8 hours in refrigerator before serving. Serves 12 or more.

Debbie Coon (Mrs. John)

MARINATED MUSHROOMS

Marinade
  1 teaspoon salt
  ¼ teaspoon cayenne
    pepper
  3 tablespoons vinegar
  1 drop tabasco sauce
  3 cloves garlic, mashed
  1 cup warm oil (suggest
    half olive oil, half
    vegetable oil)
  ½ teaspoon pepper
  ¼ teaspoon oregano
  ¼ teaspoon dry mustard
  1 tablespoon lemon juice
3 4-ounce cans whole
  mushrooms
1 onion, chopped
1 green pepper, chopped

Mix marinade ingredients and shake vigorously. Add mushrooms, onion, and pepper; mix. Chill at least four hours.

Amelia Wilson (Mrs. Henry M.)

EASY SANGRIA

1 1.5-liter bottle Spanada
   wine
1 16-ounce bottle 7-Up
Ice cubes
2 oranges or lemons, cut up

Put ingredients in a pitcher and serve.

Clara Remolina (Mrs. Rodrigo)

CRANBERRY TEA

1 1-pound package frozen
   or fresh whole cranberries
2 quarts water
2 cups water
2 cups sugar
3 cinnamon sticks
1 cup pineapple juice
2 cups orange juice
2 tablespoons lemon juice

Cook cranberries in two quarts water for 20 minutes. Strain and save the juice. Combine the two cups water, sugar and cinnamon sticks; boil for 30 minutes. Add to the cranberry juice with the pineapple, orange, and lemon juices. Serve hot. Makes 12 or more servings.

Debbie Coon (Mrs. John)

STRAWBERRY SMACK (COCKTAIL)

1 12-ounce can frozen
   lemonade
12 ounces light rum
12 ounces water
1 10-ounce package frozen
   strawberries

Place frozen lemonade, rum, water, and strawberries into a blender. Blend until well mixed. Add ice chips and blend again. Pour into frosted glasses. Garnish with fresh strawberries. Makes about six servings.

Beth Shay (Mrs. Thanad)

HOT BUTTERED RUM
Great on a cold wintry night! Brrr!

1 pound dark brown sugar
1 cup butter, softened
1 pint vanilla ice cream
½ teaspoon cinnamon
½ teaspoon allspice
¼ teaspoon nutmeg
Rum
Cinnamon sticks, optional

Mix all ingredients, except rum and cinnamon sticks, together in a large bowl. Blend until smooth. Put in containers and store in freezer. To prepare each drink, put 1 heaping tablespoon of ice cream batter and 1 ½ ounces of rum into each mug. Fill mug with boiling water. Stir well. Can be served with cinnamon stick if desired. Yield: 1 quart batter

Marianne Wright (Mrs. Robert)

FRANK'S RUM CIDER PUNCH
A real hit at winter parties!

Apple cider
Rum
2 to 3 cinnamon sticks
2 oranges
Cloves, whole
¼ to ½ cup brown sugar

Use four parts cider to one part rum. Put in crock pot or in a large pot on the stove. Add 2 or 3 cinnamon sticks. Slice oranges and stud with cloves. Add to cider. Add brown sugar. Heat to boiling and serve warm.

Pat Russo (Mrs. Frank)

MINT PUNCH

1 ½ cups sugar
1 cup water
12 bunches mint
5 lemons, extract juices and
   cut rind in squares
1 quart gingerale
crushed ice

Boil sugar and water. Pour over mint leaves, lemon juice, and rind. Let stand 2 hours at room temperature. Strain and chill. Add gingerale and ice at serving time.

Marlene Campbell (Mrs. Allen)

FRUIT PUNCH

½ gallon red fruit punch
16 ounces 7-Up
1 750 ml. bottle Cold Duck
1 750 ml. bottle burgundy
  wine
2 or 3 cups prepared orange
  juice

Pour chilled ingredients into punch bowl and serve. An ice ring may be made with the fruit punch to keep ingredients chilled.

Ella Thompson (Mrs. Robert)

CHRISTMAS PUNCH
Also nice for Valentines Day or a bridal shower!

1 12-ounce can Hawaiian
  punch, frozen
1 12-ounce can lemonade,
  frozen
½ gallon Vin Rose' or sparkling
  pink wine
1 28-ounce bottle gingerale
1 750 ml. bottle champagne
1 pint raspberry sherbet

Mix Hawaiian punch, lemonade, and wine together. Add ginger ale and champagne slowly. Spoon sherbet into punch.

Joan Leu (Mrs. Richard)

STRAWBERRY COOLER

1 cup fresh strawberries or
  1 10-ounce package frozen
  strawberries, partially
  thawed
3 cups water
2 6-ounce cans frozen pink
  lemonade concentrate,
  thawed
1 6-ounce can frozen limeade
  concentrate, thawed
1 to 1 ½ cups light rum
6 to 8 fresh pineapple chunks
  (garnish)

Puree strawberries in blender or processor until almost smooth. Mix with remaining liquids in plastic container. Cover and freeze overnight. Defrost to desired degree of slushiness and pour or scoop into serving glasses. Garnish with pineapple chunks skewered on fancy picks. 6-8 servings.

Rita Luetkemeyer (Mrs. Richard)

Soups and Sandwiches

AMY'S FAVORITE CORN CHOWDER

1 medium potato, peeled
  and diced
1 small onion, chopped
1 cup water
1 16-ounce can cream-style
  corn
2 cups milk
2 tablespoons butter or
  margarine
Salt, and freshly ground
  pepper
1 egg, slightly beaten
Chopped fresh chives
  (garnish)

Combine first 3 ingredients in medium saucepan over medium-low heat and simmer until potatoes are tender, about 10-15 minutes. Add corn, milk, and butter and blend well. Season with salt and pepper. Bring to a boil. Remove from heat. Stir some of the chowder into egg. Add mixture to saucepan and blend well. Simmer until heated through, about 1 minute. Ladle into bowls, garnish with chives and serve. Serves 4.

Barbara Grawey (Mrs. Gerald W.)

VEGETARIAN SPLIT PEA SOUP
A good substitute for split pea with ham soup

1 cup green split peas,
  soaked overnight in 4 cups
  water
2 tablespoons oil
8 peppercorns
½ teaspoon dill seeds
½ teaspoon coriander seeds
½ teaspoon cumin seeds
1 small onion, finely diced
1 carrot, finely diced
2 to 3 teaspoons salt
1 teaspoon garlic powder
1 teaspoon grated fresh
  ginger
1 teaspoon lemon juice
1 teaspoon sugar

Cook the split peas until very tender. In a separate saucepan heat the oil until hot. Sizzle all the whole seeds until fragrant and brown (about one minute). Add onions and carrots and saute, covered, until brown. Reduce heat to medium and cook 5 minutes. Add the cooked split peas, salt, and remaining ingredients. Bring to a boil, reduce heat, and simmer 10 minutes. Add more water if too thick. Should taste very savory.

Jennie Shah (Mrs. K. G.)

AVOCADO SOUP

1 13 ¾-ounce can chicken
broth or equal amount of
homemade
2 medium avocados, peeled,
seeded, and cut into
chunks (save ¼ to ½ for
garnish)
2 tablespoons dry sherry
½ teaspoon salt
¼ teaspoon onion powder
⅛ teaspoon dried dillweed
¾ cup light cream

In blender or food processor, combine chicken broth, avocado chunks, dry sherry, salt, onion, powder, and dillweed. Cover; blend until mixture is smooth. Stir in light cream. Pour into a refrigerator container. Cover. Chill well. Top each serving with a slice of avocado or a dollop of sour cream. Serves 6.

Laura Rager (Mrs. Donald)

ONION WINE SOUP

¼ cup butter
5 large onions, chopped
5 cups beef broth
½ cup celery leaves
(pack cup)
2 large potatoes, peeled and
diced
1 cup dry white wine
1 tablespoon vinegar
1 teaspoon sugar
1 cup light cream
1 tablespoon minced
parsley

Melt butter in large saucepan. Add chopped onion, saute until tender. Add beef broth, celery leaves, and potatoes. Bring to a boil. Cover and simmer 30 minutes. Puree mixture in blender. Return to saucepan and blend in wine, vinegar and sugar. Bring to a boil and simmer 5-10 minutes. Stir in cream, parsley, salt and pepper to taste. Heat and serve; do not boil. Serves 6-8.

Irene Ireland (Mrs. Harry J.)

BEER CHEESE SOUP

½ cup butter
½ cup celery, chopped
½ cup carrots, chopped
½ cup onions, chopped
½ cup flour
½ teaspoon dry mustard
2 ½ pints chicken broth
6 ounces cheddar cheese, grated
2 tablespoons Parmesan cheese, grated
1 12-ounce bottle beer
¼ teaspoon M.S.G.

Saute vegetables in butter until done, but not browned. Blend in flour, dry mustard and chicken stock, and cook 5 minutes. Add cheeses and beer. Let soup simmer for 10 minutes. Season with salt and pepper and M.S.G. Serve with French bread.

Sharlyn Munns (Mrs. James)

BORSCHT
A hearty soup that is a meal in itself!

2 pounds short ribs
2 medium onions, chopped
6 cups beef stock
1 27-ounce can sauerkraut (or less to taste)
1 small head cabbage, chopped
2 cloves garlic, minced
1 16-ounce can julienne beets (or less to taste)
⅓ cup sugar
⅓ cup vinegar
salt, pepper, dill weed
2 tablespoons cornstarch
½ cup red wine
sour cream

Place first six ingredients in soup kettle. Bring to a boil. Skim fat from top. Reduce heat and simmer two hours. Add beets, sugar, vinegar, and adjust seasonings to taste. Cook 15 minutes. Remove meat from bones if desired and return to pot. Mix cornstarch into red wine and add, stirring until heated through. Serve with sour cream. Soup may be made ahead one day and reheated. Serve with French bread and boiled potatoes.

Alice Sullivan (Mrs. E.A.)

BROCCOLI SOUP

1 10-ounce package frozen broccoli
1 cup combined vegetable water and milk
½ teaspoon salt
⅛ teaspoon pepper
¼ teaspoon dry mustard
1 10 ½-ounce can cream of chicken soup
1 cup heavy cream

Cook broccoli; drain vegetable water into 1 cup measure and add milk to make one cup. Place the broccoli, milk mixture and seasonings in blender. Cover and blend about 30 seconds. Add chicken soup to broccoli and mix in saucepan; heat and add heavy cream. Heat again to serving temperature, but **do not boil.** Cauliflower may be used instead of broccoli, if desired.

Sharlyn Munns (Mrs. James)

VEGETABLE SOUP

Soup bones
4 carrots, peeled and sliced
2 medium potatoes, peeled and diced
2 medium onions, chopped
1 cup cabbage, chopped
4 stalks celery, chopped
½ green pepper, seeded and chopped
1 28-ounce can tomatoes, undrained and chunked
1 16-ounce can green beans
¼ cup barley
1 teaspoon onion salt
½ tablespoon parsley
1 tablespoon beef bouillon
2 tablespoons sugar
1 tablespoon garlic salt
1 teaspoon garlic powder
½ teaspoon minced garlic
2 bay leaves (remove when done)
¼ teaspoon thyme
Salt and pepper to taste

In large pot put 3 quarts water, add soup bone and chunked meat if desired. Bring to boil. Reduce heat and simmer and cook for 1 hour, until meat is tender. Take out soup bone and debone. Let liquid cool and skim fat off top (place in refrigerator for easier skimming). Put meat back into the liquid and add vegetables and spices and simmer for 3-4 hours.

Ruth Giunta (Mrs. Edward)

CIOPPINO
A San Francisco treat!

2 medium onions, sliced
1 green pepper, chopped
2 cloves garlic, minced
¼ cup olive or salad oil
1 28-ounce can tomatoes
1 8-ounce can tomato sauce
1 ½ cups water
1 ½ cups red or dry white
    wine
¼ cup parsley, chopped
2 teaspoons salt
1 ½ teaspoons basil
½ teaspoon oregano
1 ½ pounds fish fillets (cod,
    halibut, grouper or bass)
1 dozen clams in shells
Any combination of these
    options:
    12 ounces split crab legs
    ½ pound shrimps in shell
    ½ pound scallops

Saute onion, green pepper, and garlic in oil. Add undrained tomatoes, tomato sauce, water, wine and seasonings. Cover and simmer 30 minutes. Scrub fresh clams well. Add clams and crab to soup. Cover and simmer 10 minutes. Clean shrimp and cut down the back with knife or scissors to remove veins. Cut fish into one-inch chunks. Add scallops, shrimp and fish and cook 5-10 minutes more or until shrimp turns pink, fish flakes with a fork and clam shells open (if any of the clams do not open, discard unopened ones because this is a sign of spoilage). Serve in bowls with French, Italian, or sourdough bread and tossed green salad. Serves 8-10.

Jo Dorsch (Mrs. Thomas)

CRAB BISQUE
Easy and delicious. Good served as a first course with standing rib roast.

2 10 ½-ounce cans cream
    of celery soup
2 cups half and half
2 teaspoons onion, grated
2 teaspoons parsley,
    shredded
½ teaspoon salt
½ teaspoon pepper
2 7 ½-ounce cans crab meat,
    or 2 cups fresh or frozen
    crab meat
2 small ripe avocados, diced

Heat all ingredients except avocados to just under boiling. Add avocados just before serving. Serves 6.

Marilyn Bauer (Mrs. James)

CHEESE SOUP
Hearty enough for a full meal!

½ cup margarine
¾ cup fresh cauliflower, diced
½ cup carrots, chopped
1 cup onion, chopped
1 cup celery, chopped
1 cup potatoes, diced
1 pound cheddar cheese, grated
2 tablespoons cornstarch
2 cups boiling water
1 13-ounce can evaporated milk
¾ cup cooked ham, chicken, or turkey, chopped
1 teaspoon Worcestershire sauce
½ teaspoon pepper

Melt margarine. Saute chopped vegetables in melted margarine until tender. In saucepan (not over heat) combine cheese and cornstarch. Pour 2 cups of boiling water over this mixture, stirring until dissolved. Over low heat, add sauteed vegetables, evaporated milk, chopped ham, chicken or turkey, and seasonings. May add garlic powder to taste. Simmer until thoroughly warmed.

Marie Johnson (Mrs. David)

PIZZA SOUP

5 10 ½-ounce cans minestrone soup
2 ½ cans water
1 ½-2 pounds Italian sausage, fried, drained of grease
1 package frozen spinach
1 16-ounce can tomatoes, undrained
1 teaspoon garlic salt
1 teaspoon oregano
Mozzarella cheese
Parmesan cheese

Heat all ingredients except cheeses. Simmer gently for about 15 minutes. Sprinkle with shredded Mozzarella cheese and Parmesan cheese before serving.

Dottie Flores (Mrs. Richard)

NEW BRUNSWICK SOUP
Soup and a slice of health bread makes a good light supper. Just what the Doctor ordered!

1 3-pound chicken, cup up
2 quarts water
1 small onion, chopped
1 bay leaf
1 teaspoon salt
1 28-ounce can tomatoes
1 10-ounce package frozen corn
1 10-ounce package frozen lima beans
1 teaspoon basil, crushed
1 teaspoon salt
½ teaspoon pepper

Place chicken in Dutch oven or heavy sauce pan. Add water, salt, onion, and bay leaf. Cover and simmer, do not boil, until tender, about 1 hour. Remove chicken from broth. Cool and remove from bones. Add tomatoes, corn, lima beans, basil, salt, and pepper to broth. Cover and simmer for 1 hour. Add cut up chicken and heat through. Remove bay leaf and serve.

Lois Berg (Mrs. Ben C.)

BROCCOLI AND CHEESE SOUP

4 tablespoons margarine
1 medium onion, chopped
5 cups water
5 chicken bouillon cubes, or 5 teaspoons instant chicken bouillon
2 10-ounce packages frozen chopped broccoli
½ to ¾ of 12-ounce package egg noodles
5 cups milk
2 pounds Velveeta cheese, chunked

Melt margarine in large kettle and saute onions until tender. Add water and bouillon. Bring to boil. Add broccoli and simmer 5 minutes. Add noodles and simmer 5 minutes. Add milk and Velveeta. Simmer until cheese is melted.

Joan Leu (Mrs. Richard H.)

POTATO CELERY SOUP
Low in calories

1 potato, peeled
  and diced
2 cups water
4 outer stalks of celery
  with leaves, chopped
1 teaspoon salt
1/16 teaspoon black pepper
1 cup milk

Cook diced potato in the water in a 2-quart saucepan, covered. When tender, add celery, salt, and pepper. When celery is tender (about 10 minutes), add milk. Cook until celery is well cooked and potatoes are very soft. Add more milk, water, or salt if desired. Simmer again and serve. Good left over. Serves 4.

Jennie Shah (Mrs. K. G.)

BROWN RICE-LENTIL SOUP

2 tablespoons olive oil
1 tablespoon butter
1-2 stalks celery, chopped
2 carrots, chopped
2 onions, diced
3 cloves garlic, minced
1 tablespoon parsley
1 28-ounce can tomatoes
1/3 cup brown rice
1 ½ cups lentils
6 cups water

Melt olive oil and butter in large kettle and saute vegetables for 5 minutes. Add remaining ingredients. Bring to boil. Cover and simmer for 1 hour.

Maryann Bugaieski (Mrs. Stanley)

PORTUGUESE BEAN SOUP
A vegetable soup with a new twist!

24 ounces Portuguese
sausage, sliced in ¼-inch
pieces, or substitute with
hot Italian sausage and
smoked sausage
½ cup smoked ham, diced
½ cup onions, diced
½ cup carrots, diced
½ cup celery, diced
½ cup cabbage, diced
½ cup bell peppers, diced
1 cup potatoes, diced
3 cups canned red beans
2 quarts tomato juice
2 quarts water
2 bay leaves
Salt, pepper, liquid smoke
to taste

Saute all meat, then vegetables. Add red beans, liquid and spices. Cook slowly for 2 hours. Remove bay leaves.

Brenda Schneider (Mrs. Barry)

MARY'S BRANDIED TOMATO SOUP
Soooo good!!

½ pound butter
1 ½ cups onion, chopped
3 16-ounce cans tomato
sauce
2 ½ teaspoons sweet basil
½ teaspoon salt
½ teaspoon pepper
2 ½ pints heavy whipping
cream or half and half
2 ½ teaspoons brown sugar
½ cup brandy

Melt butter; saute onions. Add tomato sauce, basil, salt and pepper. Simmer 30 minutes. Heat cream and sugar separately until very hot. Add to tomato mixture, stirring quickly and constantly. Add brandy and serve. This soup tastes better if made ahead and allowed to mellow.

Dolores Sheen (Mrs. John E.)

CREAM OF PUMPKIN SOUP
An original creation

3 tablespoons clarified butter or oil
½ teaspoon each black mustard seeds, coriander seeds, and cumin seeds
6 peppercorns
2 whole cloves or ¼ teaspoon ground cloves
1 small piece of cinnamon bark or ¼ teaspoon ground cinnamon
1 pint fresh pureed pumpkin pulp (or frozen, thawed) not canned
1 teaspoon tumeric
1 teaspoon cumin/coriander powder
½ teaspoon cayenne pepper
1 ½ teaspoons salt
⅛ cup sugar
1 ½ cups milk
½ cup water, optional
seeds from 4 pods of cardamom, hulled and crushed

Heat clarified butter in a 3-quart saucepan. Sizzle whole seeds, peppercorns, and cinnamon bark. When seeds begin to pop and fragrance escapes, quickly add pureed pulp. Add all powdered spices, salt, and sugar. Stir; cover and simmer for 5 minutes. Add milk and simmer (do not boil) for 10 minutes. Thin soup with water if desired. Add fresh ground cardamom, stir, and taste. Should be yellow and creamy, slightly sweet. For salty taste, leave out cardamom and adjust salt. Serves 6-8.

Jennie Shah (Mrs. K. G.)

ZUCCHINI TOMATO SOUP ALA ITALY

3 tablespoons oil
½ teaspoon dill seeds
3 medium zucchinis, cubed
2 teaspoons salt
1 pint or 1 16-ounce can tomatoes, skinned and mashed
1 teaspoon each tumeric and garlic powder
1 teaspoon each leaves of oregano, basil and dill
1 teaspoon sugar

Heat oil in a 4-quart saucepan. Cook dill seeds until they sizzle. Quickly add the zucchini and salt. Stir and cover. Cook on medium high for 5 minutes, stirring occasionally. Pour in the tomatoes and remaining ingredients. Let simmer until zucchini is soft. Makes a savory, colorful chunky soup for six. Good served on white rice.

Jennie Shah (Mrs. K. G.)

TUNA CHEESE BUNS

¼ pound cheddar cheese, cubed
3 hard-boiled eggs, chopped
1 7-ounce can tuna, drained
1 teaspoon green pepper, minced
3 teaspoons olives, chopped
2 teaspoons pickle relish
½ cup mayonnaise
8 hamburger buns

Combine first seven ingredients and spread on buns. Wrap in foil and heat for 15 minutes at 300°. May be frozen for several weeks.

Pat Russo (Mrs. Frank)

CORN DOGS
Great for kids' parties!

1 cup biscuit mix
2 tablespoons yellow corn meal
¼ teaspoon paprika
½ teaspoon dry mustard
⅛ teaspoon cayenne
1 egg
¼ cup milk
8 to 10 hot dogs
8 to 10 wooden sticks

Heat deep frying fat to 375°. Mix biscuit mix, corn meal, paprika, dry mustard, and cayenne. Stir in egg and milk until well blended. Put hot dogs on sticks and dip into batter. Fry until brown, 2 to 3 minutes.

Pat Russo (Mrs. Frank)

ITALIAN BEEF

1 5 pound rump roast
3 cups water
1 stalk celery
1 medium onion, sliced
2-3 cloves garlic, minced
2 teaspoons oregano
2 beef boullion cubes
dash red pepper
1 tablespoon soy sauce
1 tablespoon Worchestershire sauce

Combine all ingredients in a dutch oven and simmer for 3 hours. Salt and pepper to taste near end of cooking. Save juices and wrap meat in foil. Refrigerate overnight. Slice meat paper thin and layer with juices in a 9 x 13 inch pan. Cover and refrigerate 24 hours. When ready to serve reheat meat, covered in a 325° oven for ½ hour. Serve on buns. Freezes well.

Sandy Rivan (Mrs. Robert)

GROUND BEEF SANDWICHES

1 ½ pounds ground beef
½ cup onion, chopped
1 tablespoon prepared
  mustard
½ teaspoon salt
¾ teaspoon Accent
½ teaspoon pepper
2 tablespoons catsup
2 tablespoons Worcestershire
  sauce
⅔ to 1 cup sour cream
Mozzarella cheese

Brown and drain ground beef. Add remaining ingredients to beef. Just before serving, stir in ⅔ to 1 cup sour cream. Spread mixture on slice of French bread or ½ hamburger bun. Sprinkle with grated mozzarella cheese. Broil until cheese melts.

Ella Thompson (Mrs. Robert)

HOT TUNA SALAD SANDWICH

2 7-ounce cans water-
  packed tuna, drained and
  flaked with a fork
¼ cup mayonnaise
½ cup sour cream
3 tablespoons parsley flakes
1 teaspoon lemon juice
½ teaspoon garlic salt
6 French bread rolls
6 slices Swiss cheese

Combine all ingredients for tuna salad and mix well. Split and butter French rolls and sprinkle with a little garlic salt. Spread a thin layer of tuna salad on bottom of rolls. Top with a slice of Swiss cheese. Place tops and bottoms on a cookie sheet and broil until cheese is melted and tops are nicely toasted. Delicious! This tuna spread is also good served as an appetizer in a hollowed-out pineapple served on a tray surounded with party rye. Serves 6.

Marianne Wright (Mrs. Robert)

TUNA PUFFS PARMIGIANA
Excellent for lunch!

Parmesan Cheese Puffs:
  1 cup water
  ½ cup margarine
  1 cup flour
  ¼ teaspoon salt
  4 eggs
  **½ cup grated Parmesan
    cheese**
  1 tablespoon cornmeal
Tuna Filling:
  **2 6 ½-ounce cans tuna,
    drained and flaked**
  1 ½ cups celery, chopped
  **1 8-ounce can water
    chestnuts, drained and
    sliced**
  **2 tablespoons onion,
    chopped**
  ¾ cup mayonnaise
  **¼ cup Parmesan cheese,
    grated**
  ¼ teaspoon dill weed

Parmesan cheese puffs: Bring water and margarine to a boil. Add flour and salt. Stir vigorously over low heat until mixture forms a ball. Remove from heat. Cool five minutes. Add eggs, one at a time, beating well after each addition. Coat each ¼ cup of batter in combined cheese and cornmeal and place on a greased cookie sheet. Bake at 400° for 40 to 45 minutes until golden brown. Remove immediately from cookie sheet. Cool. Fill with tuna filling. Makes 12.

Tuna filling: Mix all ingredients and chill. Fill Parmesan cheese puffs and serve.

Rita Luetkemeyer (Mrs. Richard)

ITALIAN BEEF SANDWICHES
Serve with plenty of napkins — it's juicy!

1 envelope onion soup mix
3 cups water
3 beef bouillon cubes
2 teaspoons basil
2 teaspoons oregano
**1 teaspoon hot peppers
  (optional)**
5-pound rump roast
salt and pepper

Combine the onion soup, water, bouillon cubes, basil, oregano and peppers in the bottom of a roasting pan. Lightly salt and pepper rump roast and place in liquid on a low rack. Roast, covered, for 4 to 5 hours at 250°. Remove fat. To serve, dip halves (do not immerse) of Italian rolls in the gravy, layer with the thinly sliced beef and top with the other half gravy-dipped roll. *For authentic Italian sandwich, offer green pepper strips fried in vegetable oil to layer on the sandwich. Serves 12-15.

Dottie Flores (Mrs. Richard)
Eleanor Pflederer (Mrs. Robert A.)

RED CABBAGE SLOPPY JOES
An original vegetarian recipe

4 tablespoons oil
½ teaspoon cumin seeds
¼ teaspoon black mustard
  seeds (rai)
1 head red cabbage, shredded
  in food processor
2 teaspoons salt
2 teaspoons curry powder
½ teaspoon each: cayenne,
  garlic powder and onion
  powder
1 teaspoon sugar
1 teaspoon lemon juice
6 onion rolls
ketchup and mayonnaise

Heat the oil over high heat in a 4-quart saucepan. Add the seeds and fry until popped and fragrant. Add the shredded cabbage. Turn cabbage, add the salt, and cover. Stir and turn frequently, keeping pot covered. Reduce heat to medium high. Add remaiing spices, sugar, and lemon juice. Cook 20 minutes. Toast onion roll halves. Spoon cabbage onto the bottom of the onion roll and spread top half with ketchup and mayonnaise. Serve immediately. Makes 6 sandwiches.

Jennie Shah (Mrs. K. G.)

INDIVIDUAL RIBBON SANDWICH
For one sandwich

4 slices sandwich bread,
  minus crust
egg salad
tomato slice
mayonnaise
ham salad or tuna salad
cream cheese
half and half
pimiento stuffed
  olives and parsley

Butter 3 slices of bread. On bottom layer, spread egg salad. Second layer, place a tomato, sliced thin and peeled, which has been drained on paper towel, salted, and topped with a little mayonnaise. Third layer, ham salad or tuna salad. Put 4th slice of bread on top. Beat softened cream cheese with enough half and half to frost 4 sides and top of sandwich. Decorate top with slices of olives and parsley. Serve on a leaf of lettuce. Good with any kind of fruit salad.

Bernice Whittaker (Mrs. Lorin)

BARBECUE

3 pounds ground beef
2 large onions, chopped
½ cup brown sugar
2 teaspoons salt
1 ½ cup barbecue sauce
1 to 1 ½ teaspoons barbecue
spice
2 tablespoons vinegar
1 6-ounce can tomato paste
3 6-ounce cans water

Combine beef and onions. Brown and drain. Add remaining ingredients. Simmer for one hour uncovered. Stir frequently. Makes 20-24 barbecues. Divide and put in small quantities into freezer for later use if desired.

Ruth Giunta (Mrs. Edward)

Brunches

BRUNCH EGG CASSEROLE

8 slices bread, decrusted
  and cubed
⅔ pound Velveeta cheese,
  cubed or 8 ounces cheddar
  cheese, shredded
8 eggs, slightly beaten
4 cups milk
1 teaspoon salt
1 teaspoon prepared mustard
1 teaspoon onion powder
1/16 teaspoon pepper
6-8 slices bacon

Place bread cubes in bottom of a 9 x 13-inch pan. Layer cheese on bread cubes. Blend milk, eggs, and spices; pour over bread and cheese. May refrigerate overnight. Fry bacon and crumble; sprinkle over mixture. Bake at 325° for one hour or until knife comes out clean. Garnish with bacon curls if desired. (May also use ham or crabmeat. Top with chopped chives or parsley). Serves 12.

Pam Albers (Mrs. William)

BREAKFAST CASSEROLE
Nice dish for Sunday brunch!

2 ½ cups plain croutons
1 pound bulk sausage,
  browned and drained
1 cup cheddar cheese,
  shredded
4 eggs, beaten
2 ¼ cups milk
1 can cream of mushroom
  soup
½ soup can milk

Mix together croutons, sausage, and cheddar cheese. Add eggs and milk. Place in a 9 x 13-inch pan and refrigerate overnight. Before baking, combine mushroom soup and milk and pour over casserole. Bake at 325° for 1½ hours. May be frozen uncooked. If so, thaw in refrigerator day before using.

Sharlyn Munns (Mrs. James)

FANCY EGG SCRAMBLE
A good breakfast or brunch casserole

1 cup Canadian bacon or
  sausage links, diced
¼ cup green onion, chopped
3 tablespoons butter or
  margarine
12 eggs, beaten
1 3-ounce can mushrooms,
  drained
1 recipe cheese sauce (below)
2 tablespoons butter, melted
2 ¼ cups soft bread crumbs
⅛ teaspoon paprika

In large skillet saute meat and onion in 3 tablespoons butter or margarine until onion is tender but not brown. Add beaten eggs and scramble just until set. Fold cooked eggs and mushrooms into cheese sauce. Pour into buttered 12 x 7 x 2-inch baking dish. Combine remaining melted butter, soft bread crumbs and paprika. Sprinkle on top of eggs. Cover. Chill overnight. Bake uncovered in a 350° oven for 30 minutes.

Cheese Sauce

2 tablespoons margarine
2 tablespoons flour
½ teaspoon salt
⅛ teaspoon pepper
2 cups milk
1 cup (4 ounces) shredded
  process American cheese

Melt margarine. Add flour, salt, pepper. Add milk. Cook and stir until bubbling. Stir in cheese until melted.

Eleanor Pflederer (Mrs. Robert A.)

FRITTATA

½ pound fresh mushrooms,
  sliced
2 onions, chopped
1 10-ounce package frozen
  spinach
6 eggs
½ to ¾ teaspoon salt
1/16 teaspoon nutmeg
2 6-ounce jars marinated
  artichoke hearts, drained,
  cut up
1 ½ cups cheddar cheese,
  grated

Saute mushrooms and onions in small amount of vegetable oil. Thaw spinach and drain well. Beat eggs lightly and add salt and nutmeg. Mix with mushrooms, spinach, artichoke hearts, and cheese. Bake in a buttered casserole at 350° for 45 minutes. Serves 6.

Goldijean Turow (Mrs. Alan)

CHEESE CASSEROLE
Good for brunch or Sunday night supper.

2 4-ounce cans green chilies, drained
1 pound monterey jack cheese, coarsely grated
1 pound cheddar cheese, coarsely grated
4 egg whites
4 egg yolks
⅔ cup evaporated milk, undiluted
1 tablespoon flour
½ teaspoon salt
⅛ teaspoon pepper
2 medium tomatoes, sliced

Preheat oven to 325°. Remove seeds from chilies and dice. In a large bowl combine the grated cheeses and the green chilies. Turn into a well greased shallow 2-quart casserole (12 x 8 x 2). In a large bowl beat egg whites just until stiff peaks form when beater is lifted. In a small bowl combine egg yolks, milk, flour, salt and pepper. Mix until well blended. Using a rubber scraper, gently fold beaten egg whites into egg yolk mixture. Pour egg mixture over cheese mixture in casserole. With a fork, ooze it through the cheese. Bake 30 minutes. Remove it from the oven and arrange tomato slices, overlapping, around edge of casserole. Bake 30 minutes longer or until brown.

Marie Adland (Mrs. Moris)

CHEESE AND CANADIAN BACON CASSEROLE

16 slices bread, crust removed
8 slices Canadian bacon
8 slices sharp cheddar cheese
6 eggs, slightly beaten
3 cups milk
½-¾ teaspoon salt
½-¾ teaspoon dry mustard
1 cup crushed potato chips
¼ pound butter, melted

Place 8 slices of bread flat in buttered 9 x 13-inch baking dish. Put on each slice of bread a slice of Canadian bacon and a slice of cheese. Top with a slice of bread. Combine and mix well eggs, milk, salt and mustard. Pour over above and let stand overnight or about 8 hours. Before baking, top with potato chips and melted butter. Bake at 350° for 1 hour. Perfect dish for brunch or easy supper.

Boots Eastman (Mrs. Ward)

VEGETABLE QUICHE
Served at Medical Auxiliary President's Luncheon

2 medium-size cauliflower
(about 1 pound each)
2 medium-size bunches
broccoli (about 1 ½ pounds
each)
2 tablespoons butter or
margarine
2 medium onions, chopped
3 cloves garlic, minced or
pressed
1 ½ teaspoons each dry basil,
oregano, and salt
½ teaspoon each pepper and
liquid hot pepper seasoning
4 tomatoes, chopped
8 eggs
⅔ cup half and half (light
cream) or milk
½ cup Parmesan cheese,
grated
2 ½ cups Swiss cheese,
shredded

Wash and trim cauliflower and broccoli into flowerets. In a 5-quart saucepan bring salted water to a boil. Add vegetables; turn off heat and soak until tender, about 6 to 8 minutes. Drain well, coarsely chop, and set aside.

In a wide frying pan, melt butter over medium heat. Saute onions and garlic until tender. Add cooked vegetables, basil, oregano, salt, pepper, liquid hot pepper seasoning, and tomatoes. Cook, stirring occasionally, until mixture is heated through, about 4 minutes. Remove from heat. In a large bowl, beat eggs and half and half just to blend. Stir in vegetable mixture, Parmesan cheese, and 2 cups of Swiss cheese. Pour into a greased 15-inch jelly-roll pan and spread evenly. Top with remaining cheese. Bake in a 375° oven for 30 to 35 minutes or until a knife inserted in the center comes out clean. Let stand 10 minutes. Makes 12 to 18 servings.

The Committee

QUICHE

2-4 Italian sausages, chopped
1 onion, chopped
1 10-ounce box frozen spinach
4 eggs, beaten
1 cup half and half
dash nutmeg
salt and pepper, to taste
1 pound Monterey Jack
cheese, grated
½ pound Swiss cheese,
grated
1 9-inch pie shell

Brown sausage and onion. Drain grease. Cook spinach, and squeeze out liquid. Beat the 4 eggs and scald the half and half. Combine eggs and half and half together with nutmeg, salt, and pepper. Place sausage and onion in bottom of pie crust. Cover with ⅓ of cheese, then layer spinach, then second ⅓ of cheese, then egg, then half and half mixture. Top with remaining cheese. Cook at 350° for 45 minutes to 1 hour. Let cool 15 minutes. Great!

Carol Nelson (Mrs. John)

EASY CRAB QUICHE
Rich!

1 9-inch deep dish pie shell
1 cup (4 ounces) Swiss
   cheese, shredded
½ cup Parmesan cheese,
   grated
3 tablespoons flour
1 ½ cups milk
4 eggs
¼ teaspoon nutmeg
1 6-ounce package frozen
   snow crab meat, thawed
   and drained
½ 10-ounce package frozen
   chopped spinach, thawed
   and drained (5 ounces)

Preheat oven and cookie sheet to 425°. Toss cheese and flour. Combine milk, eggs, and nutmeg. Add crab, cheese mixture and spinach to the milk mixture. Pour into pie shell. Bake on preheated cookie sheet for 15 minutes. Reduce oven temperature to 350° and bake an additional 30 to 35 minutes. Serves six. A salad with a Caeser salad dressing base really enhances the crab flavor.

Irene Crane (Mrs. Donald)

CRUSTLESS SPINACH QUICHE

4 cups cottage cheese
8 ounces cheddar cheese,
   grated
8 ounces mozzarella cheese,
   grated
½ cup green onions, minced
6 eggs, beaten
6 tablespoons flour
½ teaspoon salt
dash Tabasco or cayenne
⅛ teaspoon nutmeg
1 10-ounce package chopped
   spinach, defrosted and
   drained well
2 tablespoons butter
Paprika, for garnish

Preheat oven to 350° and grease a large quiche pan or two 9-inch pie plates. Combine all ingredients except spinach and butter. Pour egg-cheese mixture in prepared pan and spread spinach on top. Dot spinach with bits of butter and sprinkle with paprika. Bake 45 to 50 minutes or until puffed and set. Let cool a few minutes before cutting.

Dolores Sheen (Mrs. John)

ITALIAN ZUCCHINI CRESCENT PIE

4 cups zucchini, thinly sliced
1 cup onion, chopped
¼ to ½ cup margarine
½ cup parsley, chopped or 2 tablespoons parsley flakes
½ teaspoon salt
½ teaspoon pepper
¼ teaspoon garlic powder
¼ teaspoon basil
¼ teaspoon oregano
2 eggs, beaten
8 ounces (2 cups) Muenster cheese, shredded
1 8-ounce can refrigerated crescent dinner rolls
2 teaspoons mustard

Cook and stir zucchini and onion in margarine for 10 minutes. Stir in parsley or parsley flakes, salt, pepper, garlic powder, basil and oregano. Combine eggs and cheese. Stir in zucchini mixture. Separate crescent rolls into 8 triangles. Place in ungreased 10-inch pie pan; press over bottom and up sides to form crust. Spread crust with mustard. Pour vegetable mixture into crust. Bake in preheated 375° oven for 18-20 minutes or until center is set. (Cover with foil during last 10 minutes of baking.) Let stand 10 minutes before serving. Serves 6.

Rita Luetkemeyer (Mrs. Richard)

BLINTZ SOUFFLE

12 cheese or fruit blintzes, defrosted
½ cup butter
4 eggs
1 ½ cups sour cream
¼ cup sugar
¼ teaspoon salt
1 teaspoon vanilla
¼ cup orange juice
Cinnamon (optional)

Melt butter in 2-quart casserole in oven, and place blintzes over butter in one layer. Beat eggs and add all other ingredients. Pour over blintzes. Bake 45 minutes at 350° until top starts to brown. If desired, with frozen blintzes, bake 1 ½ hours. Serve with powdered sugar, strawberries, raspberries, or sour cream. Enjoy!

Jennifer Dolin (Mrs. Ben)

TOO LATE FOR BREAKFAST COOKIES
Yummy and nutritious too!

¼ pound margarine or butter
1 egg
¾ cup sugar
¼ teaspoon soda
1 cup flour
½ cup bacon bits, crisp, well-drained (½ pound before cooking; ½ cup Canadian bacon, finely chopped or ½ cup cooked ham may be substituted)
2 cups cornflakes, grapenut flakes, or raisin bran

Cream margarine, egg, sugar and soda. Mix with flour. Stir in bacon and cereal. Drop by tablespoons 2 inches apart on ungreased baking sheet. Bake in 350° oven for 13 to 15 minutes or until cookies are lightly browned and still soft. Cool slightly before removing. Makes 2 dozen.

Alice Sullivan (Mrs. E.A.)

OATMEAL BANNOCKS
Nice change from pancakes

1 cup all-purpose flour, lightly spooned
1 teaspoon baking soda
1 teaspoon cream of tartar
½ teaspoon salt
1 cup quick oatmeal
2 eggs
1 tablespoon honey
1 ½ cups milk

Sift flour, baking soda, and cream of tartar into a medium bowl. Stir in the salt and oatmeal. Beat the eggs, honey, and milk in a small bowl until well mixed. Make a well in the center of the dry ingredients and add the liquids. Beat until smooth. Grease the griddle lightly; heat over low to medium heat. When griddle is hot, drop batter by spoonfuls without crowding. When bubbles form, turn and cook the other side for two to three minutes. Serve warm with butter and honey. Makes about 24 three-inch bannocks.

Chris Palagallo (Mrs. Gerald)

SCALLOPED PINEAPPLE
A special addition to either a full meal or a brunch.

1 cup butter or margarine
2 cups sugar
4 to 6 eggs
¼ cup milk
5 to 7 slices fresh bread, torn
1 to 2 16-ounce cans crushed
   pineapple, drained

Beat together with a spoon the butter or margarine, sugar, and eggs. Add the remaining ingredients. Pour into a 1 ½-quart baking dish. Bake at 350° for one hour. Serves 4 to 6.

Sandra Neu (Mrs. M.T.)

RHUBARB COMPOTE

1 ½ pounds rhubarb, cut in
   small pieces
4 ounces dates, chopped
½ pound brown sugar
1 banana, sliced

Combine rhubarb, dates, and brown sugar. Add sliced banana. Bake in covered casserole at 350° for one hour. Serve warm. May serve with cream.

Janet Shipley (Mrs. William)

HOT PEACH COMPOTE
Great with chicken or meat.

1 29-ounce can sliced peaches,
   drained
1 cup cornflakes
½ cup brown sugar
½ teaspoon cinnamon
butter or margarine

Layer peaches in a 1-quart casserole dish. Crumble corn flakes, mix with brown sugar and cinnamon. Put on top of peaches. Dot with butter. Bake uncovered in a 350° oven for 30 minutes. Serves 4.

Jennifer Dolin (Mrs. Ben)

RUM BAKED FRUIT
Nice for a winter holiday brunch.

1 29-ounce can pear halves
1 29-ounce can peach halves
1 29-ounce can apricot halves
1 16½-ounce can pitted bing
    cherries
2 10-ounce boxes frozen
    strawberries, thawed
1 cup brown sugar, firmly
    packed
½ cup rum
2 cups sour cream (optional)

Drain fruits, reserving ½ cup of any juice. Layer fruits in a 2-quart ovenproof baking dish. Top with strawberries. Sprinkle brown sugar over top. Drizzle with juice mixed with rum. Bake at 350° for 20 minutes. Remove from oven and cool slightly. May top with dollop of sour cream. Serves 8 plus.

Kathleen Palmer (Mrs. Ron)

HOT CURRIED FRUITS

1 16-ounce can peach halves
1 16-ounce can pear halves
1 16-ounce can apricot halves
1 8-ounce jar maraschino
    cherries (optional)
¾ cup butter, melted
1 cup brown sugar
2 teaspoons curry powder

Drain fruits well, overnight if possible. Arrange in a shallow glass casserole. Combine butter, brown sugar, and curry powder. Pour over fruit. Cover and bake at 300° for 1 hour. Serves 8.

Lois Berg (Mrs. Ben)

CURRIED FRUIT

1 29-ounce can peach halves,
    drained
1 29-ounce can pear halves,
    drained
1 20-ounce can pineapple
    chunks, drained
⅓ cup butter, melted
⅔ cup brown sugar
2 ½ teaspoons curry powder
3 tablespoons cornstarch

Place fruit in a shallow baking dish, placing peaches and pears hollow side up. Mix butter, brown sugar, curry powder, and cornstarch and top fruit. Bake at 325° for 1 hour. Better if made a day ahead! Reheat at 350° for 30 minutes.

Chris Palagallo (Mrs. Gerald)

NOTES

Salads and Salad Dressings

CHICKEN SALAD WITH GRAPES
Lovely salad for a luncheon.

3 cups cooked chicken, diced
1 ½ cups celery, diced
3 tablespoons lemon juice
1 ½ cups fresh seedless green grapes
¾ cup slivered almonds, toasted
Dressing:
1 cup commercial mayonnaise
¼ cup light cream
1 ½ teaspoons salt
1/16 teaspoon pepper
1 teaspoon dry mustard

Combine chicken, celery, and lemon juice and chill at least one hour. Then add grapes and almonds. Mix ingredients for the dressing and combine with chicken mixture. Serves 8-10. Serving suggestion: Pile salad in the center of a cantaloupe slice served on lettuce leaves.

Vivian Solomon (Mrs. Ted)

CURRIED CHICKEN SALAD

3 cups chicken, cooked and cubed
1 ½ cups celery, diced
3 tablespoons lemon juice
1 cup pineapple chunks
½ cup almonds, toasted
1 teaspoon curry powder (or to taste)
1 ½ teaspoons salt
⅛ teaspoon pepper
¼ cup light cream
1 cup mayonnaise

Cook chicken the day before it is to be served. After cooking, let chicken stand in broth until cool. Cut up chicken, leaving in chunks. Combine chicken, celery, and lemon juice. Chill one hour. Add pineapple and almonds. Combine remaining ingredients and add to mixture. Serves 4-6. Try this with turkey and grapefruit segments after the holidays.

Marilyn Leyland (Mrs. John)

CRANBERRY CHICKEN SALAD
One of my most favorites, ranks in my "top 10"!

2 cups chicken, diced
2 hardcooked eggs, chopped
1 ½ cups celery,
   finely chopped
1 tablespoon onion, minced
1 cup whole salted cashews
½ cup mayonnaise
1 cup minus 2 tablespoons
   cranberry juice
1 cup minus 2 tablespoons
   canned, whole cranberry
   sauce
1 3-ounce package raspberry
   gelatin

Combine chicken, eggs, celery, onion, cashews and mayonnaise and press into the bottom of an 8 x 8-inch pan. Heat cranberry juice and cranberry sauce to boiling and stir in gelatin until dissolved. Refrigerate the cranberry-gelatin mixture until it just begins to thicken. Spoon this very gently over the chicken salad. Chill for at least 8 hours. Serve on lettuce leaf with warm bread sticks. Serves 6.

Kathleen Heinzen (Mrs. Frederick)

TUNA & CRANBERRY SALAD

1 envelope Knox gelatin
¼ cup cold water
½ cup boiling water
2 7-ounce cans white tuna,
   drained and flaked
2 hard boiled eggs, chopped
½ cup green olives, chopped
1 cup celery, chopped
1 tablespoon onion, grated
1 cup mayonnaise
½ teaspoon salt
Topping:
1 3-ounce package lemon jello
¾ cup boiling water
½ cup orange juice
1 can jellied cranberry sauce

Mix gelatin with cold water to soften. Add ½ cup boiling water to dissolve. Combine gelatin with other ingredients and pour into a 7 x 11 inch pan and chill. When set cover with topping.
Topping: Dissolve jello in boiling water and add orange juice. Beat cranberry sauce until runny and mix together. When cool pour over tuna mixture. Chill to set. To serve cut in squares and serve on lettuce leaf.

Bertha Dean (Mrs. Robert)

HOT CHICKEN SALAD

2 small packages of potato chips
2 cups cooked chicken, diced
3 hard-boiled eggs, chopped
1 cup onion, minced
1 tablespoon lemon juice
1 2-ounce jar pimientos
¾ cup mayonnaise
½ cup chopped pecans, or ground almonds
1 can mushroom soup

Place 1 package potato chips, crushed, on the bottom of a 9 x 12-inch baking dish (greased). Add other ingredients and top with remaining potato chips, crushed. Bake at 450° for 10 minutes. Serves 8.

Mary Owen (Mrs. Walter)

HOT CHICKEN SALAD

10 cooked chicken breasts, cut in cubes or strips
1 cup cooked rice
2 cans cream of chicken soup, undiluted
1 cup mayonnaise
1 cup frozen peas
2 cups celery, chopped
½ cup onion, chopped
1 5-ounce can water chestnuts, drained
1 8 ½-ounce can artichoke hearts, drained
½ cup sliced olives, black or green
6 hard-boiled eggs, chopped
Topping:
   2 cups grated cheese (Cheddar, Swiss, Parmesan, whatever you have on hand)
   1 can Chinese rice noodles

Toss all ingredients together. Bake at 450° for 10 minutes. Add cheese and noodle topping and continue baking until cheese has melted. Serves 12.

Clara Remolina (Mrs. Rodrigo)

PASTA MAGNIFICO

4 cups chicken, cooked and cubed (turkey or ham)
4 cups tiny shell macaroni, cooked and cooled
1 10-ounce package frozen peas, thawed
1 cup green onions, sliced
1 cup ripe olives, sliced
1 teaspoon salt
½ teaspoon oregano
1 cup Italian dressing
½ teaspoon thyme
1 2-ounce jar pimiento, sliced
⅔ cup mayonnaise

Combine and toss all ingredients except mayonnaise; marinate overnight. Before serving, stir in the mayonnaise and arrange in salad bowl, lined with leaves of romaine lettuce. Serves 8-10.

Joyce Rashid (Mrs. Ameel)

NUTTY LETTUCE SALAD

3 ounces almonds, sliced
4 tablespoons sesame seeds
1 head of lettuce, torn
5 slices of bacon, cooked and crumbled
½ cup chow mein noodles
Dressing:
4 tablespoons sugar
1 teaspoon salt
1 teaspoon Accent
¼ teaspoon pepper
½ cup oil
2 tablespoons white vinegar

Toast almonds and seeds for 15 minutes at 300°. Mix all ingredients. Shake all dressing ingredients together. Just before serving, add dressing and toss.

Marie Johnson (Mrs. David)

SPINACH SALAD
Our favorite salad! The dressing is outstanding!

Dressing:
1 cup vegetable oil
2 tablespoons sugar
5 tablespoons red wine
  vinegar
4 tablespoons sour cream
1 ½ teaspoons salt
½ teaspoon dry mustard
¼ teaspoon black pepper,
  coarsely ground
2 teaspoons parsley, chopped
2 cloves garlic, crushed
Salad:
1 bag fresh spinach, remove
  stems and wash
½ head lettuce, torn
8 slices bacon, fried, drained,
  and crumbled
4 hard-boiled eggs, sliced
croutons

Put ingredients for dressing in a bowl and mix with a wire whisk. Mix dressing at least 6 hours before serving. Toss salad ingredients in a large salad bowl. Pour dressing over salad. Toss again and serve.

Marianne Wright (Mrs. Robert)

SPINACH SALAD

1 package spinach, cleaned
  and torn
½ 8-ounce can water chestnuts, drained and sliced
2 large hard-boiled eggs, diced
5 strips bacon, fried and
  crumbled
1 green onion, sliced
Dressing:
  ½ cup vinegar
  ½ cup catsup
  1 cup oil
  ½ cup sugar
  2 tablespoons Worcester-
    shire sauce

Combine salad ingredients and toss together. Shake dressing ingredients together in a jar. Pour over spinach mixture, toss, and serve.

Bernadette Shekleton (Mrs. Michael)

SPINACH SALAD

2 pounds raw spinach
2 hard-boiled eggs, chopped
1 or 2 8-ounce cans water
   chestnuts, sliced
½ pound fresh mushrooms,
   sliced
6 slices bacon, crisply fried
   and crumbled
Dressing:
½ cup oil
¼ cup sugar
¼ cup vinegar
1 tablespoon Worcestershire
   sauce
1 medium onion, chopped

Mix dressing ingredients in blender. Pour dressing over other ingredients just before serving.

Jane Myrna (Mrs. Ted)

SPRING FRUIT SALAD WITH POPPY SEED DRESSING
Served at the Medical Auxiliary President's Luncheon

¾ cup sugar
⅓ cup vinegar
1 teaspoon dry mustard
1 teaspoon salt
1 ½ tablespoons grated onion
1 cup salad oil
1 ½ tablespoons poppy
   seeds
4 heads bibb lettuce
2 avocados, sliced
2 grapefruit, sectioned
1 pint fresh strawberries

Blend sugar, vinegar, mustard, salt and onion; add oil slowly through top of blender. Add poppy seeds last. Combine last 4 ingredients and pour dressing over. Toss gently and serve.

The Committee

MODERN CAESAR SALAD

½ cup salad oil
¼ cup red wine vinegar
1 clove garlic, crushed
2 teaspoons Worcestershire
  sauce
¼ teaspoon salt
1/16 teaspoon pepper
3 slices bread (in croutons)
½ cup Parmesan cheese
1 ounce blue cheese, crumbled
1 medium head romaine, in
  bite-size pieces
1 egg

Shake together first six ingredients. Chill a few hours. Sprinkle cheese over lettuce. Add croutons. Add egg to dressing. Shake until well blended. Add dressing to salad. Makes 6-8 servings.

Carolyn Jakopin (Mrs. Robert)

MARINATED VEGETABLE SALAD

1 16-ounce can shoe peg or
  white corn
1 16-ounce can French
  green beans
1 16-ounce can tiny peas
1 4-ounce jar chopped
  pimientos
½ cup celery, diced
½ cup onion, diced or cut in
  rings
1 small green pepper, chopped
½ cup oil
½ cup sugar
½ cup white vinegar

Drain vegetables and mix together with celery, onion, and green pepper. Mix oil, sugar, and vinegar together. Pour over vegetables; marinate overnight.

Joan Berney (Mrs. John)
Chris Palagallo (Mrs. Gerald)

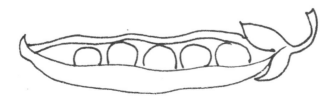

COLESLAW FOR FREEZING

1 head of cabbage, shredded
1 teaspoon salt
1 carrot, grated
1 green pepper, chopped
1 medium onion, chopped
Dressing:
  1 cup vinegar
  ¼ cup water
  2 cups granulated sugar
  1 teaspoon mustard seed
  1 teaspoon celery seeds

Mix salt with cabbage, let stand one hour then squeeze out excess moisture. Add carrots, onion, and pepper to cabbage. Combine dressing ingredients and boil for 1 minute. Cool to lukewarm and add to cabbage. Mix well. Put in freezer containers to freeze. Thaws in a short time. May be refrozen.

Ann Nace (Mrs. William)

COLESLAW

6 cups cabbage, sliced thinly
¼ cup sugar
1 cup carrots, shredded finely
½ teaspoon salt
¼ teaspoon pepper
½ cup milk
Dressing:
  1 cup mayonnaise
  ½ cup dairy buttermilk (can use powdered)
  ½ teaspoon celery seeds
  2-3 drops hot pepper sauce
  3 tablespoons dry, minced onions

Toss cabbage with sugar, carrots, salt, and pepper. Drench mixture in milk. Cover and refrigerate about 15-20 minutes. Combine mayonnaise, buttermilk, celery seeds, hot pepper sauce, and minced onions. Mix well with cabbage mixture. Refrigerate again for at least an hour before serving. Drain some of the dressing off first and serve it separately for those who wish a juicier slaw. To maintain freshness, keep covered tightly and refrigerate up to 5 days.

Rita Luetkemeyer (Mrs. Richard)

CARROT SALAD

1 pound carrots, cooked just
  until tender
½ onion
lemon juice
1 green pepper
1 tomato
Dressing:
  1 shallot
  several sprigs of fresh
    parsley
  ½ teaspoon dry mustard
  1/16 teaspoon pepper
  ½ teaspoon salt
  2 tablespoons tomato paste
  2 tablespoons brown sugar
    (or honey)
  4 tablespoons vinegar
  8 tablespoons oil

Slice the cooked carrots (using the medium serrated slicing disc of food processor if you have one) and transfer to a salad bowl. Chop the green pepper and onion (use lemon juice to rub into onion to cut bitterness).

Prepare the dressing by mincing the shallot and parsley first, then adding all the seasonings and liquids, processing until smooth (use either a blender or food processor). If very thick, add a little water. Pour over salad.

Cut the tomato into tiny chunks; toss with the rest of the salad and chill over night.

Jo Dorsch (Mrs. Thomas)

COLD RICE SALAD

1 package chicken flavored
  Rice-a-Roni
12 large black olives, sliced
4 green onions, sliced
1 small green pepper,
  chopped
1 or 2 jars marinated artichoke hearts, cut up
⅓ cup marinade from artichokes
⅓ cup mayonnaise
¾ teaspoon curry powder

Cook Rice-a-Roni according to package directions and cool slightly. Add olives, onions, green pepper, artichoke hearts and mix. Mix together the marinade, mayonnaise, and curry powder. Add this dressing to the rice mixture and stir well. Refrigerate before serving.

Marg Norris (Mrs. Paul)

CRUNCHY CAULIFLOWER SALAD

1 medium head of cauliflower
1 cup radishes, sliced
½ cup green onions, sliced
1 8-ounce can water chest-
    nuts, sliced & drained
¾ cup sour cream
¾ cup mayonnaise
2 teaspoons caraway seeds
1 package buttermilk salad
    dressing mix

Wash cauliflower and break into flower-ettes. Combine with next three ingredients in mixing bowl. Stir together remaining ingredients and pour over vegetables. Stir well. Spoon into serving bowl. Cover and chill.

Berenice Consigny (Mrs. Paul)

CREAMY POTATO SALAD

8 medium potatoes
⅓ cup Italian dressing
¾ cup celery, sliced
⅓ cup green onions and tops,
    sliced
4 hard boiled eggs, chopped
1 cup mayonnaise
½ cup dairy sour cream
1 ½ teaspoons horseradish
    mustard or Dijon
few drops yellow food color-
    ing (optional)
parsley to garnish

Cook potatoes in jackets; peel and slice when done. While potatoes are still warm, pour on Italian dressing. Chill 2 hours. Add celery, green onions and tops, and hard boiled eggs. Mix mayonnaise, sour cream, and mustard. May add a few drops of yellow food coloring for good eye appeal. The addition of food coloring makes the mayonnaise mixture look homemade. Mix into potato mixture. Chill several hours. Garnish with parsley and serve.

Marianne Wright (Mrs. Robert)

MARY'S SPECIAL POTATO SALAD

4-5 large or 6 medium red
    potatoes, boiled in skins
1 24-ounce carton small curd
    cottage cheese
¾ cup mayonnaise
1 small onion, thinly sliced
1 teaspoon celery seed
salt and pepper to taste in
    cottage cheese

Peel warm potatoes and slice into serving dish. Combine remaining ingredients. Layer potatoes with cottage cheese and mayonnaise mixture (about 4 layers). Begin with potatoes and end with cottage cheese mixture. Cover tightly and refrigerate at least 24 hours before serving.

Mary Ward (Mrs. Clarence V. Ward, Jr.)

SU NO MONO (VINEGARED BROCCOLI SALAD)

1 pound broccoli
4 radish roses (Garnish)
Dressing:
  ½ cup rice vinegar
  1 tablespoon sugar
  ¼ teaspoon dry mustard

Divide broccoli into flowerettes. Trim stalks to one inch. Bring large pot of salted water to a rapid boil over high heat. Add broccoli and cook until crisp-tender, 5 to 6 minutes. Drain and rinse with cold running water. Drain well and pat dry with paper towels. Refrigerate. When ready to serve, spoon dressing over top. Garnish with radish roses. Serves 4.

Jo Dorsch (Mrs. Tom)

TOMATO BROCCOLI SALAD

2 pounds broccoli, cut into
  flowerettes, cooked & cooled
2 small onions, chopped
2 cloves garlic, crushed
¼ cup butter
2 tablespoons vegetable oil
4 medium tomatoes, chopped
2 teaspoons sugar
1 teaspoon basil leaves,
  crushed
1 teaspoon oregano leaves
1 cup mayonnaise
few cherry tomatoes

Saute onion and garlic in butter and oil until transparent. Stir in tomatoes, sugar and spices. Simmer, uncovered, over medium heat for 15 minutes. Cool slightly. Stir in mayonnaise. Combine with broccoli. Refrigerate 3-4 hours. Garnish with cherry tomatoes.

Julie Horvath (Mrs. Fred)

ZUCCHINI-BLUE CHEESE SALAD

1 head lettuce
1 small head romaine or
   boston lettuce
¼ cup olive oil
2 medium zucchini, sliced
1 cup radishes, sliced
3 or 4 green onions, sliced
4 tablespoons blue cheese,
   crumbled (more if desired)
2 tablespoons tarragon or
   white vinegar
¾ teaspoon salt
1 small clove garlic, crushed
¼ teaspoon pepper

Tear greens in bite-size pieces. Toss with oil. Add zucchini, radishes, onions, and cheese. Mix vinegar, salt, garlic, and pepper. Pour over lettuce and toss. Serves 6-8.

Joan Berney (Mrs. John)

ZUCCHINI SALAD

4 small zucchini
1 6-ounce jar ripe olives
1 8-ounce can bamboo shoots
2 4-ounce cans mushrooms
1 8-ounce bottle Italian
   salad dressing
½ envelope ranch style
   dressing

Cut zucchini into bite-size pieces. Cut olives in half. Drain all vegetables and mix together. Mix Italian dressing with ranch dressing. Pour over vegetables. Let stand covered in refrigerator overnight.

Joan Leu (Mrs. Richard)

CUCUMBER MOUSSE
An elegant jello salad; tastes good with anything.

¾ cup boiling water
1 3-ounce package lime Jello
1 cup small-curd cottage cheese
1 cup mayonnaise
2 tablespoons onion, grated
1 cup unpeeled cucumber, grated
1 cup slivered almonds (optional)

Pour boiling water on Jello; dissolve and cool. Add remaining ingredients and blend. Pour into mold and refrigerate until set. Unmold. Serve on lettuce leaf or from a platter for buffet.

Bernadette Shekleton (Mrs. Michael)

GRANNY'S CREAM CHEESE SALAD
A holiday favorite at our house!

1 6-ounce (large) package lemon gelatin
¼ cup water
1 3-ounce package cream cheese, softened
½ cup sugar
1 cup crushed pineapple, well drained (save juice)
1 5-ounce bottle maraschino cherries, drained, finely chopped and blotted on paper toweling
¼ cup green pepper, finely chopped (optional)
½ pint whipping cream, whipped

Soak lemon gelatin in the ¼ cup water. Drain juice from pineapple and add enough water to make 1-¾ cups liquid. Bring liquid to boil and add the cream cheese and sugar, which have been beaten together. Boil until sugar-cheese combination is dissolved. Add gelatin, stirring until well mixed. When cool, add pineapple, cherries, and green pepper. Refrigerate until slightly set. Whip cream and fold into gelatin mixture. Pour into quart-sized mold or dish. Refrigerate until set. Unmold or cut into slices and serve on lettuce leaves. Serves 8. Great for Christmas using lime gelatin in place of lemon.

Kathleen Heinzen (Mrs. Frederick)

FROZEN FRUIT SALAD

1 6-ounce can frozen orange
   juice, thawed
1 6-ounce can water
1 cup sugar
1 8-ounce can crushed
   pineapple
1 16-ounce can apricots,
   drained & cut into pieces
2 bananas, cut up (not mashed)

Mix orange juice with water and sugar. Add pineapple, apricots and bananas. Put in baking paper cups in muffin pan. When frozen, it can be taken out of tins and put in plastic bag for storage in freezer. Serves 14.

Kathryn Cohen (Mrs. A.E.)

FRUIT SALAD O'BRIAN
Excellent accompaniment to fowl and pork. A nice addition to a buffet table.

2 20-ounce cans pineapple
   chunks, well drained
1 10-ounce bar mild cheddar
   cheese, cut in 1/4-inch squares
1 1/2 cups miniature marshmallows
1 10-ounce jar maraschino
   cherries, drained
1/2 cup pecan halves
Sauce:
Pineapple juice, drained from
   the 2 20-ounce cans pineapple chunks
2 eggs
1 tablespoon plus 2 tea-
   spoons flour
Pinch of salt
3/4 cup sugar

In a large bowl, gently stir the drained pineapple chunks, cheese squares, marshmallows, drained cherries and pecan halves.

Sauce: In a 2-quart saucepan, beat the pineapple juice and eggs together. Mix the flour, salt and sugar together and add to the juice-egg combination, stirring well. Bring to a boil, over medium heat, stirring frequently so it doesn't burn. Cook until thickened. Cool sauce and stir into fruit mixture. Refrigerate. May be served in a large bowl for buffet or on a lettuce leaf for individual salads. This can be made the day before. Serves 10.

Kathleen Heinzen (Mrs. Frederick)

FROZEN PINEAPPLE SALAD (OR DESSERT)
Great to have on hand for last-minute company.

1 15-ounce can crushed
  pineapple
1 3-ounce package lime
  gelatin
1 8-ounce package butter
  mints
1 10-ounce container Cool
  Whip

Pour undrained pineapple in a bowl; sprinkle gelatin on top. Refrigerate overnight. Crush mints in blender; add mints and Cool Whip to gelatin mixture and mix well. Place in shallow pan and freeze.

Pat Russo (Mrs. Frank)

FINGER JELLO
Kids love this! Can eat with their fingers, and it won't melt!

3 envelopes Knox gelatin
1 cup cold water
3 3-ounce boxes cherry Jello
½ cup sugar
½ 3-ounce package lemon
  Jello
4 cups water

Mix Knox gelatin with 1 cup cold water. Add cherry jello and sugar. Stir in lemon Jello and mix well. Heat 4 cups water to almost boiling; pour into Jello mixture and mix well. Pour into a 9 x 13-inch pan and chill. Cut in small squares. For Valentine's Day try cutting Jello with heart-shaped cookie cutter. For St. Patrick's Day, use lime Jello and shamrock cookie cutter. Nutritious treat for school parties.

Rita Luetkemeyer (Mrs. Richard)

SUNSHINE SALAD
A tasty pick up, summer or winter

1 20-ounce can pineapple chunks, including the juice
4 apples, unpeeled, diced
4 bananas, sliced
5 oranges, sectioned and sliced with any juices from oranges
½ cup coconut, shredded
½ cup pecans, chopped
1 ½ teaspoons vanilla

Combine all ingredients in a large 2-quart tupperware bowl. Seal container and invert for 1-2 minutes. Refrigerate right side up.

Irene Crane (Mrs. Donald)

7-UP JELLO SALAD

1 3-ounce package lemon Jello
1 cup boiling water
1 cup 7-Up (instead of cold water)
1 8-ounce can crushed pineapple, drained
2 bananas, diced
1 cup miniature marshmallows
Whipped cream or Cool Whip

Mix Jello with hot water and then add 7-Up. Add drained pineapple, bananas, and marshmallows. When set, frost with whipped cream or Cool Whip.

Mary Ann Smith (Mrs. Edward)

STRAWBERRY SALAD

1 6-ounce box strawberry gelatin
2 cups boiling water
1 10-ounce package frozen strawberries
2 bananas, mashed
1 8-ounce can crushed pineapple and juice
1 cup (½ pint) sour cream

Dissolve gelatin in boiling water. Add frozen strawberries. When strawberries are well thawed, add bananas and pineapple with juice. Let set partially. Pour half in mold, spread with sour cream and pour rest of gelatin on top.

Barbara Malcolm (Mrs. Robert)

LEMON LIME FRUIT JELLO SALAD
Goes well with chicken and noodle casserole or individual ribbon sandwiches.

½ of 3-ounce box lemon Jello
½ of 3-ounce box lime Jello
1 ½ cups pineapple juice, unsweetened (can use juice from crushed pineapple)
Lemon juice to taste (few drops)
1 16-ounce carton small curd cottage cheese, drained well in sieve
1 8-ounce can crushed pineapple, unsweetened, drained well in sieve
¼ cup celery, chopped fine
2 green onions, chopped fine
2 slices cucumber, seeds removed, chopped fine
¼ to ½ cup seedless green grapes, sliced lengthwise

Mix lemon and lime Jellos. Add boiling pineapple juice. Stir until dissolved. When cool, add lemon juice to taste. Whirl cottage cheese in a blender. Add Jello and whirl both together. Pour into a 6 x 10-inch Pyrex dish and add remaining ingredients. Chill until firm. Serve on lettuce leaves. Serves 6 to 8.

Bernice Whittaker (Mrs. Lorin)

RAINBOW RIBBON SQUARES
Takes some time, but it's well worth it.

5 3-ounce packages fruit flavored gelatin (any 5 different flavors)
6 ¼ cups boiling water
1 cup sour cream or plain or vanilla yogurt

Dissolve 1 package gelatin in 1¼ cups boiling water. Pour ¾ cup into a 9-inch square pan. Chill until set but not firm, about 15 minutes. Chill the remaining gelatin in bowl; gradually blend in 3 tablespoons of sour cream and spoon over gelatin in pan. Chill until set but not firm. Repeat for each remaining flavor of gelatin. Chill at least 2 hours. Cut into squares to serve to show off the rainbow colors.

Pat Russo (Mrs. Frank)

CELERY SEED DRESSING

2 teaspoons dry mustard
¾ cup sugar
1 ½ teaspoons salt
¼ medium-size onion, grated
2 teaspoons paprika
½ cup vinegar
2 cups salad oil
1 egg yolk
1 tablespoon celery seed

Chill vinegar and oil. Whip all ingredients until thick. Add celery seeds to above ingredients. Store in refrigerator.

Rhoda Turow (Mrs. I.L.)

MOTHER'S BLUE CHEESE DRESSING
Once you taste homemade dressing, you'll never serve store-bought again!

2 tablespoons white vinegar
1 4-ounce package blue
  cheese
½ teaspoon Accent, optional
½ teaspoon black pepper
1 teaspoon salt
½ cup green onions, finely
  chopped
1 8-ounce carton sour cream
1 cup mayonnaise

Mash together vinegar and blue cheese with a fork. Then mix all ingredients. Let sit about 2 hours in refrigerator before serving. Great on salads or as a dip for raw vegetables or chips.

Marianne Wright (Mrs. Robert)

CURRY SALAD DRESSING

¼ cup vegetable oil
1 small onion, minced
1 stalk celery, minced
½ green pepper, minced
1 tablespoon curry powder
1 cup water
¼ to 1 cup mayonnaise

Heat vegetable oil. Saute onion, celery, and green pepper until soft. Add curry powder and water. Bring to a boil; reduce heat and simmer 15 minutes. Sieve and let cool. Add ¼ to 1 cup mayonnaise to taste.

Joan Berney (Mrs. John)

CHEDDAR CHEESE SALAD DRESSING

1 ½ cups mayonnaise
½ cup buttermilk
½ cup cheddar cheese,
  finely shredded
dash Worcestershire sauce
dash red wine vinegar
1/16 teaspoon salt
1/16 teaspoon pepper

Combine all ingredients in medium bowl and blend thoroughly. Store tightly covered in refrigerator.

Dottie Flores (Mrs. Richard)

FRUIT SALAD DRESSING
Good on any fruit salad, especially romaine and fresh pineapple.

1 tablespoon flour
1 cup sugar
½ cup pineapple juice
¼ cup orange juice
¼ cup lemon juice
2 eggs, beaten
Whipped cream or sour cream

Mix flour, sugar, juices. Add eggs. Cook on top of double boiler until smooth and thick. Add whipped or sour cream to a little of it as you use it. Keeps well in refrigerator.

Dottie Flores (Mrs. Richard)

POPPY SEED SALAD DRESSING

¾ cup sugar
1 cup vegetable oil
⅓ cup cider vinegar
⅛ teaspoon grated onion
1 teaspoon salt
1 teaspoon dry mustard
1 ½ tablespoons poppy
  seeds

Combine all ingredients except poppy seeds in blender; process on high until well blended. Stir in poppy seeds. Chill thoroughly; stir well before serving. Yield: 1 ¾ cups.

Julie Horvath (Mrs. Fred)

WESTERN SALAD DRESSING MIX

Master Mix
2 tablespoons salt
2 teaspoons MSG
2 teaspoons parsley flakes
1 teaspoon garlic powder
1 teaspoon black pepper
½ teaspoon onion powder

Stir all of the above ingredients together and store in an airtight container. Makes 4 pints of dressing by using the following recipes.

1. Western Dressing
3 ⅛ teaspoons Western
   Salad Dressing Master Mix
1 cup mayonnaise
1 cup buttermilk

Use a wire whisk to mix in a medium bowl. Cover and refrigerate 24 hours before serving.

2. Creamy Herb Dressing
3 ⅛ teaspoons Western
   Salad Dressing Master Mix
1 cup mayonnaise
1 cup buttermilk
1 tablespoon chopped chives
½ teaspoon dried tarragon
   leaves, crushed

Prepare as directed for Western Dressing. Cover and chill 24 hours.

3. Creamy Italian Dressing
3 ⅛ teaspoons Western
   Salad Dressing Master Mix
1 cup mayonnaise
1 cup buttermilk
1/16 teaspoon cayenne
1 teaspoon dried Italian
   seasoning, crushed

Prepare as directed for Western Salad Dressing. Cover and chill for 24 hours.

Kristy Gorenz (Mrs. David)

WHITE WINE FRENCH DRESSING

4 tablespoons white wine
4 tablespoons lemon juice
1 cup salad oil
1 teaspoon salt
¼ teaspoon sugar
1 teaspoon dry mustard
1 garlic clove, optional

Combine all ingredients in food processor or jar with tight-fitting lid; mix. Refrigerate until ready to use.

Marilyn Wood (Mrs. John)

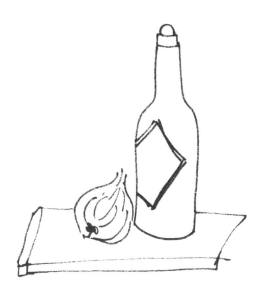

NOTES

Entrees

BROILED BEEF TENDERLOIN WITH MUSHROOM SAUCE
Elegant—your guests will rave!

1 beef tenderloin, 5 to 6
  pounds
⅓ cup butter
1 large clove garlic
½ pound fresh mushrooms,
  sliced
2 medium onions, sliced
Ground trimmings from meat
  or ¼ pound hamburger
2 tablespoons chili sauce
1 tablespoon Diable Sauce
pinch dried marjoram
pinch dried thyme
pinch hickory smoked salt
4 drops Tabasco
2 dashes Worcestershire
  sauce
5 ounces dry red wine
2 ounces condensed beef
  bouillon
salt and pepper
1 tablespoon flour

Sauce: Melt the butter in a large skillet. Cut garlic lengthwise into slivers and saute with mushrooms and onions in hot butter until the onions are limp. Add the ground meat and break up with a fork while stirring constantly. After 4 or 5 minutes add remaining ingredients and stir well. Simmer until ready to pour over tederloin when it is placed in a roaster.

To cook tenderloin: Preheat the oven and broiling pan for 15 minutes at 550° (broil). Have the tenderloin at room temperature and place on the broiling pan not more than 2 inches from the heat. Cook 8 minutes. Turn and cook for 7 minutes. Remove from the broiler and place in a roaster. Pour the sauce over the tenderloin and cook in a 350° oven for about 15 to 20 minutes. Pour the sauce from the roaster over the meat and serve.

Helen Schendl (Mrs. Raymond)
Dolores Sheen (Mrs. John)

THOMPSON'S FAVORITE ROAST BEEF
Recipe from one of Peoria's leading supermarkets.

⅓ cup dry mustard
2 cloves garlic, finely
  chopped
½ teaspoon pepper
¼ teaspoon onion salt
1 teaspoon Worcestershire
  sauce
2 teaspoons lemon juice
3 tablespoons butter, melted
4-5 pound boneless rolled
  chuck roast
6 strips bacon

Mix mustard, garlic, pepper, onion salt, Worcestershire sauce, lemon juice, and butter into a paste and rub into roast. Let stand about 30 minutes. Preheat oven to 425°. Place 6 strips of bacon over roast. Place in oven and reduce heat to 350°. Cook 15 minutes per pound for rare, 20 minutes per pound for medium. Let stand 15 minutes before carving.

The Committee

BEEF WELLINGTON

Don't be afraid to try this—it's surprisingly easy! A great dinner party entree because all the work can be done in advance.

PASTRY (1)
4 cups flour
1 cup unsalted butter, room temperature, cut into pieces
6 tablespoons shortening
1 teaspoon salt
1 teaspoon lemon juice
10 to 12 tablespoons ice water

MEAT (2)
3 to 4 pound beef tenderloin
3 tablespoons soft butter
⅓ cup cognac

DUXELLES (3)
½ cup butter
2 green onions, finely chopped
1 pound mushrooms, finely chopped
salt

ASSEMBLY (4)
salt
1 egg white, lightly beaten
1 egg yolk
1 teaspoon cream or milk

1. Make pastry in advance and refrigerate: In large bowl mix together flour, butter, shortening and salt until mixture resembles coarse meal. Pour lemon juice and 10 tablespoons (½ cup plus 2 tablespoons) ice water over mixture and toss lightly. Gather into a ball. Wrap and refrigerate until ready to use.

2. Preheat oven to 450°. Trim filet if needed. Rub with butter and pepper. Place meat thermometer into filet. Roast on a rack until thermometer reads 120° (about 20-25 minutes). Remove from oven. Flame with cognac. Cool on a rack, then refrigerate.

3. While meat is cooling, prepare the duxelles: Melt butter in large skillet. Saute green onions until translucent. Add mushrooms. Cook slowly over low heat until mushrooms lose moisture, turn dark, and develop a dry look. Add salt to taste. Chill.

4. Roll pastry out ¼-inch thick, large enough to envelop meat completely, allowing an overlap at bottom and ends. Spread pastry with chilled duxelles. Place filet in the center. Sprinkle with salt. Bring edges of pastry together, paint with egg white and secure. Place seam side down on a baking sheet. Cut small decorations from leftover pastry and fasten to roll with egg white. Mix yolk and cream and brush roll completely. Let dry several minutes. Refrigerate until ready to complete baking.

All of the above can be done the day before.

SAUCE ESPAGNOLE (5)

¼ cup butter
½ cup onion, finely chopped
½ cup carrots, finely chopped
2 tablespoons parsley, finely chopped
½ teaspoon thyme
½ bay leaf
¼ cup flour
2 ½ cups beef broth or bouillon
1 cup dry white wine
1 tablespoon tomato paste
salt and pepper to taste
1 4-ounce can mushrooms, drained (optional)

5. Prepare Sauce Espagnole: Melt butter in saucepan. Add next five ingredients and cook over low heat, stirring constantly, until vegetables are soft and begin to brown. Remove from heat and blend in flour. Increase heat to medium and continue cooking, stirring constantly, until roux turns brown. Stir in broth and wine. Bring to boiling point and simmer 30-40 minutes. Add tomato paste and salt and pepper to taste. Add mushrooms if desired. Can prepare day ahead and reheat just before using.

6. Preheat oven to 425°. Place filet on cookie sheet and bake 10 minutes. Reduce heat to 375° and bake 20-25 minutes longer (at 20 minutes meat will be quite rare). Remove from oven and let stand 10 minutes before carving. Serve with Sauce Espagnole. Makes 6 to 8 servings.

Marilyn Bauer (Mrs. James)

SAUERBRATEN RHINELAND
Serve with noodles, potato dumplings, or spatzle.

1 ½ cups vinegar
1 ½ cups water
2 bay leaves
12 whole cloves
¼ teaspoon pepper
½ teaspoon mace
1 ½ teaspoons salt
1 tablespoon sugar
2 large onions, sliced thin
3 to 4 pounds beef, heel of
   round, rump or arm roast
½ cup all-purpose flour
4 tablespoons shortening or
   oil

Heat vinegar, water, bay leaves, cloves, pepper, mace, salt and sugar to boiling point. Pour over sliced onions and allow to stand to cool. Place meat in crock or large casserole (not aluminum). Pour marinade over the meat and cover. Place in refrigerator for 5 days, turning meat once a day so it will pickle evenly. Remove meat from marinade. Strain, but save the liquid. Wipe meat dry. Dredge with flour and season with salt and pepper and paprika. Brown meat on all sides in hot shortening. When brown, add 1 cup strained marinade. Cover. Bring to steaming point, then reduce heat to simmer. Continue adding marinade as needed and pour more water through strained spices and onions if extra liquid is required (even for the gravy). Cook until tender (usually about 2 or 2 ½ hours). Remove meat to hot platter and keep warm. Make brown gravy: If there should be much fat remaining on top of pan liquid, skim. Mix 3 tablespoons flour in ½ cup extra marinade or water and add to liquid in pan, stirring constantly. Add any remaining marinade and water to make 2 or 2 ½ cups total gravy. Cook until thickened and smooth. Serves 10. (You may use smaller quantity of meat but suggest you still use same amount of marinade and cut down cooking time.)

Kathleen Heinzen (Mrs. Frederick J.)

ELAINE'S BEEF BRISKET

Beef brisket (any size)
Worcestershire sauce
Paprika
Garlic Powder
Nature's Seasoning
Dry mustard
Roast Meat Seasoning*
Lawry's salt
Ground pepper

Coat the brisket and season well with all of the remaining ingredients. Place in a large roasting pan and add water to near top of meat. Do not cover. Brown in a 400° oven for ½ hour. Cover pan with foil and continue baking at 350° until tender, about 3 hours. Remove meat from the broth, cool, slice, and return to broth and reheat. Broth may also be thickened. Serve with mashed potatoes or grits and candied sliced carrots. Excellent when sliced and used for sandwiches with barbecue sauce.

* Available at Hickory Farms

Joyce Rashid (Mrs. Ameel)

BEEF BRISKET

Beef brisket
1 package dry onion
  soup
¼ to ½ cup barbecue
  sauce
½ cup sherry

Place beef brisket in the center of a large piece of aluminum foil. Combine remaining ingredients and pour over brisket. Close wrap tightly. Bake at 350° for 3 hours or until fork tender. Let cool. Let fat come to the top of gravy and skim off (may hasten this process by refrigerating). Cut meat thinly across the grain. Add gravy and rewarm.

Goldijean Turow (Mrs. Alan)

EASY DELICIOUS ROAST BEEF

2 to 3 pound eye of round roast
1 16-ounce bottle Italian salad dressing

Marinate roast in dressing for 3 to 6 hours. Put roast in shallow baking dish. Preheat oven to 450°. Sear roast in hot oven for 30 minutes. Reduce oven to 250° and cook for 2 hours. Delicious sliced for dinner or sandwiches.

Rebecca Whittaker (Mrs. Lorin D., Jr.)

BAVARIAN-STYLE POT ROAST
This is a great change of pace pot roast. The gravy is fantastic!

2 tablespoons all-purpose flour
2 teaspoons salt
¼ teaspoon pepper
1 3-4 pound blade-cut chuck roast
2 tablespoons vegetable oil
2 medium onions, quartered
1 bay leaf
½-1 teaspoon caraway seeds
2 tablespoons white vinegar
¼ cup water

Combine flour, salt, and pepper; mix well. Dredge roast in seasoned flour, reserving excess flour. Brown roast on all sides in hot oil in a large Dutch oven; drain off drippings. Add remaining ingredients to roast; cover and simmer 3 hours or until meat is tender. If gravy is desired, thicken pan liquid with reserved seasoned flour. I usually use Wondra flour to thicken the gravy because it doesn't turn lumpy.

Marianne Wright (Mrs. Robert)

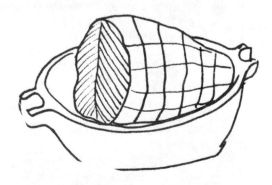

COLD MARINATED BEEF DELUXE
Great for picnics or tailgates

2 cups water
few drops lemon juice
¼ teaspoon salt
1 large onion, sliced in
  rings
15 large mushrooms, sliced
1 ½-2 pounds cold roast beef,
  cooked rare and thinly
  sliced
½ cup red wine vinegar
2 teaspoons Dijon mustard
1 teaspoon salt
¼ teaspoon crushed marjoram
¼ teaspoon pepper
1 cup salad oil or ½ cup
  salad and ½ cup olive oil
2 tablespoons chopped
  parsley

Bring to boil the water, lemon juice, and salt. Drop in onion rings; remove immediately and drain. Place onions and mushrooms on top of meat slices. Mix together the remaining ingredients, except the parsley, and pour over the meat. Refrigerate until time to serve; then sprinkle with parsley. Serves 6-8. I usually serve with French bread or Kaiser rolls.

Marianne Wright (Mrs. Robert)

EASY BEEF BRISKET
Tastes even better a day later!

1 3 to 4-pound beef brisket
1 8-ounce bottle Italian
  dressing
1 cup burgundy or rose wine
1 4-ounce can mushrooms,
  sliced and drained

Place brisket in shallow baking pan. Pour dressing and wine over brisket. Cover and marinate overnight in refrigerator. Roast in a 325° oven, covered, for 3 hours. Remove from oven. Slice thin and return to oven. Add the mushrooms, making sure the meat slices are submerged in marinade. Cover pan and continue baking at 325° for 45 minutes. Serves 8.

Irene Crane (Mrs. Donald)

HAWAIIAN STEAK KEBABS
Let guests assemble their own!

¾ cup canned pineapple juice, drained from 20-ounce can chunks packed in natural juices
¼ cup corn oil
3 tablespoons soy sauce
2 tablespoon brown sugar
1 teaspoon ground ginger (or less, to taste)
1 garlic clove or ⅛ teaspoon garlic powder
2 to 2 ½ pounds chuck cubes or 1 chuck roast with bone (4 pounds cut into cubes)
vegetables*

Combine all ingredients except pineapple chunks, meat, and vegetables. Remove fat from meat and cut in uniform-sized cubes. Place cubes in a glass or china bowl; pour marinade over them. Cover bowl and refrigerate overnight. Remove meat from marinade and place on metal skewers with pineapple chunks and vegetables.* Place skewers on grill; cook 4-5 minutes on each side.
*Choose from any combination of onion, green pepper, mushrooms, cherry tomatoes.

Jo Dorsch (Mrs. Thomas)

BEEF-GREEN PEPPER-TOMATO

1 pound sirloin or round steak, cut in thin strips
4 beef bouillon cubes
4 cups boiling water
salt, pepper, garlic salt to taste
1 teaspoon sugar
1 tablespoon soy sauce
2 green peppers, cut in chunks
3 green onions, cut in small pieces
4 tablespoons cornstarch
¼ cup cold water
3 tomatoes, cut in wedges

Brown meat in a little oil. Add bouillon cubes, water, sugar and soy sauce, along with salt, pepper and garlic salt. Simmer 45 to 60 minutes or until tender. Add green peppers and green onions. Simmer 5 minutes more. Thicken with cornstarch, dissolved in ¼ cup cold water. Add tomatoes. Simmer just to heat tomatoes. Serve with rice. Serves 6.

Eleanor Pflederer (Mrs. Robert A.)

BLACK PEPPER STEAK

Black Pepper Sauce:
1 10½-ounce can consomme
6 tablespoons butter
2 teaspoons peppercorns,
   ground or crushed
1 cup fresh mushrooms,
   sliced or 4 ½-ounce jar
   sliced mushrooms, drained
⅔ cup water
1 ½ to 2 pounds top sirloin
3 tablespoons butter
½ cup brandy

Heat the consomme, butter, peppercorns, mushrooms, and water for pepper sauce in a saucepan. Quickly saute meat in butter in large skillet on both sides. Amount of time depends on how well done meat is preferred. When ready, add brandy to meat and flame off. When flame is gone, add the black pepper sauce to meat and simmer for 3 or 4 minutes. Serve with seasoned, browned rice or wild rice. Serves 4.

Kathleen Heinzen (Mrs. Frederick J.)

PEPPER STEAK

1 pound beef chuck or better
   quality of beef, cut into 3 x
   1-inch pieces
¼ cup vegetable oil
½ clove garlic, minced
2 tablespoons soy sauce
1 teaspoon salt
¼ cup water
1 cup green peppers, cut
   into 1-inch pieces
1 cup onions, chopped
1 cup fresh mushrooms,
   sliced in large pieces
½ cup celery, chopped
1 tablespoon cornstarch
½ cup water
2 tomatoes, cut into eighths
3 to 4 cups cooked rice

Brown beef in hot oil. Add garlic and cook until yellow. Add soy sauce, salt and water. Cover and cook 45 minutes. Add all vegetables except tomatoes. Cook 30 minutes or longer if preferred; stir in cornstarch blended with water. Add tomatoes and cook without stirring for 10 minutes. If it becomes too dry, add a little water. Serve over hot fluffy rice. Serves 4.

Judy Zimdars (Mrs. John)

ROUND STEAK ITALIANO

2 pounds round steak
8 to 10 ounces bulk Italian
sausage
1 8-ounce can tomato sauce
¾ cup apple juice
½ cup onion, chopped
½ teaspoon garlic salt
¼ teaspoon oregano
⅛ teaspoon pepper

Cut steak into eight serving pieces. Pound to tenderize and brown in small amount of cooking oil. Remove from skillet. Brown sausage and drain. Add tomato sauce, apple juice, onion, and spices. Return meat to skillet. Cover and simmer 50 to 60 minutes. Serve over noodles. Pass Parmesan cheese to sprinkle on top. Serves 8.

Kathleen Palmer (Mrs. Ron)

ENGLISH BEEF SHORT RIBS

3 to 4 pounds beef short
ribs
2 teaspoons salt
1 teaspoon thyme
½ teaspoon savory
⅛ teaspoon pepper
1 cup water
4 small onions, sliced
1 tablespoon brown sugar
1 tablespoon vinegar
1 tablespoon prepared
mustard
2 tablespoons flour
¼ cup water
½ cup buttermilk

Place ribs in heavy skillet and cover. Cook slowly for 90 minutes, turning to brown. Pour off drippings. Sprinkle with seasonings. Add 1 cup water and cook 30 minutes. Add onions on top of meat and cook 30 minutes more or until meat is tender. Remove meat to platter. Stir sugar, vinegar, and mustard into liquid in skillet. Blend flour into ¼ cup water; add gradually and continue stirring until thickened. Stir in buttermilk. Return ribs to skillet and simmer several minutes.

Amelia Wilson (Mrs. Henry)

BEEF BURGUNDY

2 to 3 pounds beef stew
  meat, trim fat
2 10 ½-ounce cans golden
  mushroom soup
1 envelope onion soup mix
1 to 1 ¼ cups Burgundy wine

Mix all ingredients. Do not brown meat or add water. Cover and leave covered. Bake in a 300° oven for 3 to 4 hours. Serve over noodles.

Berenice Consigny (Mrs. Paul)

BEEF IN WINE SAUCE

4 slices bacon
3 pounds beef stew meat
1 onion, chopped
3 tablespoons olive oil
½ 6-ounce can tomato paste
  (3 ounces)
2 ¼ cups red wine
½ teaspoon salt
pepper
2 bay leaves
2 cloves garlic, minced
¾ cup beef broth
1 ½ pounds pearl onions

Boil bacon in water for 3 minutes. Brown beef and chopped onion in olive oil. Add tomato paste and one cup of the red wine, bacon, spices, and garlic. Simmer for 1½ hours. Add remaining wine, beef broth, and pearl onions. Continue to simmer for 1½ hours or until beef is tender. Serves 6 to 8.

Barbara Adams (Mrs. Philip)

BOEUF CHABLIS
A fancy stew, rather French

2 to 3 pounds boneless beef chuck, cut in 1 ½-inch cubes
¼ pound butter or margarine
¼ cup cognac
4 carrots, quartered and cut into 2 ½-inch sticks
3 carrots, grated
2 onions, diced
6 tablespoons flour
2 cloves garlic, finely sliced
3 bay leaves
1 ½ teaspoons thyme
1 teaspoon salt
¼ teaspoon pepper
2 cups dry white wine
1 pound fresh mushrooms, halved
16 to 20 small white onions, peeled (or onions cut into small quarters)

Trim excess fat from beef. Brown beef in butter in heavy casserole or dutch oven. Heat cognac, ignite and pour over beef. Add carrot sticks, grated carrots, diced onions, flour, garlic, bay leaves, thyme, salt and pepper; mix lightly. Stir in wine. Cover and bake in moderate oven, 325°, for 1 ½ hours, stirring every 30 minutes. Add mushrooms and onions, cover and continue baking 1 hour, stirring occasionally. Adjust seasoning to taste. Remove bay leaves. Makes 6 to 8 servings.

Alice Sullivan (Mrs. E.A.)

ITALIAN BEEF STEW WITH ROSEMARY

1 ½ pounds beef stew meat in 1-inch cubes
3 tablespoons oil
1 large onion, chopped
1 cup celery, diced
2 cloves garlic, minced
1 28-ounce can tomatoes (preferably Italian), cut up, with liquid
½ cup parsley, minced
⅔ cup dry white wine
1 ½ teaspoons salt
½ teaspoon pepper
1 teaspoon rosemary

In Dutch oven, brown beef in oil. Remove. Saute onion, celery, and garlic until tender. Return beef and remaining ingredients to pot. Bring to a boil. Lower heat, cover and simmer 1 ½ to 2 hours until meat is tender. If desired stew may be thickened by mixing 1 ½ tablespoons flour in ¼ cup cold water. Add to stew and cook until thickened. Good served with a tossed salad, French bread, and a glass of wine for a complete meal.

Bernadette Shekleton (Mrs. Michael)

NO PEEK STEW

**2 to 2 ½ pounds beef
  stew meat, trimmed**
2 cups potatoes, cut up
2 cups carrots, cut up
2 cups celery, cut up
1 large onion, cut up
**2 tablespoons Minute
  Tapioca**
1 10 ½-ounce can tomato soup
1 cup water
1 teaspoon salt
½ teaspoon pepper
1 tablespoon parsley, minced
1 teaspoon Accent
½ teaspoon basil

Mix all together. Place in a 9 x 13 x 2-inch pan. Cover tightly with aluminum foil. Bake in a 350° oven for 3 hours.

Berenice Consigny (Mrs. Paul)

MEATBALLS AND SAUCE

Sauce:
1 16-ounce can whole
  cranberry sauce
¾ cup catsup
1 teaspoon lemon juice
2 tablespoons brown sugar
Meatballs:
2 pounds hamburger
1 cup corn flakes, crushed
1 tablespoon parsley
2 tablespoons soy sauce
2 eggs
½ cup catsup
1 small onion, chopped
salt and pepper

Combine sauce ingredients. Cook in saucepan until well blended. Meanwhile mix meatball mixture adding salt and pepper to taste. Form into balls and then place in covered casserole dish. Cover with sauce. Bake 1 ½ hours at 350°. This recipe can be used with pork chops also. Just brown chops. Then cover with sauce. Bake for 1 ½ hours.

Mari Jo Baker (Mrs. Donald)

BAKED MEATBALLS

2 pounds ground beef
1 cup bread crumbs
1 package dry onion
  soup mix
3 eggs
1 12-ounce bottle chili
  sauce
1 ½ cups water
1 cup light brown sugar,
  not packed
1 cup sauerkraut, drained
1 16-ounce can whole
  cranberries

Mix meat, crumbs, soup mix, and eggs. Form into small meatballs and place in a 9 x 13 x 2-inch pan. Mix sauce ingredients and simmer ½ hour. Pour over meatballs; bake 1 hour at 350°, uncovered. This recipe freezes well.

Pam Albers (Mrs. William)

MEAT BALLS STROGANOFF

1 ½ pounds lean ground beef
¾ cup milk
¾ cup packaged bread
  crumbs
½ teaspoon salt
¼ teaspoon pepper
¾ tablespoon parsley,
  snipped
¼ cup margarine
¾ cup onion, minced
½ pound mushrooms, sliced
  or medium can
¾ teaspoon paprika
2 tablespoons flour
1 can bouillon, undiluted
½ teaspoon Worcestershire
  sauce
½ cup sour cream
Hot fluffy cooked rice

Meatballs: With fork, combine meat, milk, bread crumbs, salt, pepper, and parsley. Shape into 1 ¼-inch balls; saute in two tablespoons of the margarine until browned. Set aside.

Sauce: In remaining two tablespoons margarine, saute onions, mushrooms, and paprika about 5 minutes. Sprinkle flour over mushrooms. Stir, slowly. Add bouillon, salt, and pepper. Return meatballs to sauce, cover; simmer ten minutes. Just before serving, stir in Worcestershire sauce and sour cream and heat. Serve over cooked rice, sprinkled with dill.

Kacky Heinzen (Mrs. F. J.)

A QUICK AND EASY BEEF STEW
A hearty beef stew!

3 pounds beef stew meat,
  cut into 1 ½-inch cubes
2 cans cream of mushroom
  soup
2 3- or 4-ounce cans
  mushrooms
1 envelope dry onion soup
  mix
½ cup sherry
salt and pepper to taste

Place all of the ingredients in a large casserole. Cover and bake in a 325° oven for 2 to 3 hours. Serve over rice or noodles, with a tossed salad and garlic bread. Delicious. Serves 6.

Lois Ward (Mrs. Edward)

OVEN BROWNED BBQ MEATBALLS
"Spicy"

Meatballs:
1 pound ground beef
1 teaspoon salt
¼ teaspoon pepper
¼ cup catsup or chili sauce
1 tablespoon Worchester-
   shire sauce
¼ cup onions, chopped
½ cup cornflake crumbs
Sauce:
½ cup water
1 tablespoon flour
1 tablespoon Worcester-
   shire sauce
1 teaspoon red pepper
1 teaspoon chili powder
1/16 teaspoon salt
½ teaspoon dry mustard
1 teaspoon black pepper
1 tablespoon butter
1 cup catsup
¾ cup vinegar

Mix meatball ingredients together and form meatballs. For sauce mix together water and flour, then add remaining ingredients. Bring to a boil and pour over meatballs. Bake in a 400° oven for 15 to 20 minutes.

Ella Thompson (Mrs. Robert)

STEFADO
Beef stew with onions

3 pounds beef chuck or
   round, cut into 2-inch cubes
½ pound butter
3 cloves garlic, minced
3 bay leaves
1 cinnamon stick, broken in
   half
1 teaspoon allspice
1 ½ cups red burgundy wine
1 6-ounce can tomato paste
1 cup water
3 pounds pearl onions, peeled
½ cup olive oil

Brown beef in butter in a heavy pan or Dutch oven. Add garlic, bay leaves, cinnamon, and allspice. Stir well. Add wine, tomato paste, and water. Start simmering. Meanwhile, saute whole pearl onions in olive oil until golden brown. Add to meat mixture. Cover and simmer 2 to 2 ½ hours on very low heat. During simmering, sauce should cover meat at all times. Add water if necessary. Sauce should be thick when ready to serve.

Amelia Wilson (Mrs. Henry)

MEAT LOAF

1 pound ground beef
1 egg
¼ cup onion, chopped
¼ cup green pepper, chopped
½ cup bread crumbs
1 teaspoon salt
1 tablespoon Worcester-
    shire sauce
¼ cup milk
Sauce:
1 cup catsup
1 cup water
1 ½ teaspoons chili powder
¼ cup brown sugar

Mix all of the meat loaf ingredients together. Make into 4 or 5 individual meat
loaves and put into a margarine-greased
casserole dish. Top with sauce and bake
uncovered for 45 minutes at 350°. It is
good with rice or mashed potatoes and a
cooked vegetable; carrots, corn, or green
beans. Serves 4.

Vivian Solomon (Mrs. Ted)

SAUERBRATEN MEATBALL STEW
Ground beef with a German accent

1 pound lean ground beef
1 egg, slightly beaten
½ cup gingersnap crumbs
    (about 10 cookies)
¼ teaspoon nutmeg
1 10 ½-ounce can condensed
    cream of onion soup
1 10 ½-ounce can water
¼ cup red wine vinegar
1 tablespoon sugar
2 medium carrots, sliced
    very thin
¼ cup raisins
salt to taste

Mix first four ingredients. Form into one-
inch meatballs. Makes about 24. Brown
in skillet. Pour off fat. Add remaining
ingredients. Bring to boil. Lower heat;
cover and simmer 25 to 30 minutes.
Makes 4 servings. Good over cooked
noodles.

Bernadette Shekleton (Mrs. Michael)

VEAL PAPRIKA

¾ to 1 pound thin veal cutlets
2 to 3 tablespoons margarine
  or butter
1 ½ teaspoons paprika
2 small or medium onions,
  sliced thin
½ teaspoon salt
½ teaspoon sugar
⅓ cup dry white wine
¼ cup sour cream

Dredge veal in flour and pound veal thin if necessary. Melt butter; add paprika, onions, salt and sugar. Saute until onions are tender. Remove and add veal. Brown veal, adding more butter if necessary. Add onions over veal. Combine wine and sour cream and pour over meat. Simmer until done, 20 to 30 minutes. Garnish with parsley. Serve with poppy seed noodles. Serve 3 or 4.

Jo Dorsch (Mrs. Tom)

MEDALLIONS OF BREADED VEAL IN PARMESAN AND GRATED LEMON ZEST

8 veal scallops
flour
1 ½ cups fine bread crumbs
1 cup Parmesan cheese,
  finely grated
grated rind of 2 ½ lemons
1 teaspoon salt
⅛ teaspoon pepper
2 small eggs
3 ounces cooking oil
parsley
lemon wedges

Pound veal scallops very thin. Dredge in flour and pat between your palms to give them a thin, even dusting. In a small bowl mix bread crumbs, cheese, lemon rind, salt and pepper. In another bowl beat eggs, dip each floured scallop in egg and then into bread crumb mixture. In a large skillet heat cooking oil. Saute scallops until golden brown on both sides. Serve with a garnish of parsley and lemon wedges.

Barbara Grawey (Mrs. Gerald W.)

VEAL BIRDS

½ cup celery, chopped
1 small onion, minced
2 tablespoons margarine
2 cups bread crumbs
1 teaspoon salt
½ pound sliced bacon
2 pounds veal steak, very
  thinly sliced

Cook celery and onion in margarine until crispy tender. Add crumbs, salt and pepper to taste. Add a little water to moisten. Slice veal into 2 to 3-inch wide slices and no longer than 4 inches long. Place stuffing on each strip of veal. Roll carefully and bind with 1 or ½ slice bacon. Skewer in place with toothpicks. Roll birds in flour. Brown slowly in skillet using a small amount of oil. Transfer to a lightly greased casserole. Add drippings, thinned with water. Cover and bake in 350° oven until tender, about 45 minutes.

Variation: Instead of drippings and water, add 1 10¾-ounce can of cream of mushroom soup plus ¼ cup water. Heat and pour over veal birds. Cover and bake as directed.

Genevieve McMorrow (Mrs. T. R.)

SUSAN'S VEAL SVECKOVA

1 ½ to 2 pounds veal, cubed
4 tablespoons flour
1 teaspoon salt
⅛ teaspoon pepper
4 tablespoons butter
1 cup dry white wine
1 ½ cups onions, thinly
  sliced
1 8-ounce can mushrooms
1 cup sour cream
1 tablespoon paprika
4 cups cooked, buttered
  noodles

Mix flour, salt and pepper; dredge veal in flour mixture. Melt butter in large skillet. Add veal. Brown on all sides, turning regularly, over moderate heat. Add wine. Cover skillet and cook 15 minutes over low heat. Turn meat and drippings into large casserole. Cover with onions, then mushrooms. Spread sour cream and paprika on top. Cover and bake 45 minutes at 350°. Serve over buttered noodles.

Alice Sullivan (Mrs. E. A.)

BAKED VEAL CHOPS

½ cup cornflake crumbs
¼ cup Parmesan cheese,
  grated
½ teaspoon salt
1/16 teaspoon pepper
4 veal chops
1 egg, lightly beaten
1 8-ounce can tomato sauce
½ teaspoon oregano
½ teaspoon sugar
1/16 teaspoon onion salt
4 ounces mozzarella
  cheese, grated

Combine cornflake crumbs, Parmesan cheese, salt and pepper. Dip veal chops in lightly beaten egg, then in crumb mixture. Place in a buttered baking dish. Bake at 400° for 20 minutes. Turn and bake 20 minutes more. Combine tomato sauce, oregano, sugar, and onion salt. Heat to boiling while stirring. Pour over baked chops. Top with mozzarella cheese and continue baking until browned.

Amelia Wilson (Mrs. Harry M.)

VEAL STEW
Grammy Neuhoff's Favorite

1 pound veal stew meat,
  cubed
1 bay leaf
1 small onion, sliced
several whole cloves
1/16 teaspoon salt
1/16 teaspoon pepper
1 tablespoon margarine
2 tablespoons flour
1 egg yolk
2 slices lemon
parsley for garnish

Cover veal with water. Add bay leaf, onion, cloves, salt and pepper. Bring to a boil. Simmer slowly for 1 to 1 ½ hours, or until meat is tender. Melt margarine. Add flour to make a roux. Strain liquid from cooked veal into roux to make a thick sauce. Bring to boiling point. Remove from heat. Add egg yolk and more stock if desired. Remove bay leaf and cloves. Add lemon and cooked veal. Serve over mashed poatatoes, garnished with parsley snips. Serves 4.

Betty Neuhoff (Mrs. Carl)

NOTES

PORK ROAST

3 to 4 pounds pork roast,
boned
2 medium onions, sliced
2 cloves garlic, crushed
1 small bay leaf
1 pinch dried rosemary
salt and pepper
¾ cup dry red wine
¼ cup orange juice

Trim pork roast of all fat. Tie roast to retain shape. Put onions and garlic in heavy casserole. Place meat on top. Add bay leaf and rosemary. Salt and pepper as desired. Add ¼ of the wine. Roast in 350° oven for 35 minutes. Add remaining wine and orange juice. Cover and cook for 1 ½ hours, turning meat once or twice while cooking.

Clara Remolina (Mrs. Rodrigo)

FROZEN PORK ROAST
Dottie received this recipe from Colleen Orenic, a former member of our auxiliary.

1 frozen pork roast, 6 pounds
or less
1 package Lipton onion-
mushroom soup mix
⅓ cup onion, chopped
2 ½ cups water

Put pork roast in a roasting pan. Sprinkle with soup mix and onions. Pour in water and cover with foil. Bake in a 275° oven for 8 hours.

Dottie Flores (Mrs. Richard)

PORK IN MUSHROOM SAUCE

4 to 6 pork loin chops, at
  least one-inch thick
flour
salt and pepper
1 10 ½-ounce can cream of
  mushroom soup
½ cup sour cream
⅓ cup vermouth or white wine
8 ounces mushrooms, sauted

Dredge pork chops in flour and season with salt and pepper. Brown in a small amount of shortening. Then place in a casserole. Combine mushroom soup, sour cream, and wine. Pour over pork. Cover with foil and bake at 350° for 1 ½ hours, turning the meat once. Uncover last 20 minutes and top with sauteed mushrooms just before serving. May be made ahead and reheated except for mushrooms.

Joan Berney (Mrs. John)

MOM'S HAM LOAF

2 pounds freshly ground pork
1 pound freshly ground ham
2 eggs, beaten
1/16 teaspoon baking
  powder
1 teaspoon salt
1 cup bread crumbs
1 cup tomato juice

Mix together all ingredients. Place in baking pan and bake at 350° for 30 minutes. Cover and bake an additional one hour.

Pat Callaway (Mrs. James)

BUTTERFLY CHOPS WITH CREAMY MUSTARD TOPPING
This dish is good served with sauteed mushrooms and a spinach or broccoli souffle.

4 pork loin butterfly chops, each cut ½ inch thick
½ cup mayonnaise
⅓ cup soft bread crumbs (approximately one slice of white bread without crust)
1 tablespoon chopped parsley
1 tablespoon prepared mustard (scant)
⅛ teaspoon paprika
¼ teaspoon salt

Place pork loin butterfly chops on rack in broiling pan; broil 10 minutes, turning chops once. In small bowl with fork, mix mayonnaise, bread crumbs, parsley, mustard, paprika, and salt. When pork chops are finished cooking, spread mayonnaise mixture over chops; broil 1 minute longer or until topping is hot and bubbly. Watch carefully! Serves 4. If more chops are used, double topping ingredients.

Vivian Solomon (Mrs. Ted)

SAUCY CHOPS

8 pork chops, ½-inch thick
salt and pepper
8 ½ ounces applesauce
1 cup onion, sliced
1 cup catsup
¼ cup water
1 tablespoon soy sauce
¼ teaspoon sage or thyme

Season chops with salt and pepper. Brown in skillet. Combine applesauce, onion, catsup, water, soy sauce, and sage or thyme. Pour over meat. Cover and simmer 45 minutes or until meat is tender. Serve with rice.

Jo Dorsch (Mrs. Tom)

PORK CHOPS WITH APPLE DRESSING

6 pork chops
1 teaspoon salt
¼ teaspoon pepper
3 cups bread cubes, toasted
1 ½ cups unpared apples, chopped
½ cup seedless raisins
½ cup celery, chopped
½ cup onion, chopped
1 teaspoon poultry seasoning
½ cup canned condensed beef broth or 1 beef bouillon cube dissolved in ½ cup hot water
3 tart red apples, cored and halved

Slowly brown pork chops, seasoning well with salt and pepper. Place in shallow baking dish. Toss together all dry ingredients for the dressing. Toss lightly with the broth to moisten. Cover each chop with dressing and top with apple half. Cover dish with foil and bake at 350° for one hour or until pork is well done.

Janet Shipley (Mrs. Wm. A.)

LA STRATA
Good luncheon dish

1 pound bulk pork sausage
½ cup onion, chopped
1 8-ounce can herb tomato sauce
1 2 ½-ounce can tomato paste, optional
1 teaspoon basil
1 teaspoon parsley, chopped
¼ teaspoon oregano
1/16 teaspoon garlic salt
1/16 teaspoon pepper
1 8-ounce can mushrooms, drained
1 10-ounce package frozen spinach, thawed and drained
8 ounces low fat cottage cheese
1 12-ounce package mozzarella cheese, shredded

Preheat oven to 375°. In medium skillet, saute meat and onion until onion is tender and meat is browned. Drain fat. Add tomato sauce, tomato paste, basil, parsley, oregano, garlic salt, pepper and mushrooms. Combine spinach and cottage cheese. In an 8-inch square baking dish, arrange in layers one-half the spinach mixture, meat mixture and mozzarella cheese. Repeat with other half, ending with cheese. Bake 15 or 20 minutes or until hot and bubbly. Makes four servings.

Lorraine Zwicky (Mrs. George)

RIBS

1 18-ounce bottle Open Pit
   Bar-b-que Sauce (original)
½ cup soy sauce
3 tablespoons bead molasses
1 cup brown sugar
5 pounds back ribs, cut into
   1 rib pieces

Combine ingredients. Pour over ribs and marinate overnight, mixing twice. Remove from marinade and broil until brown. Return to marinade and bake covered for 1 hour at 350°. Serves 6. Brush ribs with marinade after broiling and bake on a large cookie sheet with edge, covered with foil.

Vivian Solomon (Mrs. Ted)

MICROWAVE SWEET AND SOUR PORK OR VEAL

1 ½ pounds cubed pork or
   veal
2 tablespoons cornstarch
3 tablespoons soy sauce
¼ cup packed brown sugar
¼ cup vinegar
1 teaspoon salt
¼ teaspoon ground ginger
1 13-ounce can pineapple
   chunks, undrained
1 small onion, thinly sliced
1 medium green pepper, cut
   into strips

Toss together meat and cornstarch in a 2-quart glass casserole. Stir in remaining ingredients except green pepper. Cover with glass lid or plastic wrap. Microwave on roast for 25 minutes. Stir in green pepper. Recover and continue cooking on roast for 5-10 minutes or until meat is tender. Let stand, covered, five minutes before serving. Serves 4-6. Serve with rice or fried noodles.

Barbara Bordeaux (Mrs. Dean)

HAM AND BROCCOLI CASSEROLE
A quick recipe to use for leftover ham.

¼ cup onion, chopped
1 10-ounce package frozen chopped broccoli, thawed and drained
2 tablespoons butter or margarine
1 10 ¾-ounce can cream of chicken soup, undiluted
2 cups cooked ham, chopped
1 cup instant rice, uncooked
½ cup processed cheese spread
¼ cup milk
½ teaspoon Worcestershire sauce
⅛ to ¼ teaspoon dry mustard
paprika, optional

In large skillet, saute onion and broccoli in butter until onion is tender. Remove from heat. Stir in remaining ingredients. Spread mixture into a lightly greased 1½-quart casserole and sprinkle with paprika if desired. Bake at 350° for 25 to 30 minutes or until bubbly. Serves 6.

Andrea Lister (Mrs. Richard)

LEFTOVER HAM SUPPER

2 cups ham, cut in strips
2 tablespoons butter
1 package long grain and wild rice mix
1 16-ounce can pineapple chunks
water

Brown ham strips in butter. Add rice mixture and package of seasoning. Drain syrup trom pineapple chunks and add enough water to make 2 ½ cups liquid. Stir into skillet. Cover and cook until liquid is absorbed. Add more water if necessary to make rice soft. Add pineapple chunks and serve.

Kackie Heinzen (Mrs. F.J.)

PORK CHOP NEOPOLITAN

6 loin pork chops, 2 pounds
2 tablespoons olive oil
1 cup onion, chopped
1 clove garlic, minced
**1 16-ounce can Italian
   tomatoes, undrained**
1 teaspoon salt
½ teaspoon oregano
½ teaspoon basil leaves
**1 large green pepper, cut into
   six wedges**
1 4-ounce can mushrooms

Wipe chops with damp paper towel. In hot oil brown chops on both sides. Remove from skillet. Using one tablespoon of oil in the skillet add onion and garlic; saute 5 minutes. Add all other ingredients except mushrooms and peppers. Add pork chops to skillet. Arrange pepper wedges in between chops, spoke fashion. Simmer, covered, 1 hour 15 minutes or until chops are tender. Add mushrooms and simmer 5 minutes longer. Serves 6.

Ines Spano (Mrs. Gregory)

NOTES

ROAST CHICKEN WITH LEMON

1 whole fryer (2 ½ pounds)
1 teaspoon salt
Freshly ground pepper
2 small lemons

Wash chicken. Pat dry inside and out. Sprinkle with salt and pepper inside and out. Puncture lemons with a fork and put inside chicken. Close cavity with string and place inside roasting pan breast side down. Roast at 350° for 20 minutes. Turn, being careful not to break skin. If not broken, it will swell like a balloon. Continue roasting 20 minutes. Turn heat to 400° and roast an additional 20 minutes or until chicken is golden.

Berenice Consigny (Mrs. Paul)

LEMON CHICKEN

3 whole chicken breasts,
  boned and skinned
¼ teaspoon salt
¼ teaspoon pepper
Juice of 1 lemon
1 tablespoon sherry
4 tablespoons cornstarch
4 tablespoons flour
2 egg whites,
  beaten until foamy
Oil to deep fry
1 tablespoon ketchup
1 tablespoon soy sauce
1 tablespoon sugar
1 tablespoon vinegar
1 tablespoon vegetable oil

Slice chicken breasts lengthwise in ½-inch strips. Combine salt, pepper, lemon juice, and sherry. Marinate chicken in lemon juice mixture for 20 minutes. Mix cornstarch and flour together well. Dip chicken in cornstarch mixture, then in egg white. Fry in oil over moderate heat until lightly brown. Drain. Cut in bite-size pieces. Heat together the ketchup, soy sauce, sugar, vinegar, and 1 tablespoon oil. Pour over chicken.

Serving suggestions: This is pretty served on a large chop plate, centered with a tomato cut in wedges but not completely cut through. Surround the tomato with steamed broccoli. Alternate the chicken with 3 cups finely cut cabbage. Garnish with sliced lemon peel.

Rosella Koerner (Mrs. C.S.M.)

LEMON CHICKEN MARSALA

4 chicken breasts,
  boned and skinned
Flour
3 tablespoons vegetable oil
3 tablespoons butter
6 cloves garlic
1 pound fresh mushrooms,
  sliced
⅓ cup sweet Marsala
1 10 ½-ounce can chicken
  broth
2 lemons
1 tablespoon cornstarch
2 tablespoons water
1 teaspoon basil
1 teaspoon oregano
Salt and pepper to taste
2 tablespoons parsley,
  minced

Cut each chicken breast into 6 strips. Coat with flour. Heat oil and butter in a large skillet. Saute chicken quickly on both sides and remove from skillet. Press garlic in pan and saute quickly. Add more butter if needed and saute mushrooms. Add Marsala and cook 2 minutes. Add chicken broth and the juice of one lemon, slowly. Mix cornstarch with water and stir in. Add basil, oregano, salt and pepper. Cook 5 minutes. Return chicken to sauce. Slice remaining lemon into about 8 rounds and place on top of chicken. Sprinkle with parsley and cook on low heat for 10 minutes. This can be made ahead by eliminating the last 10 minutes of cooking and warming in a casserole. Serve with green noodles. Serves 4 to 6.

Goldijean Turow (Mrs. Alan)

LEMON LIME BAKED CHICKEN

3 broiler chickens,
  quartered
½ cup lemon juice
½ cup lime juice
1 teaspoon salt
1 teaspoon freshly ground
  pepper
1 ½ cups dry white wine
4 cloves garlic, crushed
1 teaspoon basil or Italian
  seasoning
1 cup butter, melted
3 cups potato chips, crushed

Preheat oven to 400°. Wash and dry chicken pieces. In large bowl combine juices, salt, pepper, wine, garlic, and basil. Add the chicken and marinate in refrigerator for 4 hours. Remove chicken and pat dry. Dip each piece in melted butter. Roll in crumbled chips. Arrange in flat buttered dish and bake for 1 hour.

Mimi Adland (Mrs. Moris)

SKILLET CHICKEN

1 whole frying chicken
1 onion
5 cups water (or more)
1 cup onion, minced
3 tablespoons margarine
2 teaspoons curry powder
1 7-ounce package broad
  noodles
1 green pepper, diced
1 2-ounce jar pimiento,
  drained and chopped
1 4-ounce jar mushrooms,
  drained

Cook chicken and onion in lightly salted water until tender. Reserve at least 3½ cups chicken broth. Remove bones from chicken and cut chicken in chunks. Saute 1 cup minced onion in margarine until clear. Add curry powder to the skillet. Add at least 3 ½ cups chicken broth (or more if needed). Bring to a boil and add noodles. Cover and cook slowly for 10 minutes. Add chicken, green pepper, pimiento, and mushrooms. Cook slowly, uncovered, until noodles are tender. Remove from heat, cover, and let stand for 5 minutes before serving.

Rosella Koerner (Mrs. C. S. M.)

CHICKEN N' DUMPLINGS
An old recipe from Mike Gulley's baby sitter.

1 3-pound fat fryer
3 cups flour
1 egg, beaten
½ teaspoon salt

Stew fryer and reserve broth. Sift flour into bowl making a well in the center. Add salt to beaten egg. Heat broth to boiling. Take 1 cup broth, ⅓ of which is fat, and slowly add this to egg, beating constantly. Pour egg mixture into flour well and fold into flour with a fork. Make 3 balls of dough. Wrap each in foil to keep warm. Roll out each ball until quite thin. Cut into 1-inch wide strips. Break into pieces 2 to 3 inches long, stretching as you break. Boil gently until tender, 5 minutes or less. Add boned chicken when the dumplings are tender.

Sharon Gulley (Mrs. R. Michael)

BARBECUED CHICKEN
This is good with corn on the cob and diced fried potatoes.

1 chicken fryer, cut into
    serving pieces
1 8-ounce can tomato sauce
¼ cup vegetable oil
⅓ cup vinegar
1 cup brown sugar
¾ teaspoon garlic powder
¾ teaspoon oregano
pinch each of marjoram
    and sweet basil
1 tablespoon rosemary
    (optional)

Brown fryer pieces in hot fat without flouring. Combine remaining ingredients and pour over browned chicken. Bake covered at 350° for 30 minutes. Remove cover and continue baking 30 minutes longer or until tender. Serves 4 or 5.

Vivian Solomon (Mrs. Ted)

MEXICALI CHICKEN

2 whole chicken breasts,
    boned, skinned and
    halved
1 tablespoon butter
⅓ cup sour cream
1 canned green chili,
    drained and finely
    chopped
½ cup Monterey Jack cheese,
    shredded
Avocado slices for garnish

Place chicken breasts between 2 sheets of waxed paper and pound to ¼ to ½ inch thickness. In a large skillet heat butter over medium high heat. Add half the chicken and saute about 3 minutes on each side. Remove chicken and place on a foil-lined broiler tray. Saute remaining chicken. In a small bowl mix sour cream, green chili, and cheese until well blended. Spread 1 rounded tablespoon of sour cream mixture on each chicken piece. Broil 5 minutes in a preheated broiler with oven rack about 6 inches from heat. Garnish with avocado slices. Makes 4 servings. 260 calories each, without avocados.

Carol Nelson (Mrs. John)

CHICKEN NEOPOLITAN STYLE

2 whole chicken breasts,
  cut in half (about 12-
  ounces each) or 1 fryer,
  cut up
1 ½ teaspoons salt
½ teaspoon pepper
3 tablespoons olive oil
  (no substitution)
10 small, white onions
  (jarred)
1 to 2 4-ounce jars button
  mushrooms
1 clove garlic, minced
1 can condensed tomato
  bisque
½ cup dry red wine
½ teaspoon leaf oregano,
  crumbled
½ teaspoon leaf basil,
  crumbled
3 tablespoons parsley,
  minced
6 pitted ripe olives, sliced

Sprinkle chicken with salt and pepper; let stand 5 minutes. Saute or lightly brown chicken, skin side down, in hot oil in a large skillet about 15 minutes; turn and saute other side. Add onions, mushrooms, and garlic; cook 5 minutes. Combine soup, wine, oregano, and basil in a 2-cup measure; pour over chicken. Bring to boiling; lower heat and cover. Cook about 40 minutes or until chicken is tender. Stir in parsley and olives. Serve over rice. Serves 4. Double ingredients to serve 6 to 8 people. This recipe can be prepared earlier in the day and reheated in a 325° oven before serving.

Vivian Solomon (Mrs. Ted)

HAWAIIAN CHICKEN
Quick meal that's low in calories.

4-6 chicken breasts or thighs
1 8-ounce can unsweetened
  pineapple chunks
1 11-ounce can mandarin
  oranges

Bake chicken in uncovered casserole dish for 45 minutes at 350°. Remove skins. Add pineapple and oranges with juice. Bake uncovered for 15 more minutes. Delicious served over wild rice.

Pat Russo (Mrs. Frank)

MEXICAN CHICKEN OLÉ
Ole means "wow" and that's what this recipe is! Quick, easy, raisin-rich, and thrifty!

1 3-pound chicken fryer, cut up
2 tablespoons vegetable oil
½ cup seedless raisins
1 medium onion, thinly sliced
1 clove garlic, minced
¼ teaspoon thyme
1 8-ounce can stewed tomatoes
1 7-ounce can green chilies, chopped
¼ cup dry white wine or vermouth
chopped parsley

Lightly sprinkle chicken with salt and pepper. Brown on both sides in oil in a large skillet. Add raisins, onion, garlic, and thyme. Reduce heat. Cover and simmer for 5 minutes. Add tomatoes, chilies and wine. Bring to a boil. Reduce heat. Cover and simmer for 25 minutes. Serve on a warm platter sprinkled with parsley. Accompany with hot tortillas, steaming rice and a chilled salad.

Linda Carballido (Mrs. Jorge)

STIR-FRY CHICKEN WITH MACADAMIA NUTS

1 pound boneless and skinless chicken breasts, cut into 1-inch cubes
1 8 ¾-ounce can unsweetened pineapple chunks
2 tablespoons soy sauce
1 teaspoon ginger
3 tablespoons vegetable oil
1 ½ cups carrots, thinly sliced diagonally
1 clove garlic, crushed
1 10-ounce box frozen pea pods
⅔ cup macadamia nuts, coarsely chopped
2 teaspoons cornstarch
¼ cup water

Place chicken in a snug fitting bowl. Drain pineapple, reserving ½ cup juice. Combine juice with soy sauce and ginger. Pour over chicken. Toss to coat completely. Set aside for 15 minutes. In a large skillet heat oil until hot. Add carrots; stir-fry until crisp-tender, about 3 minutes. Remove with a slotted spoon. Set aside. Drain chicken, reserving marinade. Add chicken and garlic to skillet. Stir-fry until cooked, about 3 minutes. Add pea pods. Stir-fry about 2 minutes longer. Add macadamia nuts and reserved carrots. Stir-fry 1 minute longer. Combine cornstarch, water and reserved marinade. Mix well. Add to skillet. Cook and stir until thickened, about 2 minutes. Serve with steamed rice. Serves 4.

Barbara Malcolm (Mrs. Robert)

CHICKEN KIEV

¾ cup butter or margarine
1 tablespoon parsley, chopped
1 tablespoon chives, finely cut
1 tablespoon shallots or green onions, finely minced
½ teaspoon salt
⅛ teaspoon pepper
6 whole chicken breasts, boned and skinned
salt and pepper
1 egg
1 tablespoon cold water
flour
⅔ cup packaged bread crumbs
¼ cup butter or margarine

1. Prepare chicken: Mix softened butter or margarine, parsley, chives, shallots or green onions, salt and pepper. Shape into 6 sticks. Chill or freeze until firm. Place one chicken breast between two pieces of waxed paper. Pound slightly with a mallet. Repeat with remaining breasts.
2. Place one stick of herbed butter on each breast. Roll breast so butter is completely enclosed. Close edges with wooden picks. Sprinkle lightly with salt and pepper.
3. Heat oven to 400°. Beat egg and water in pan or flat dish. Dredge breasts with flour. Dip in egg mixture. Roll in bread crumbs to coat well. Heat butter or margarine in a large skillet over medium heat. Saute breasts until golden on all sides, turning gently with two forks. Put chicken in a shallow baking pan. Bake 15-20 minutes or until tender. Serves 6. Hint: Chicken browns better if it is chilled several hours after coating, before sauteing. Can be prepared ahead several hours or a day before. Saute and bake, just before serving.

Marilyn Bauer (Mrs. James)

"COOKED" CHICKEN (MICROWAVE)
This is an easy way to prepare chicken when the recipe calls for "cooked" chicken.

2 ½-3 pounds chicken
½ onion, sliced
1 stalk celery, cut up (use leaves)
2 cups hot water
1 teaspoon salt
¼ cup white wine

Place chicken, onion, celery, water, wine, and seasonings in a 3-quart casserole. Cover. Cook on high 20 minutes. Reserve stock, bone chicken, and use in any recipe calling for "cooked" chicken. Keep in the refrigerator or freezer until ready to use.

The Committee

CHICKEN CREPES VERONIQUE

3 chicken breasts, about 12
ounces each
1 envelope instant chicken
broth, or 1 chicken
bouillon cube
1 cup water
1 recipe for crepes
6 tablespoons butter
⅓ cup flour
1 teaspoon salt
1 cup cream (half and half)
¼ cup dry sherry
1 cup seedless grapes,
halved
1 7-ounce jar pimiento,
drained and diced

Combine chicken breasts with instant broth and water in a frying pan; heat to boiling. Cover. Simmer 30 minutes or until tender. Remove chicken and cool until easy to handle. Pour broth in a 2-cup measure; add water to make 1 ½ cups. Pull skin from chicken and remove meat from bones and dice. Make crepes and keep warm. Melt butter in a pan and stir in flour and salt. Cook, stirring constantly, until bubbly. Stir in the 1 ½ cups broth, cream, and sherry; continue cooking and stirring until sauce thickens and boils 1 minute. Stir in the chicken, grapes, and pimientos. Spoon ⅓ cup chicken filling on each crepe and roll. Place in a single layer in a shallow baking dish. Spoon remaining chicken filling over top. Bake in a 350° oven for 20 minutes. Serves 8.

Marilyn Wood (Mrs. John)

CHICKEN BREASTS PARMESAN
Microwave

1 pound boneless chicken
breasts
⅓ cup crushed cereal flakes
¼ cup Parmesan cheese,
grated
1 8-ounce can tomato sauce
1 tablespoon dry spaghetti
sauce mix
½ cup monterey jack
cheese, shredded
¼ cup Parmesan cheese,
grated

Shake chicken breasts, cereal flakes, and ¼ cup Parmesan cheese together in a paper bag. Place chicken in a 1 ½-quart microwave safe pan. Cover. Microwave on medium high for 9 minutes or until chicken is done. Combine tomato sauce and spaghetti sauce mix. Pour over chicken. Sprinkle with remaining cheeses. Microwave on high for 4 minutes. Serves 2 to 4.

Shirley Bennett (Mrs. Gaylord)

CHICKEN HOW-SO

2 whole chicken breasts, boned and skinned
2 tablespoons butter or margarine
1 can golden mushroom soup
½ cup water
1 beef bouillon cube
1 tablespoon soy sauce
1 teaspoon Worcestershire sauce
½ teaspoon curry powder
½ teaspoon poppy seeds
1 8-ounce can bamboo shoots
½ cup celery, sliced
½ cup onion, sliced
1 3-ounce can mushrooms
1 small green pepper, chopped
3 tablespoons dry white wine
1 3-ounce can chow mein noodles

Cut chicken breasts into 1 ½-inch cubes. In medium skillet brown chicken in butter until golden brown. Stir in the soup, water, bouillon cube, soy sauce, Worcestershire sauce, curry powder, and poppy seeds. Mix. Cover and simmer 15 minutes, stirring occasionally. Add the bamboo shoots, celery, onion, and mushrooms. Cover and simmer 10 minutes or until tender crisp. Stir in green pepper and wine. Cover and simmer 2 to 3 minutes more. Serve over chow mein noodles. Serves 4.

Maryann Bugaieski (Mrs. Stanley)

GOOD AND GOOEY CHICKEN
The name says it all!

1 8-ounce bottle Russian dressing
1 10-ounce jar apricot preserves
1 1 ⅜-ounce package dry onion soup mix
1 2 ½-3-pound chicken, cut up
Seasoned salt and freshly ground pepper to taste

Combine dressing, preserves, and onion soup mix in a bowl. Mix well and pour into a 9 x 13 x 2inch baking dish. Sprinkle chicken with seasoned salt and pepper. Place chicken, skin side down, in baking dish. Bake at 375° for 45 minutes, basting occasionally. Turn chicken over and baste. Bake 35 minutes more, basting. Serves 4-6.

Kathryn Cohen (Mrs. A.E.)

CHICKEN CASSEROLE

1 10 ¾-ounce can cream of
mushroom soup
1 10 ¾-ounce can cream of
chicken soup
1 5-ounce jar Old English
cheese
½ cup mayonnaise
8 ounces fine noodles,
cooked
4 cups cooked chicken, diced
1 10-ounce package frozen
asparagus, thawed
⅓ cup green pepper,
chopped
1 4-ounce can mushrooms,
drained
1 cup crushed potato chips
1 2 ¼-ounce package
slivered almonds

In medium saucepan mix soups, cheese, and mayonnaise and heat slowly, stirring until cheese melts. Grease a 9 x 13-inch pan. Layer noodles, chicken, asparagus, green peppers, and mushrooms. Top with the soup mixture. Cover with crushed potato chips and almonds. Bake at 350° for 45 minutes. Can be made day before. Add chips and almonds just before baking. Serves 8.

Grace Seward (Mrs. G. R.)

CHICKEN CASSEROLE

2 cups diced chicken
1 cup celery, chopped
2 tablespoons green onion,
chopped
3 hard-boiled eggs, diced
½ cup sliced almonds
1 10 ¾-ounce cream of
chicken soup
¾ cup mayonnaise
1 2-ounce jar pimiento
crushed potato chips

Mix all ingredients together. Put in greased casserole. Top with crushed potato chips. Bake at 350° for 45 minutes.

Barbara Bordeaux (Mrs. Dean)

CHICKEN CASSEROLE

1 to 2 cups cooked chicken,
  cut into small pieces
  (or 2 chicken breasts)
1 cup celery, chopped
1 cup Minute Rice, prepared
  according to package
  directions
1 10 ½-ounce can cream of
  chicken soup, undiluted
2 tablespoons minced onion
½ cup Miracle Whip
  salad dressing
2 tablespoons lemon juice
¾ teaspoon salt
¼ teaspoon pepper

Mix all ingredients together and place in a buttered 8 x 8-inch casserole or baking dish. Top with buttered bread crumbs. Bake at 350° approximately 30 to 40 minutes until bubbly. Optional toppings: buttered crushed corn flakes or Towne House crackers; sprinkle with paprika. When doubling this recipe for larger casserole, use one can cream of chicken soup and one can cream of celery or cream of mushroom soup. Serves 4 to 6.

Pam Albers (Mrs. William)

CHICKEN AND ZUCCHINI STUFFING CASSEROLE

6 cups zucchini, thinly sliced
¼ cup onion, chopped
1 cup water, salted
1 cup carrot, grated
1 10 ½-ounce can cream of
  chicken soup
1 cup sour cream
3 cups cooked chicken,
  diced
½ cup margarine
1 box chicken-flavored
  Stove Top stuffing mix

Boil the zucchini and onion in the water for 15 minutes; drain and let stand. Blend together the carrot, soup, sour cream, and diced chicken. Mix in the zucchini mixture. Melt the margarine in a skillet. Mix in stuffing mix until margarine is absorbed. Put half the stuffing mixture in a 9 x 13-inch pan, then pour zucchini mixture on top, then top with remaining stuffing. Bake at 350° for 35 minutes. Serves 8 to 10.

Ruth Giunta (Mrs. Edward)

CHICKEN SPAGHETTI CASSEROLE

1 large roasting chicken
½ cup butter or margarine
3 medium onions, minced
2 green peppers, minced
1 cup celery, chopped
1 clove garlic, crushed, or
1/16 teaspoon garlic
   powder
2 cups canned tomatoes
1 16-ounce package
   spaghetti
¼ pound mild cheese,
   grated

Boil chicken in water until tender. Save stock. Saute onions, peppers, celery and garlic in butter. Add 1 quart stock and tomatoes. Simmer. Bone chicken and cut into rather large pieces. Add to sauce. Add spaghetti which has been cooked in the chicken stock and drained. Mix well with chicken and sauce and put into casserole. Bake covered for 40 minutes at 350°. Sprinkle with cheese and bake 20 minutes more uncovered. Serves 8-10.

Dottie Flores (Mrs. Richard)

CHICKEN BISCUIT CASSEROLE

2 cups cooked chicken or
   turkey
1 10 ¾-ounce can cream of
   chicken soup
½ cup mayonnaise
1 cup cheddar cheese,
   shredded
1 4-ounce can mushroom
   pieces, drained
1 teaspoon lemon juice
1 10-ounce can Hungry
   Jack Biscuits
2 tablespoons melted
   margarine
½ cup crushed croutons

Combine first six ingredients. Heat until bubbly. Then pour into a 9 x 13 x 2-inch baking dish. Place biscuits on top of chicken mixture. Brush with melted margarine. Sprinkle crushed croutons on top. Bake at 375° for 25-30 minutes. Serves 4. Double all ingredients except biscuits to serve 6.

Linda Clementz (Mrs. Gregory)

CREAMED CHICKEN AND HAM
This is a good luncheon dish or serve as a side dish for buffet brunch.

¼ cup butter or margarine
¼ cup onion, chopped
¼ cup all purpose flour
1 tablespoon prepared mustard
½ teaspoon salt
dash pepper
1 14-ounce can (1 ⅔ cups) evaporated milk
1 cup water
1 3-ounce can broiled, sliced mushrooms, undrained
1 cup cooked chicken, cubed
1 cup baked ham, cubed
¼ cup black olives, sliced

Melt butter in large saucepan; add onion and saute until tender. Blend in flour, mustard, salt and pepper. Add milk, water and liquid from mushrooms. Bring to a boil and cook two minutes, stirring constantly until mixture thickens. Stir in mushrooms, chicken, ham, and olives. Heat. Serve over Pepperidge Farm pastry shells with centers removed. Serves 6.

Vivian Solomon (Mrs. Ted)

CHICKEN STEW
Microwave

8 ounces frozen lima beans
¼ cup water
1 pound boneless chicken breast
1 onion, sliced
garlic powder, salt and pepper to taste
1 bay leaf
¼ cup water
1 16-ounce can zucchini with tomatoes

Place lima beans and ¼ cup water in microwave dish. Cover. Microwave on high for 6 minutes. Set aside. Combine chicken, onion, seasonings and ¼ cup water in a 3-quart pan. Cover and microwave on high for 8 minutes. Add lima beans and zucchini with tomatoes. Microwave on high for 8 minutes, then medium low for 3 minutes. Serves 4.

Shirley Bennett (Mrs. Gaylord)

DR. ANGELA BOWEN'S CHICKEN BREASTS IN ORANGE SAUCE

1 ½ pounds chicken breasts, deboned and skinned
1 teaspoon salt
½ teaspoon paprika
4 teaspoons margarine
1 cup orange juice
1 tablespoon orange rind, grated
1 teaspoon tarragon
1 orange, sliced

Sprinkle chicken breasts with salt and paprika. Brown lightly in margarine. Add orange juice, rind and tarragon. Cook, covered in a 325° oven for 30 minutes. When done, remove chicken and cook sauce over high heat to reduce volume. Serve sauce over chicken and/or steamed rice. Garnish with orange slices. Four servings. Suitable for diabetics.

Rosella Koerner (Mrs. C.S.M.)

RICE STUFFED PHEASANT

2 2 ½ pound pheasants
2 teaspoons salt
1 ½ cups long grain rice
3 cups water
½ cup butter or margarine
1 cup celery, finely chopped
3 tablespoons onion, minced
½ cup mushrooms, sliced or canned mushrooms, drained
⅛ teaspoon crushed sage
⅛ teaspoon crushed thyme
⅛ teaspoon crushed savory
melted butter or margarine
6 slices of bacon

Rub 1 teaspoon salt into cavities. Brown rice in frying pan. Transfer rice to saucepan, add water and 1 teaspoon salt. Cook until tender. Melt butter in frying pan, add celery, onion, mushrooms and cook 10 minutes. Add to rice along with herbs. Stuff birds lightly, truss, brush with melted butter and place bacon across breasts. Roast at 300° for 2 hours basting frequently.

Bonnie Adams (Mrs. Carl)

DUCK AND WILD RICE CASSEROLE
Chicken may be substituted for duck.

2 medium ducks (3 cups
  cubed meat)
3 stalks celery
1 onion, halved
2 tablespoons margarine
½ cup chopped onion
¼ cup flour
4-ounce can mushrooms,
  sliced
1 ½ cups half and half
1 tablespoon chopped
  parsley
1 6-ounce package seasoned
  wild long-grain rice
1 ½ teaspoon salt
¼ teaspoon pepper

Boil ducks until tender, one hour or more, in water to cover, with celery, onion halves, salt and pepper to taste. Remove ducks. Cool and cube meat; reserve broth. Cook rice according to package directions. Melt margarine; saute chopped onion. Stir in flour. Drain mushrooms, reserving broth. Add mushrooms to onion mixture. Add enough duck broth to mushroom liquid to make 1½ cups liquid. Stir into onion mixture. Add remaining ingredients. Put into a greased 2-quart casserole. Sprinkle slivered almonds on top. Bake covered at 350° for 15-20 minutes. Uncover and bake for 5-10 more minutes or until very hot.

Barbara Shekleton (Mrs. Thomas)

WILD DUCK IN ORANGE SAUCE

½ cup olive oil
¼ cup dry white wine
2 onions, thinly sliced
Few sprigs parsley
Salt and pepper to taste
4 wild duck breasts
3 tablespoons butter
Orange sauce:
1 tablespoon cornstarch
1 cup orange juice
3 tablespoons sugar
1 tablespoon orange rind,
  grated
2 tablespoons Curacao or
  Grand Marnier

Combine oil, wine, onions, parsley, salt and pepper. Marinate the duck breasts in this mixture. Drain and wipe the breasts dry with a paper towel. Saute the breasts gently in butter until tender (20-30 minutes). Arrange breasts on a hot platter. Pour hot orange sauce over breasts, garnish with orange slices and sprigs of lemon verbena. Orange Sauce: Mix cornstarch with a little orange juice in a saucepan. Add the rest of the juice and the sugar. Cook until thick and clear, stirring as it cooks. Add the orange rind and the liqueur. Serve hot.

Bonnie Adams (Mrs. Carl)

SEAFOOD SHELLS
Very easy!!

1 16-ounce can Spanish rice, drained
1 tablespoon mayonnaise
1 7-ounce can solid white tuna, drained
1 7-ounce can medium shrimp, drained
Dry bread crumbs or
Pepperidge Farm stuffing

Combine rice and mayonnaise. Flake tuna. Cut shrimp in half. Add to rice and mayonnaise. Fill 4 individual baking shells and sprinkle with dry bread crumbs or Pepperidge Farm stuffing. Bake at 350° until hot. Makes 4 servings.

Kay Bickerman (Mrs. Ray)

SEAFOOD CASSEROLE

1 ½ cups rice, uncooked
½ cup celery, diced
¼ cup onion, chopped
1 green pepper, diced
1 2-ounce jar pimiento
3 tablespoons butter
3 tablespoons flour
1 ½ cups milk
Salt and paprika
1 6-ounce can crab
1 4 ½-ounce can shrimp
1 cup mayonnaise
1 10-ounce package frozen peas
Crushed potato chips

Cook rice in your favorite fashion. Saute celery, onion, pepper, and pimiento in butter. Add flour. Stir in milk slowly and heat until thickened. Season with salt and paprika to taste. Combine all remaining ingredients except peas and potato chips. Heat peas slightly, then fold into mixture. Put into greased 2-quart casserole. Sprinkle with crushed potato chips. Bake at 350° for 30 to 40 minutes. Serves 8.

Betty Neuhoff (Mrs. Carl)

SEAFOOD CASSEROLE

2 cups cooked rice
½ cup green pepper, finely chopped
½ cup celery, finely chopped
½ cup onion, finely chopped
4 ½-ounce can water chestnuts, drained and sliced
1 cup mayonnaise
¼ teaspoon salt
1 cup tomato juice
⅛ teaspoon pepper
½ pound shelled shrimp, cooked
7 ½-ounce can Alaska king crab, drained
½ pound fresh sea scallops
¼ cup sliced unblanched almonds
1 cup cheddar cheese, grated

Combine rice, green pepper, celery, onion, and water chestnuts. Combine mayonnaise, tomato juice, salt and pepper. Place half of rice mixture in buttered 2-quart casserole. Arrange half of shrimp, large pieces of crab and scallops over rice. Pour half of tomato mixture over above. Repeat. Combine nuts and cheese and arrange over top. Bake covered at 350° 25-30 minutes. Serves 6. May be frozen.

Pat Callaway (Mrs. James)

BAKED FISH WITH SEASONED STUFFING

1 16-ounce package frozen cod fillets
1 small onion, chopped
1 celery rib, chopped
1 tablespoon butter
1 cup water
1 8-ounce package Pepperidge Farm Seasoned Stuffing
¼ cup mayonnaise
2 teaspoons lemon juice
¼ teaspoon salt
1/16 teaspoon pepper
1/16 teaspoon paprika

Thaw frozen fillets for ten minutes and cut into four pieces. Saute onion and celery in butter. Add water; bring to boil. Pour over stuffing mix. Cover and let stand five minutes. Spoon dressing into four individual ovenproof dishes or a shallow one-quart casserole. Top with fish. Spread with mayonnaise, lemon juice, salt, pepper, and paprika. Cover with foil. Bake at 375° for 20 minutes. Remove foil. Bake 2 to 3 minutes more until mayonnaise is browned. Garnish with lemon and parsley. Substitute diet margarine and Weight Watchers mayonnaise for a leaner meal.

Mary Dickison (Mrs. George)

FAVORITE FISH CASSEROLE

1 pound frozen haddock or
   cod fillets thawed, or 1
   pound fresh
2 tablespoons butter or
   margarine
¼ cup onion, finely chopped
2 tablespoons flour
¼ teaspoon salt
⅛ teaspoon pepper
1 cup milk
1 cup sharp processed
   American cheese, shredded
½ cup milk
1 envelope sour cream
   sauce mix
1 4-ounce can mushroom
   stems and pieces, drained
1 cup frozen peas, thawed
1 cup soft bread crumbs,
   optional
2 tablespoons butter,
   melted, optional

Simmer fish gently in water for 10-12 minutes. Drain. Break into bite-size pieces. Set aside. Cook onion in butter until tender. Blend in flour, salt, and pepper. Add 1 cup milk all at once and stir until smooth and thickened. Add cheese and stir until melted. Use ½ cup milk to make sour cream sauce in small bowl. In 2-quart casserole combine cheese sauce, sour cream sauce, fish, mushrooms, and peas. Top with buttered crumbs if desired (combine bread crumbs with melted butter). Bake at 400° for 15 to 20 minutes.

Bernadette Shekleton (Mrs. Michael)

POOR MAN'S LOBSTER
A good recipe for using those block packages of frozen fish.

2 one-pound blocks of frozen
   haddock or cod fillets,
   thawed enough to cut
   (about 1 hour at room
   temperature)
2 cups water
3 tablespoons cider or wine
   vinegar
2 teaspoons salt
6 tablespoons butter
½ teaspoon paprika
lemon wedges

Cut each block of fillets into 12 equal chunks, each about 1 ¼ inches square. In medium saucepan bring water, vinegar, and salt to a boil. Add fish. Reduce heat to moderate and simmer 15 minutes. Choose a broiler proof pan large enough to hold fish in a single layer and melt butter in it. Remove fish from liquid with a slotted spoon and add to butter. Sprinkle with paprika and spoon butter over. Broil about 5 inches from heat for about 5 minutes, spooning butter over fish once. Serve with lemon wedges.

Bernadette Shekleton (Mrs. Michael)

JANE'S SHRIMP & ARTICHOKE

1 ½ pounds fresh mush-
  rooms, sliced
3 tablespoons butter
2 pounds shrimp, raw
1 10-ounce package frozen
  artichoke hearts, cut in
  half
¾ cup butter
9 tablespoons flour
1 ½ cups milk
1 ½ cups cream
½ cup dry sherry
2 tablespoons Worcester-
  shire sauce
½ cup Parmesan cheese,
  grated
Paprika

Cook sliced mushrooms in 3 tablespoons butter for 6 minutes. Scatter shrimp and artichoke hearts in a 9 x 12-inch baking dish. Add mushrooms. In saucepan melt ¾ cup butter. Add flour, milk and cream. Stir until thickened and smooth. Add sherry and Worcestershire sauce. Pour over shrimp mixture. Sprinkle with cheese and paprika. Bake in a 375° oven for 30 minutes. Enjoy!

Joyce Cashman (Mrs. Michael)

NEW ORLEANS BAR-B-QUE SHRIMP

1 cup butter or margarine,
  melted
½ teaspoon celery seed
¼ teaspoon red pepper
2 teaspoons paprika
2 teaspoons dry mustard
¼ teaspoon ginger
⅛ teaspoon black pepper
3 cloves or ½ teaspoon
  ground cloves
3 pods garlic, chopped or
  1 ½ teaspoons garlic powder
3 teaspoons salt
1 lemon, sliced
2 bay leaves, crushed
Salt, garlic powder, and
  pepper may be added
  according to taste.
8 pounds raw shrimp, in
  shells, deheaded

Mix seasonings in melted butter. Let mixture cool a little and add shrimp. Marinate 1 hour and cook over medium heat until shrimp are done. This doesn't take very long; be careful not to overcook the shrimp. Serve with hot French bread. Serves 4-6 persons as a main course. May also be served as an appetizer.

Mary Putman (Mrs. Harrison C. III)

SHRIMP THERMIDOR BAKE
Reduced calorie recipe—257 calories per serving.

¼ cup chopped onion
¼ cup chopped celery
1 10 ¾-ounce can condensed cheddar cheese soup
½ cup skim milk
2 tablespoons dry sherry
¾ pound fresh or frozen shrimp, shelled and cooked
2 tablespoons parsley, snipped
Dash hot pepper sauce
¾ cup soft bread crumbs
1 tablespoon butter or margarine, melted
Dash paprika

In a covered saucepan cook onion and celery in a small amount of water for 5 minutes; drain. Stir soup, milk, and sherry into saucepan with vegetables. Heat. Stir in shrimp, parsley, and hot pepper sauce. Spoon mixture into four individual casseroles or baking shells. Toss together bread crumbs, melted butter or margarine, and paprika. Sprinkle on top of each casserole. Bake in a 375° oven 15 to 20 minutes. Serves 4. More shrimp or bread crumbs may be added, but it also increases the calories.

Helene Easton (Mrs. Willard)

SAGANAKI
Baked Shrimp with Feta Cheese

2 medium onions, thinly sliced
½ cup olive oil
2 pounds tomatoes, peeled and chopped
½ cup parsley, chopped
2 teaspoons salt
¼ teaspoon pepper
2 cloves garlic, minced
2 pounds shrimp, shelled and deveined
½ pound feta cheese

Saute onions in olive oil until tender. Add tomatoes, parsley, salt, pepper and garlic. Cover and simmer 30 to 60 minutes, stirring occasionally. Put sauce and shrimp into 6 individual ovenproof dishes. Crumble feta cheese over top. Bake uncovered in a 425° oven, for 10 to 15 minutes, until shrimp is cooked and cheese is melted.

Amelia Wilson (Mrs. Henry)

SHRIMP CASSEROLE

1 ½ pounds shrimp, deveined
  and shelled
1 tablespoon lemon juice
 3 tablespoons vegetable oil
 ¾ cup long grain rice
 ¼ cup green pepper, diced
 ¼ cup onion, diced
2 tablespoons butter
1 teaspoon salt
⅛ teaspoon pepper
⅛ teaspoon mace
dash cayenne
1 10 ½-ounce can tomato
  soup
1 cup cream
½ cup sherry
¾ cup slivered almonds

Boil shrimp and drain. Sprinkle with lemon juice mixed with oil. Refrigerate 1 hour. Cook long grain rice (wash several times first); drain and refrigerate 1 hour. Heat oven to 350°. Saute green pepper and onion for 5 minutes in butter. Add remaining ingredients, except almonds. Stir in rice and shrimp (save a few shrimp for top). Top with remaining shrimp and slivered almonds. Bake 20 minutes.

Joan Berney (Mrs. John)

SHRIMP CASSEROLE

6 eggs
3 cups milk
2 tablespoons parsley,
  minced
¾ teaspoon dry mustard
½ teaspoon salt
10 slices white bread,
  decrusted and cubed
2 cups cheddar cheese,
  shredded
2 cups shrimp, cleaned

Beat eggs, milk and seasonings. Combine with bread cubes, cheese and shrimp. Pour into a greased 7 ½ x 11 ½ x 1 ½ dish. Bake uncovered for one hour or until center is set in a 325° oven.

Mary Ellen DeBord (Mrs. Alan)

SHRIMP SCAMPI

¼ cup butter or margarine
¼ cup salad or olive oil
2 tablespoons parsley, chopped
1 tablespoon garlic powder
½ teaspoon salt
1/16 teaspoon cayenne pepper
2 tablespoons lemon juice
1 pound large fresh shrimp, shelled and deveined, tails on
lemon wedges

Preheat oven to 400°. In large skillet with a metal handle, or heatproof serving dish, melt butter. Add oil, half the parsley, garlic powder, salt, cayenne, and lemon juice. Mix well. Add shrimp, tossing gently with butter mixture. Arrange in skillet in a single layer. Bake 8 to 10 minutes or just until tender. Sprinkle with remaining parsley. Serve with lemon wedges.

Carol Nelson (Mrs. John)

LOBSTER CASSEROLE

2 10½-ounce cans condensed cream of mushroom soup
1 cup mayonnaise
¼ cup sherry
½ cup milk
1 ½ pounds boneless lobster or crab meat, uncooked
3 cups packaged seasoned croutons
2 5-ounce cans water chestnuts, drained and sliced
½ cup green onions, minced
1 cup cheddar cheese, grated

Mix soup, mayonnaise, and sherry. Stir in milk. Combine with remaining ingredients except cheese. Turn into a 3-quart baking dish; top with cheese. Bake at 350° for 40 minutes. If made ahead and refrigerated, bake 1 hour. May substitute crab for lobster. Serves 8.

Marianne Wright (Mrs. Robert)

CRAB AND ARTICHOKE CASSEROLE

½ cup butter
3 tablespoons onion,
   minced
½ cup flour
1 quart cream, heated to
   boiling point
½ cup Madeira wine
2 tablespoons fresh lemon
   juice
4 cups fresh or frozen
   crabmeat
3 9-ounce packages frozen
   artichoke hearts, cooked
   to package directions
2 ½ cups shell macaroni,
   cooked and drained
2 cups Gruyere cheese or
   Swiss cheese, grated
Paprika

Preheat oven to 350°. Melt butter in large heavy skillet. When it sizzles add onions and saute until golden. Stir in flour and cook over low heat until flour is pale yellow. Remove from heat. Add cream, stirring vigorously. Return to moderate heat. Stir until sauce comes to a boil. Reduce heat. Add Madeira. Season with salt and pepper. Pour lemon juice over crabmeat; toss lightly. Combine crabmeat, artichoke hearts, macaroni, and sauce together in a 5-quart buttered casserole. Sprinkle cheese over casserole and dust with paprika. Bake 25 to 30 minutes, or until heated through. Casserole may be prepared day before and refrigerated. Bring to room temperature before placing in preheated oven. Serves 10.

Laura Rager (Mrs. Donald)

CRAB MEAT CASSEROLE STYLE

1 pound lump crabmeat
   (or shrimp and crabmeat
   combined)
½ teaspoon dry mustard
heavy dash of cayenne
   pepper
1 tablespoon white onion,
   finely chopped
½ cup celery, chopped,
   steamed until almost
   tender and cooled
¼ cup green pepper, diced
1 teaspoon lemon juice
mayonnaise
buttered bread crumbs

Combine all ingredients. Add enough mayonnaise to moisten. Place in greased casserole dish. Top with buttered bread crumbs. Bake at 350° until bubbly and crumbs are toasty. Serves 4 to 6.

Julie Horvath (Mrs. Fredric)

CRAB STRUDEL

½ cup chopped green onion
½ cup butter
1 cup dry vermouth
2 6 ½-ounce cans crabmeat, drained and flaked
8 ounces cream cheese, softened
4 anchovy fillets, finely chopped
¼ cup parsley, chopped
4 egg yolks
1 teaspoon salt
1 teaspoon pepper
1 teaspoon garlic powder
8 filo leaves
4 tablespoons melted butter
1 egg, beaten

Cook onion in butter until golden. Add vermouth; boil 4 minutes and remove from heat. Add crabmeat, cream cheese, anchovies, parsley, egg yolks, salt, pepper, and garlic powder; stir until cream cheese melts. Put 1 filo leaf on kitchen towel, and brush with melted butter; repeat until 4 leaves are stacked. Put ½ crab mixture on filo lengthwise and roll. Put on buttered pan; make 2nd strudel. Brush tops with melted butter, then beaten egg. Bake 15 mintues at 350°; increase to 450° for 5-10 minutes. May be frozen. To serve, heat frozen strudel at 350° for 20-30 mintues. Serve with lemon slices if desired. Serves 24 slices.

Bonnie Fenton (Mrs. Craig)

EASY SALMON PIE
Microwave

2 eggs
1 ½ cups cooked rice
6 green onions, finely chopped
1 1-pound can salmon, undrained
1 6 ½-ounce can solid packed tuna in water
½ cup butter or margarine, melted
¼ teaspoon thyme
1 cup fine dry bread crumbs
shredded cheddar or American cheese

In large bowl beat eggs. Add rice and onions. Remove bones and skin from salmon. Add salmon and tuna undrained to rice mixture. Add melted butter along with thyme and crumbs. Mix well. Spread mixture into round glass pie plate or microwave baking dish. Sprinkle shredded cheese over top. Cover with waxed paper. A few toothpicks in top will prevent cheese from melting onto waxed paper. Microwave on high for 9-11 minutes, rotating dish ½ turn after 5 minutes. Garnish with tomato slices and parsley. Serve in wedges.

Andrea Lister (Mrs. Richard)

TUNA CHOW MEIN CASSEROLE

1 cup celery, chopped
¼ cup onion, chopped
2 tablespoons green
  pepper, chopped
1 tablespoon butter
1 7-ounce can tuna,
  drained
1 10 ½-ounce can cream of
  mushroom soup
¼ cup milk
¼ cup water
3 ounces chow mein noodles
¾ cup cashew nuts, optional
½ teaspoon seasoned salt
1 teaspoon soy sauce

Heat oven to 350°. Saute celery, onion and green pepper in butter. Combine with remaining ingredients, reserving ⅓ cup chow mein noodles. Sprinkle remaining chow mein noodles over dish. Bake, uncovered, 30 minutes. Serves 4-6.

Jo Dorsch (Mrs. Thomas)

AMERICANIZED PAELLA
The Near East Spanish Rice has blended spices which make this a very tasty paella.

2 cups uncooked chicken
  breast, deboned, cubed
1 small onion, diced
2 tablespoons butter
1 pound small shrimp,
  cleaned and boiled for
  2 minutes
½ pound mild Italian sausage,
  sliced thin and cooked
8 to 10 pimiento-stuffed
  olives, sliced thin
1 10-ounce package frozen
  green peas, thawed
1 box Near East Spanish
  Rice Pilaf

Saute the chicken breast with the diced onion in butter. The chicken, shrimp and Italian sausage may all be cooked one or two days ahead and stored individually in the refrigerator. Prepare the Near East Spanish rice as directed on the box. While the rice is cooking, remove the chicken, shrimp, and sausage from the refrigerator. Add chicken, onions, shrimp, and sausage. Cover and simmer until thoroughly heated. Add chopped olives and peas. Continue cooking until hot. Serves 6.

Irene Crane (Mrs. Donald)

INDIVIDUAL PIZZAS

**6-8 frozen flour tortillas
(7-8 inches in diameter)**
1 ¼-1 ½ cups pizza sauce
½ pound sausage
**8 ounces fresh mushrooms,
sliced**
1 medium onion, chopped
**12 ounces mozzarella
cheese, grated**

Preheat oven to 375°. Thaw and separate tortillas. Place on cookie sheets. Spoon three tablespoons pizza sauce on each tortilla. Bake for 8 minutes. While baking, brown sausage, mushrooms, and onions together over medium heat until lightly browned. Drain well. Spoon mixture on the paritally baked tortillas. Top with grated cheese. Bake for an additional 15-20 minutes until cheese is golden and bubbly. Makes 6-8 pizzas.

Barbara Corley (Mrs. Richard)

SAUSAGE LASAGNA

6 lasagna noodles
1 pound smoked sausage
3 slices mozzarella cheese
1 16-ounce jar Italian
  cooking sauce
Parmesan cheese

Cook and drain noodles. Divide sausage into six pieces. Then split sausage lengthwise. Stuff each with one-half slice cheese. Wrap each sausage with a noodle. Place in baking dish and cover with Italian cooking sauce. Bake for 30 minutes at 350°. Serve with Parmesan cheese. Makes 4-6 servings.

Linda Clementz (Mrs. Gregory)

SPAGHETTI

Meatballs:
3 pounds ground beef
½ onion, chopped
⅛ teaspoon sweet rosemary
⅛ teaspoon sweet basil
1 teaspoon garlic salt
⅓ teaspoon garlic powder
⅛ teaspoon marjoram leaves
Dash oregano
½ cup milk
1 teaspoon dry parsley
1 egg
½ package crackers, crushed
Dash salt and pepper
Sauce:
2 8-ounce cans tomato paste
1 ½ teaspoons garlic salt
Dash pepper
5 tablespoons sugar
4 8-ounce cans water
½ teaspoon salt
1 teaspoon garlic powder
2 bay leaves

Mix ingredients for meatballs together and make into small balls. Brown meatballs in small amount of cooking oil. Drain meatballs. Mix together all ingredients for sauce, add meatballs and simmer for one hour.

Ruth Giunta (Mrs. Edward)

MRS. CHAPMAN'S SPAGHETTI

1 pound ground beef
1 clove garlic, minced
2 large onions, cut fine
3 tablespoons olive oil or
butter
1 12-ounce can tomato
juice
1 6-ounce can tomato paste
1 cup consomme (Campbell's)
¼ teaspoon cloves
¼ teaspoon cinnamon
salt and pepper
1 cup mushrooms, sliced
or button
4 tablespoons Parmesan
cheese
8 ounces spaghetti

Brown meat and garlic in 1½ tablespoons olive oil or butter. Saute onions in remaining 1½ tablespoons oil until translucent. Combine and add all ingredients except mushrooms, Parmesan cheese, and spaghetti. Cook at a very low temperature 1½ hours. Add more juice or consomme if it cooks down too much (should be consistency of heavy cream). Add mushrooms last ten minutes of cooking and add cheese just before serving. Stir. Cook spaghetti until tender and serve with sauce. Pass extra cheese.

Joan Berney (Mrs. John)

SPAGHETTI WITH BROCCOLI, TOMATOES AND WALNUTS

1 pound thin spaghetti
½ cup walnuts, coarsely
  chopped
¼ cup butter or margarine
2 tablespoons olive or
  vegetable oil
1 pint cherry tomatoes,
  stems removed
1 large garlic clove, minced
½ teaspoon salt
1/16 teaspoon red pepper
  flakes
1 teaspoon leaf basil,
  crumbled
1 medium-sized bunch
  broccoli, cut into 1-inch
  pieces, about 6 cups
½ to 1 cup chicken broth
½ cup freshly grated
  Parmesan cheese
¼ cup fresh parsley,
  chopped

Cook pasta according to directions on box. Toast walnuts for 5 minutes at 350°. Melt 2 tablespoons butter and oil over moderate heat in a medium-sized skillet. Add the tomatoes. Cook, stirring often, about 5 minutes or until tomatoes are tender but still hold their shape. Stir in the garlic, salt, pepper, basil and cook 2 minutes longer. Remove from heat. Cover to keep warm. Add broccoli to pasta during last five minutes of cooking time. Drain pasta and broccoli. Melt two tablespoons butter in pasta kettle. Put pasta and broccoli in kettle. Toss to coat with butter. Add tomato mixture, ½ cup of the broth, the cheese and parsley. Toss to blend, adding more broth if mixture seems dry. Divide into four servings. Sprinkle each serving with ¼ of the nuts. Serve immediately with more Parmesan cheese.

Chris Palagallo (Mrs. Gerald L.)

FRANK'S LASAGNA

1 pound lasagna noodles
2 quarts spaghetti sauce
2 to 2 ½ pounds ricotta
  cheese
1 pound mozzarella cheese,
  grated
1 to 2 ounces Parmesan
  cheese, grated
1 to 2 ounces romano
  cheese, grated

Cook noodles as directed. Heat spaghetti sauce. Cover bottom of a 9 x 12-inch pan with sauce. Place one layer of noodles over sauce. Spread ricotta, mozzarella, Parmesan, and romano cheeses over noodles. Then cover with sauce. Repeat three or four times, ending with a layer of noodles, top with cheeses and sauce. Bake at 350° for 45 to 60 minutes. May be frozen.

Pat Russo (Mrs. Frank)

CANNELLONI

Filling:
2 tablespoons olive oil
¼ cup onion, chopped
1 teaspoon garlic, chopped
1 10-ounce package frozen, chopped spinach, thawed and drained
2 tablespoons butter
1 pound ground round steak
2 chicken livers
5 tablespoons grated Parmesan cheese
2 tablespoons heavy cream
2 eggs, lightly beaten
½ teaspoon oregano
Salt and pepper
Besciamella:
4 tablespoons butter
4 tablespoons flour
1 cup milk
1 cup heavy cream
1 teaspoon salt
⅛ teaspoon white pepper
Tomato Sauce:
4 tablespoons olive oil
1 cup onions, finely chopped
4 cups coarsely chopped tomatoes, undrained
6 tablespoons tomato paste
2 teaspoons dried basil
2 teaspoons sugar
1 teaspoon salt
Pepper
Manicotti noodles
4 tablespoons Parmesan cheese, grated
2 tablespoons butter

Filling: Heat olive oil in a skillet. Add the onions and garlic and cook over moderate heat, stirring frequently, for 7 or 8 minutes, until they are soft but not brown. Stir in the spinach and cook, stirring constantly, for 3 or 4 minutes. When all the moisture has boiled away, transfer to a large mixing bowl. Melt 1 tablespoon butter in the same skillet and lightly brown the ground meat, stirring constantly to break up any lumps. Add the meat to the onion-spinach mixture. Then melt 1 more tablespoon of butter in the skillet and cook the livers, turning them frequently for 3 or 4 minutes until they are somewhat firm, lightly browned but still pink inside. Chop them coarsely. Then add them to the meat mixture in the bowl along with the Parmesan cheese, cream, eggs, and oregano. With a wooden spoon, mix the ingredients together gently but thoroughly. Season with salt and pepper.

For Besciamella: In a heavy saucepan melt the butter over moderate heat. Remove the pan from the heat and stir in the flour. Pour in the milk and cream all at once, whisking until flour is partially dissolved. Then return pan to high heat and cook, stirring constantly with the whisk. When sauce comes to a boil and is smooth, reduce heat. Simmer, stirring, for 2 or 3 minutes longer, or until the sauce is thick enough to coat the wires of the whisk heavily. Remove sauce from heat and season with salt and pepper.

Tomato Sauce: Cook onions in olive oil; add remaining ingredients and simmer.

Assembling and baking Cannelloni: Pre-

Continued next page

Cannelloni continued

heat oven to 375°. Cook 1 box manicotti noodles. Stuff noodles with filling. Pour just a film of the tomato sauce into two 10 x 14-inch shallow baking dishes. Lay the cannelloni side by side in one layer on the tomato sauce. Pour the besciamella over it and spoon the rest of the tomato sauce on top. Scatter in 4 tablespoons Parmesan cheese and dot with 2 table-spoons butter. Bake the Cannelloni un-covered for 20 minutes or until the cheese is melted and the sauce bubbling.

Sharlyn Munns (Mrs. James)

SUPER STIR-FRY

2 tablespoons vegetable oil
Pork, chicken, turkey, or beef cut in thin strips (any amount)
2 cloves garlic, minced
2 tablespoons vegetable oil
2 cups broccoli stems and flowerets, thinly sliced
2 onions, cut in thin wedges
1 carrot, thinly sliced
mushrooms, sliced (any amount)
Sauce:
2 tablespoons cornstarch
1 ¼ cups water or chicken broth
⅓ cup soy sauce
⅓ cup dark corn syrup
Dash of crushed or ground red pepper

Heat oil over medium high heat in a large skillet or wok. Add meat and garlic. Stir fry 2 or 3 minutes until hot. Remove from skillet (if you use raw meat, stir fry until tender). Heat 2 tablespoons vegetable oil. Add broccoli, onions, and carrot. Stir fry 2 minutes. Add mushrooms. Stir fry 1 minute. Return meat to skillet. Add sauce and stir. Bring to boil over medium heat. Serve with rice. Makes 4 to 6 servings.

Sauce: Mix cornstarch and water in a bowl until smooth. Stir in soy sauce, corn syrup, and red pepper. This can be made ahead and kept cold. Stir just before using.

Jean Millikin (Mrs. Paul)

EASY ITALIAN CASSEROLE

1 pound ground beef
½ cup onion, chopped
1 clove garlic, crushed
1 15-ounce can tomato sauce
1 4-ounce can mushroom
  stems and pieces, drained
1 teaspoon sugar
½ teaspoon dried oregano
  leaves
½ teaspoon dried basil
  leaves
¼ teaspoon salt
¼ teaspoon pepper
2 cups Bisquick mix
½ cup milk
1 egg
8 slices (¾ ounce each)
  process American cheese
¼ cup Parmesan cheese,
  grated

Cook and stir ground beef, onion, and garlic in 10-inch skillet over medium heat until beef is brown; drain. Stir in tomato suace, mushrooms, sugar, oregano, basil, salt and pepper. Heat to boiling, stirring constantly. Reduce heat. Simmer, uncovered, stirring occasionally, 10 minutes. Heat oven to 400°. Grease a 9 x 9 x 2-inch pan. Mix baking mix, milk, and egg. Spread half of mixture in pan. Top with 4 of the cheese slices. Spoon beef mixture over cheese. Top with remaining cheese slices and sprinkle with Parmesan cheese. Drop remaining dough by spoonfuls onto cheese. Sprinkle with paprika if desired. Bake uncovered until light brown, about 20 minutes. Serves 6.

Lois Berg (Mrs. Ben)

CHEESE ENCHILADAS

1 package corn tortillas
1 16-ounce can tomato sauce
1 teaspoon garlic powder
1 teaspoon cumin
1 teaspoon oregano
1 small onion, chopped
12 ounces longhorn cheese,
  grated
12 ounces Monterey Jack
  cheese, grated
1 3 ½-ounce can black olives,
  chopped

Dip tortillas in warm cooking oil, then dip in tomato sauce seasoned with garlic powder, cumin and oregano. Spread with chopped onion, both cheeses, reserving about one cup for later use, and olives. Roll and layer in shallow baking dish. Pour a little sauce over each layer and sprinkle with cheese. Cover. Bake at 350°for 30 minutes. Serves 6.

Pat Russo (Mrs. Frank)

ITALIAN MEAT PIE

1 ½ pounds ground pork or beef
2 bunches green onions, chopped finely
2 tablespoons fennel
1 teaspoon chicken bouillon or poultry seasoning
pinch of sage
1 pound ricotta cheese
½ pound mozzarella cheese, shredded
½ pound provolone cheese, shredded
¼ cup parmesan cheese, grated
¼ cup parsley, chopped
3 eggs
1 box Pillsbury hot roll mix
⅓ cup granulated sugar, approximately
1 tablespoon soft margarine

Preheat oven to 350°. Brown pork in a large skillet and drain. Add onion, fennel, chicken bouillon, and sage. Simmer covered 20 minutes. In a large bowl mix all cheeses, parsley, eggs, 2 tablespoons sugar, salt and pepper to taste. Mix well. Add meat mixture and mix well. Mix hot roll mix according to pizza recipe on box. Spread ½ of dough on bottom and sides of a 9 x 13 greased pan. Spread filling evenly over dough. Spread rest of dough over top, meeting edge of bottom crust. Spread top of crust with 1 tablespoon soft margarine and sprinkle with remaining sugar. Punch several holes in top with a fork. Bake at 350° for 45 minutes or until top is nicely browned. May be cut in squares and served cold as an appetizer or served hot cut in large squares as a main course.

Lenore Juco (Mrs. Francisco)

FAGOTTINI DI CARNE
In Spanish "Empanadas"

½ pound lean ground beef
¼ pound ground pork
1 cup onion, chopped
1 cup green pepper, chopped
1 cup drained tomatoes, chopped
1 clove garlic, chopped
1 ½ teaspoons cornstarch
salt and pepper
Pastry:
3 cups unsifted flour
1 teaspoon salt
1 teaspoon baking powder
¾ cup oil
½ cup cold water

Brown meats. Add next 4 ingredients. Cook 10 minutes, stirring. Stir in cornstarch. Remove from heat. Cool. Prepare pastry as follows: combine flour, salt and baking powder. Combine oil and water. Add to flour mixture. Stir until soft dough forms. Divide pastry into 12 balls. Roll each ball into a 5-inch circle between wax paper. Place 3 tablespoons of meat mixture in center of each circle. Fold circle in half and seal edges with fork. Bake at 425° 12-15 minutes. Serve hot or cold. Excellent for picnics.

Ines Spano (Mrs. Gregory)

CHILI

2 pounds ground beef
1 16-ounce can tomatoes
1 6-ounce can tomato paste
1 small onion, chopped
6 ounces water
1 teaspoon (scant) chili
  powder
1 dash hot sauce
1 envelope Chili-O-Mix
1 16-ounce can fancy red
  kidney beans, drained
salt and pepper to taste

Brown meat in large skillet or pot. Add rest of ingredients and mix well, adding Chili-O and beans last. Cook slowly about one hour, stirring occasionally. Cool chili and refrigerate for later use. Recipe may be doubled and leftover chili frozen. If doubling, watch the amount of chili powder added.

Vivian Solomon (Mrs. Ted)

TOM'S TEXAS CHILI

3 pounds boneless chuck,
  cut in 1-inch cubes
2 tablespoons vegetable oil
4 tablespoons chili powder
2 teaspoon ground cumin
3 tablespoons flour
1 tablespoon leaf oregano
1 10 ¾-ounce can beef broth
1 teaspoon salt
¼ teaspoon pepper
1 cup dairy sour cream
1 lime cut into wedges
avocado slices

Heat oil in a 4-quart kettle on medium heat. Add beef, stirring until the meat changes color, but not brown. Lower heat. Combine chili powder, cumin, and flour. Sprinkle over meat, stir to coat. Crumble oregano over meat and add beef broth, stirring to blend. Add salt and pepper. Bring to a boil, stirring occasionally. Reduce heat and simmer, partially covered, over low heat for two hours. Stir occasionally. Cool thoroughly. Cover and refrigerate over night to ripen flavor. Before serving, reheat chili and simmer uncovered until meat is almost falling apart and sauce is thickened, 1 or 2 more hours. Garnish with sour cream, lime to squeeze, and slices of avocado. Serve with Mexicali corn bread, romaine salad, and caramel flan for dessert.

Joyce Rashid (Mrs. Ameel)

SWEET AND SOUR PORK
Good as Yen Ching's!

8 ounces boneless pork
½ teaspoon salt
1 teaspoon light soy sauce
flour
egg yolk, beaten
1 firm 3-inch tomato
1 3-inch onion
green pepper
1 dozen pineapple chunks
½ cup sweet and sour
  sauce (recipe below)

Cut pork into ¾-inch or ½-inch cubes. Season with salt and light soy sauce. Roll in flour; roll again in egg yolk, then flour. Deep fry until done at 320° for 2 to 3 minutes. Cut tomato into 8 parts. Cut onion the same way. Chop green pepper into ¾-inch squares. When pork is done, drain. Brown onion and pepper in one tablespoon oil for 30 seconds. Add ½ cup sweet and sour sauce. Cook one minute. Add tomato and pineapple chunks. Cook for 5 seconds. Add the deep fried pork and remove from heat. Mix well and serve immediately.

Sweet and sour sauce:

½ cup orange juice, preferably fresh, but frozen is
  acceptable
1 cup white vinegar
1 cup sugar
1 ½ teaspoons salt
½ cup pineapple juice
½ cup tomato paste
2 tablespoons cornstarch
4 tablespoons water

Combine above ingredients except cornstarch and water and bring to a boil slowly. Simmer for 10 minutes. Adjust seasoning to taste if needed. Blend cornstarch and water together and add to thicken. To store, keep this sauce in a large mouthed jar, covered loosely. Keep in a cool dark place. Keeps well for months!

Rita Luetkemeyer (Mrs. Richard)

Vegetables, Rice, and Pasta

SCALLOPED ASPARAGUS

2 cups soft bread crumbs or cracker crumbs, buttered
4 tablespoons butter
6 tablespoons flour
1 teaspoon salt
¼ teaspoon paprika
3 cups milk
1 cup American cheese, grated
4 hard-boiled eggs, sliced
1 2-ounce jar pimiento, sliced and drained
1 3½-ounce can mushrooms, whole or sliced, drained
2 or 3 15-ounce cans asparagus, drained

Place half of the crumbs in greased 2 to 2 ½-quart baking dish. Make a white sauce of butter, flour, milk and salt; add cheese and blend. Place alternate layers of asparagus, egg, pimiento, mushrooms, and cheese sauce. Cover top with remaining crumbs. Bake at 350° for 30 minutes. This can be made ahead of time and refrigerated until ready to bake.

Kacky Heinzen (Mrs. F. J.)
Lois Ward (Mrs. Edward)

GREEN BEANS WITH WALNUTS

1 pound green beans
⅔ cup water
1 tablespoon instant minced onion
2 teaspoons dry mustard
3 tablespoon butter
½ cup walnuts, toasted
½ cup radishes, coarsely grated (Optional)

Wash, trim, and cut beans in thin diagonal slices. Turn into a large skillet with boiling water, onion, mustard, and salt. Cover tightly and cook over moderate heat 10 to 15 minutes, or until tender and crisp. Add water if needed to keep from sticking. When beans are tender, liquid should be almost gone. Meanwhile, melt butter; add walnuts. Toss with cooked beans. Turn into serving dish and top with grated radish.

Jo Dorsch (Mrs. Thomas)

LIMA BEAN CASSEROLE

8 slices bacon, cut in small strips
2 10-ounce packages frozen baby lima beans
½ cup onion, chopped
½ cup celery, chopped
1 ½ cups Monterey Jack or mild cheddar cheese, shredded
¼ teaspoon pepper
Dash of Worchestershire sauce

Fry bacon until half done. Save 3 tablespoons of the drippings. Cook the lima beans in 1 ½ cups boiling, salted water until tender. Drain, reserving ½ cup of the liquid. Mix all of the ingredients except the bacon in lightly greased 2-quart casserole. Sprinkle with bacon. Bake uncovered at 350° for 25 minutes.

Gennie McMorrow (Mrs. T. R.)

BEST IN THE WEST BARBECUE BEAN BAKE

1 pound ground beef
1 pound bacon, chopped
1 onion, chopped
½ cup ketchup
½ cup barbecue sauce
1 teaspoon salt
4 tablespoons prepared mustard
4 tablespoons molasses (or honey)
1 teaspoon chili powder
½ teaspoon pepper
2 16-ounce cans red kidney beans
2 16-ounce cans pork and beans
2 16-ounce cans butter beans

Brown beef, bacon and onion. Drain excess fat. Combine with all other ingredients except beans; stir well. Add beans and combine thoroughly. Bake for 1 hour at 350°. Makes 20-24 servings.

Bertha Dean (Mrs. Robert)

CALIFORNIA BEANS

2 16-ounce can kidney beans
2 16-ounce cans pork and
  beans
6 slices bacon, cooked and
  crumbled
½ cup catsup
½ cup brown sugar
½ teaspoon chili powder
½ teaspoon cumin
1 onion, chopped
1 cup cheddar cheese,
  grated

Drain kidney beans; combine all ingredients except cheese. Bake at 400° in an uncovered bean pot for 45 minutes. Sprinkle cheese over top; cover and continue baking 15 minutes.

Marianne Wright (Mrs. Robert)

BROCCOLI CASSEROLE DIVAN
Excellent at Thanksgiving served with turkey!

2 10-ounce packages frozen
  chopped broccoli
Pepper
Monosodium glutamate
1 10 ½-ounce can cream of
  chicken soup, undiluted
Juice of 1 lemon
½ cup mayonnaise
6 slices American cheese
½ cup bread crumbs
2 tablespoons butter,
  melted
1 teaspoon seasoned salt

Cook broccoli as package directs, but cook just 5 minutes. Put in greased 9 x 13-inch casserole. Sprinkle with pepper and monosodium glutamate. Mix soup, lemon juice and mayonnaise. Spread over broccoli. Top with cheese. Sprinkle with crumbs. Drizzle with butter. Sprinkle with seasoned salt. Bake at 350° about 30 minutes. Serves 6-8.

Mary Owen (Mrs. Walter E.)

BROCCOLI CHEESE BAKE
Even broccoli haters like this. Makes a good side dish for a roast or a cold meat salad.

6 tablespoons butter
4 tablespoons onion, chopped
2 tablespoons flour
½ teaspoon salt
¼ teaspoon pepper
½ cup water
½ pound Velveeta cheese, cubed
3 eggs, slightly beaten
2 10-ounce packages chopped broccoli, thawed and drained
½ cup fine dry bread crumbs
1 tablespoon butter, melted

In saucepan melt butter. Saute onion until tender. Blend in flour, salt and pepper. Stir in water. Add cubed cheese and stir until melted. Combine eggs and broccoli. Add cheese sauce to broccoli mixture. Place in 2-quart shallow baking dish. Combine crumbs and melted butter. Sprinkle over top. Bake at 325° for 45 minutes or until done. Makes 8 servings.

Bernadette Shekleton (Mrs. Michael)

SESAME BROCCOLI

1 pound broccoli spears, cooked
1 tablespoon soy sauce
1 tablespoon champagne vinegar
1 package (individual) diet sweetener
1 tablespoon toasted sesame seeds
1 tablespoon margarine (optional)

Mix together soy sauce, vinegar, sweetener, sesame seeds, and margarine (if desired). Add to broccoli. Serves 4 to 6.

Shirley Bennett (Mrs. Gaylord)

RED CABBAGE AND WINE

1 head red cabbage, shredded
1 medium onion, chopped fine
4 tablespoons butter or
  drippings
1 medium apple, grated
¼ cup vinegar
½ cup red wine
½ of a 10-ounce jar of currant
  jelly
1 tablespoon honey
1 teaspoon salt
1/16 teaspoon pepper
1 tablespoon cornstarch

Combine all ingredients except cornstarch in a large pot. Simmer mixture until tender, stirring occasionally. Before serving add the cornstarch, dissolved in 2 tablespoons of water.

Phyllis Lowy (Mrs. Howard)

BAKED CINNAMON CARROTS

½ cup granulated sugar
4 tablespoons margarine
1 heaping teaspoon cinnamon
1 pound carrots, peeled, cut
  lengthwise in ⅜-inch
  strips about 2-inches long

In a 1 ½ to 2-quart casserole, melt sugar and margarine. Add cinnamon. Lay carrots on top. Add boiling water to cover. Bake at 350° for 1 hour and 30 minutes. Serve with slotted spoon.

Berenice Consigny (Mrs. Paul)

BAKED LIMAS WITH SOUR CREAM

2 cups dried limas, soaked
  overnight
½ teaspoon salt
¾ teaspoon prepared
  mustard
½ cup brown sugar
⅛ teaspoon pepper
1 cup sour cream
Bacon strips

Cook limas, in enough water to cover, with salt and mustard until tender. Drain. Place in a 2-quart baking dish. Add brown sugar and pepper and mix well. Pour over 1 cup sour cream and enough hot water to cover. Cover and bake 1 hour at 300°. Remove cover and place bacon strips on top and return to oven to crisp bacon. Very good!!

Sharlyn Munns (Mrs. James R.)

DELICIOUS CARROTS

1 16-ounce bag frozen carrots, whole
½ tablespoon cornstarch
½ tablespoon Tang
  (orange drink powder)
⅛ teaspoon salt
1/16 teaspoon nutmeg
1 tablespoon butter
Chopped parsley

Cook carrots according to package directions. Drain and save ½ cup of the liquid.
Blend in the remaining ingredients. Bring
to a boil to thicken. Add carrots. Sprinkle
chopped parsley over to garnish.

Berenice Consigny (Mrs. Paul)

GLAZED CARROTS

4 medium-sized carrots,
  peeled and sliced as coins
  or strips
1 tablespoon undiluted
  frozen orange juice
1 tablespoon brown sugar
2 tablespoons butter

Cook carrots until tender in boiling, lightly
salted water. Drain well. Combine carrots
with other ingredients in a large skillet.
Stir and heat until carrots are glazed.
This may be done in the oven. Also can
use frozen or canned carrots if desired.
Serve 4.

Dottie Flores (Mrs. Richard)

COMPANY CAULIFLOWER

1 medium cauliflower
½ pound mushrooms, sliced
¼ cup green pepper, sliced
¼ cup butter
¼ cup flour
2 cups milk
1 teaspoon salt
6 slices American cheese
Dash of paprika

Separate cauliflower in medium pieces.
Cook, covered, in boiling salted water
about 10 to 15 minutes. Drain. Meanwhile, saute mushrooms and green pepper
lightly in butter. Blend in flour; gradually
stir in milk and cook, stirring constantly
until thick. Add salt. Place half of the
cauliflower in a 1 ½-quart casserole. Cover
with cheese slices, then half of the sauce.
Repeat layers and sprinkle with paprika.
Bake at 350° about 15 minutes. Serves 6
to 8. Can be made ahead and refrigerated.
Increase baking time accordingly.

Kathleen Palmer (Mrs. Ronald)

CELERY-CARROT CASSEROLE

2 cups celery, sliced
  diagonally
2 cups carrots, sliced
1 8-ounce can water
  chestnuts, sliced
1 10 ½-ounce can cream of
  chicken soup
1 roll Ritz crackers
¼ pound butter or
  margarine, melted
Toasted almonds, slivered

Cook celery and carrots on simmer until crisp but not overdone. Add sliced water chestnuts and mix into chicken soup which has been slightly diluted. Put into a buttered casserole dish. Roll out crackers and mix crumbs into melted butter or margarine. Crumble over casserole and add toasted almond slivers. Bake at 350° until bubbly, about 20 minutes.

Ruth Easton (Mrs. Robert)

CREAMED CELERY WITH PECANS

4 cups celery, cut diagonally
  in ½-inch pieces
2 tablespoons butter
2 tablespoons flour
2 cups milk
½ teaspoon salt
¾ cup pecans, coarsely
  chopped
buttered bread or cracker
  crumbs

Grease a 1 ½-quart casserole. Boil celery until tender in enough water to cover. Drain (do not overcook). Melt butter over medium heat; stir in flour and add milk slowly to make cream sauce, stirring until thick and smooth. Add salt, well-drained celery, and pecans. Spoon into prepared cassrole and top with buttered crumbs. Bake at 400° for 15 minutes. (If baking other things at 350°, this can be baked at 350° for a longer period of time.)

Margaret Norris (Mrs. Paul)

CORN CASSEROLE

1 small onion, diced
1 medium green pepper, diced
½ cup butter
1 16-ounce can whole kernel corn, undrained
1 16-ounce can cream-style corn
1 8 ¾-ounce package Jiffy Corn Muffin Mix
3 eggs
1 teaspoon sugar
salt and pepper to taste
1 cup sour cream
1 ½ cups cheddar cheese, grated

Saute onion and pepper in butter. Add remaining ingredients. Pour into greased 2-quart casserole. Top with sour cream and cheese. Bake at 350° for 45 minutes or until golden brown.

Rita Luetkemeyer (Mrs. Richard)

EASY SCALLOPED CORN

2 17-ounce cans cream-style corn
1 small onion, chopped
salt to taste
pepper to taste
2 tablespoons butter
crackers
1 egg
½ can milk (using corn can as measure)
paprika

Butter a deep 1-quart baking dish. Layer 1 can of corn, ½ of the onion, ½ of the salt, ½ of the pepper, and butter. Break enough of the crackers to completely cover. Repeat layers and another layer of crackers. Beat egg and combine with milk. Pour over top. Pierce the casserole with fork in several places to allow milk mixture to mix into casserole. Sprinkle with paprika. Bake at 400° for 30 minutes. Serve hot. Casserole will puff up in center.

Liz Cram (Mrs. Richard)

MEXICAN CORN

1 16-ounce can creamed
  corn
1 cup Bisquick
1 egg, beaten
2 tablespoons butter,
  melted
1 tablespoon sugar
½ cup milk
1 3-ounce can chopped
  green chilies
1 cup Monterey jack cheese,
  shredded
Paprika

Combine corn, Bisquick, egg, butter, sugar, and milk. Pour half of this mixture in an 8 x 8-inch greased pan. Top with green chilies and Monterey jack cheese. Top with remaining corn mixture. Dust with paprika. Bake at 400° for 30 minutes.

Joan Berney (Mrs. John)

EGGPLANT PARMESAN

1 medium eggplant
2 eggs, beaten
1 cup bread crumbs
½ cup vegetable oil
1 ½ cups tomato sauce
1 teaspoon oregano
⅛ teaspoon garlic powder
Salt and pepper
½ cup Parmesan cheese
½ pound mozzarella cheese,
  grated

Peel eggplant and slice into ½-inch slices. Dip in beaten egg, then in crumbs. Saute in the oil until brown. Mix tomato sauce with oregano and garlic powder. Layer in a buttered casserole: eggplant, salt and pepper, Parmesan cheese, half the tomato sauce, and half the mozzarella cheese. Repeat. Bake at 350° for 30 minutes.

Joan Berney (Mrs. John)

LENTILS CREOLE

1 ½ cups lentils
4 cups water
1 bay leaf
1 cup onion, chopped
½ cup carrots, chopped
½ cup celery, chopped
2 tablespoons butter or
 margarine
2 16-ounce cans stewed
 tomatoes
1 6-ounce can hot V-8
1 10-ounce package frozen
 cut okra, partially thawed
½ teaspoon salt
½ teaspoon sugar
¼ teaspoon pepper
Few drops hot pepper sauce
Ground French thyme, basil,
 marjoram to taste

Rinse lentils. Bring to a boil in 4 cups water with bay leaf and simmer 30 minutes. In a medium saucepan saute onion, carrots, and celery in butter until lightly browned. Add remaining ingredients, including cooked lentils. Cover; stirring occasionally, simmer 45 minutes or more until okra is tender. Additional water may be added for desired consistency. Serve over brown rice.

Joyce Rashid (Mrs. Ameel)

MUSHROOM ONION CASSEROLE

2 ½ pounds onions, sliced
 (about 3 large)
6 tablespoons butter
2 tablespoons flour
½ cup cream
1 cup milk
8 ounces Monterey jack or
 Swiss cheese, grated
2 ounce jar pimiento,
 chopped
2 tablespoons sherry
1 ½ cups mushrooms, sliced
½ teaspoon marjoram
1 teaspoon thyme
1 ½ cups fine cracker
 crumbs
Slivered almonds

Saute onions in 2 tablespoons butter until tender; drain. Set aside. Melt 4 tablespoons butter in a saucepan. Add flour and stir well. Stir in cream and milk and cook over medium heat until thickened. Add cheese, pimiento, sherry, mushrooms, and seasonings. Grease a 2-quart casserole. Layer onions, cheese sauce, and cracker crumbs. Repeat. Top with slivered almonds. Bake in a 325° oven for one hour. Serves 8.

Joan Berney (Mrs. John)

OKRA MEDLEY

1 10-ounce box frozen okra
1 16-ounce can corn (whole kernel)
1 16-ounce can tomatoes

Cook okra as directed on package. Drain; cut pods in half. Add to corn and tomatoes. Heat in pan on top of stove. Good with fish dinner.

Kay Bickerman (Mrs. Ray)

ONION RINGS

4 cups onion rings, sliced ¼-inch thick
1 tablespoon salt
flour
Batter:
1 teaspoon basil powder
1 teaspoon pepper
½ teaspoon garlic salt
3 cups packaged pancake mix
3 cups club soda or beer

Place onion rings in container with lid. Sprinkle on salt and cover. Refrigerate 1 hour. Dredge the onion rings lightly in plain flour and allow to dry on waxed paper 4 to 5 minutes. Combine all ingredients for batter. Then dip onion rings in the batter to coat. Fry in deep fat at 375° to 400° until lightly browned.

Rita Luetkemeyer (Mrs. Richard)

STUFFED ONIONS

6 large onions
6 slices bacon
1 10 ¾-ounce can condensed cream of mushroom soup
1 10-ounce package frozen chopped spinach, cooked and drained
1 tablespoon vinegar
1 tablespoon brown sugar

Cut top off onions and scoop out leaving about ⅛-inch thick shell. Chop the scooped out onions. Cook bacon until crisp. Cook the chopped onions in the bacon drippings until tender. Stir in the soup, spinach, vinegar, brown sugar and bacon. Mix well and fill the onion shells with this mixture. Place the stuffed onions in a 2-quart shallow baking dish and cover with foil. Bake at 375° for 30 minutes or until tender. Larger onions may take longer. Makes 6 servings.

Ann Zolin (Mrs. William)

ORIENTAL PEAS

2 10-ounce packages frozen
  peas, cooked
1 cup water chestnuts,
  sliced
1 cup fresh bean sprouts
½ pound mushrooms,
  sauteed
1 cup Bechamel Sauce
  (Recipe below)
Soy sauce to taste

Mix all ingredients and bake at 350° for 30 minutes. Serves 8.

Bechamel Sauce:
4 tablespoons butter
4 tablespoons flour
1 cup milk
1 cup heavy cream
1 teaspoon salt

Melt butter, stir in flour. Add milk and cream. Stir, bringing to a boil. Simmer 2 to 3 minutes. Add salt.

Kathleen Palmer (Mrs. Ronald)

SWISS GREEN BEANS

4 tablespoons butter
2 tablespoons flour
1 teaspoon salt
1 teaspoon pepper
1 teaspoon sugar
½ teaspoon onion, grated
1 cup sour cream
4 cups French-style green
  beans, cooked
½ pound Swiss cheese,
  shredded
2 cups cornflakes, crushed

Melt half the butter and stir in flour, salt, pepper, sugar, and onion. Stir in sour cream and cook, stirring until sauce is hot and thickened. Fold in beans and cheese. Pour into baking dish. Melt remaining butter and stir in cornflakes. Sprinkle on top of casserole and bake at 400° for 20 minutes. Serves 6.

Marianne Wright (Mrs. Robert)

POTATO CASSEROLE

2 pounds frozen hash brown
  potatoes, thawed
½ cup melted margarine
1 teaspoon salt
¼ teaspoon pepper
½ cup onion, chopped or 2
  tablespoons instant onion
1 10-ounce can cream of
  chicken soup
1 pint sour cream
2 cups Cheddar cheese,
  shredded
Topping:
2 cups crushed cornflakes
¼ cup melted butter

Mix the first 8 ingredients and place in a greased 9 x 13 x 2-inch pan. Place corn-flakes on top and pour melted butter over all. Bake at 350° for 45 minutes. This casserole can be made the day before. Serves 16.

Marie Johnson (Mrs. David)
Pat Russo (Mrs. Frank)

IRISH POTATO CASSEROLE

8 to 10 medium-sized
  potatoes
1 8-ounce package cream
  cheese (softened)
1 8-ounce container sour
  cream
½ cup margarine or butter,
  melted
¼ cup chopped chives
1 small onion, grated or garlic
  to taste
paprika

Cook potatoes in boiling salted water until done. Drain and mash. Beat cream cheese with electric beater until smooth. Add potatoes and remaining ingredients except paprika. Beat just until combined. Spoon mixture into lightly buttered 2-quart casserole. Sprinkle with paprika. Cover with aluminum foil and refrigerate over night. Remove from refrigerator 15 minutes before baking. Uncover. Bake at 350° for 30 minutes, or until brown. Makes 8 servings.

Irene Ireland (Mrs. Harry)

SWISS POTATOES

5 medium potatoes, thinly
  sliced
1/16 teaspoon garlic powder
1 cup whipping cream
salt and pepper
2 ½ cups grated Gruyere
  cheese

Butter a 9 x 13-inch glass baking dish. Layer in several layers, ending with cheese as the last layer. Bake at 400° for 55 minutes.

Joyce Rashid (Mrs. Ameel)

CASSEROLE POTATOES

6 medium potatoes, peeled
  and diced
⅓ cup butter, melted
salt and pepper

Place diced potatoes in buttered 2-quart casserole. Add salt and pepper and melted butter. Toss lightly. Cover and bake at 325° about 45 minutes.

Gennie McMorrow (Mrs. T.R.)

ROASTED POTATOES

¼ cup cooking oil
2 teaspoons seasoned salt
⅛ teaspoon garlic powder
4 medium potatoes

Preheat oven to 350°. In a bowl combine oil, seasoned salt, and garlic powder. Quarter potatoes. Toss in seasoned oil. Place cut side up in small baking dish. Bake at 350° for one hour.

Bonnie Fenton (Mrs. Craig)

HOT DEVILED POTATOES
These are especially good in the summer served with grilled steaks.

Instant mashed potatoes, enough for 4 servings
½ cup dairy sour cream
2 teaspoons prepared mustard
½ teaspoon salt
½ teaspoon sugar
2 tablespoons green onion, chopped
paprika, for garnish

Prepare potatoes according to package directions. Heat sour cream (do not boil), add mustard, salt and sugar; stir. Stir into hot potatoes; add onion and stir. Spoon into foil potato shells. Heat in a 350° oven for 25 to 30 minutes. May be prepared ahead and stored in refrigerator.

Marianne Wright (Mrs. Robert)

MICROWAVE SAUERKRAUT

2 medium apples, chopped (about 2 ½ cups)
1 tablespoon butter or margarine
1 tablespoon flour
1 16-ounce can sauerkraut, rinsed and well drained
4 tablespoons brown sugar, divided
½ teaspoon caraway seed
⅓ cup pecans, chopped (optional)

Combine apples and butter in a 2-quart casserole. Cover; microwave on High 2 to 3 minutes or until tender. Remove half the mixture to a small bowl; set aside. Stir flour into remaining mixture. Add sauerkraut, 2 tablespoons brown sugar and caraway seeds. Cover; microwave on High 5 to 6 minutes or until heated through, stirring after half the cooking time. Combine the reserved apple-butter mixture with 2 tablespoons brown sugar and pecans. Sprinkle over sauerkraut. Microwave uncovered on High 1 to 3 minutes or until topping melts.

Rita Luetkemeyer (Mrs. Richard)

SAUERKRAUT WITH APPLES

1 27-ounce can sauerkraut
1 medium onion, sliced
1 tablespoon bacon drippings
   or cooking oil
3 medium apples, peeled,
   cored and sliced
1 large potato, peeled and
   shredded
1 cup chicken broth
2 tablespoons packed
   brown sugar
1 teaspoon salt
1 teaspoon caraway seed

Drain sauerkraut. Cook onion in oil until tender. Add sauerkraut, apples, potatoes, broth, brown sugar, salt and caraway seeds. Mix well. Cover and cook 20 minutes. Add more broth if needed. Sprinkle more brown sugar if desired. Serves 8-10. May add cooked, smoked ham hocks or bratwurst, to make complete meal.

Alice Sullivan (Mrs. E.A.)

SPINACH CHEESE BAKE
Good for brunch or as a side dish with main entree.

1 tablespoon butter
2 eggs
¾ cup skim milk
¼ cup flour
½ teaspoon baking powder
¼ teaspoon salt
⅛ teaspoon nutmeg
1 10-ounce package frozen
   chopped spinach, thawed
   and drained
2 cups (½ pound) shredded
   Monterey Jack cheese

Preheat oven to 350°. Place butter in 8-inch square dish and melt. Coat dish with butter. Beat eggs lightly; stir in milk. Add flour, baking powder, salt, and nutmeg. Beat until smooth. Stir in spinach and cheese. Pour into dish. Bake 30 to 35 minutes or until knife comes out clean. Serve immediately.

Carol Nelson (Mrs. John)

SPINACH CASSEROLE

3 to 4 10-ounce packages chopped frozen spinach
1 envelope onion soup mix
2 cups sour cream
1 cup Pepperidge Farm stuffing mix
½ cup melted butter

Cook spinach according to package directions. Drain **well**. Mix spinach with sour cream and onion soup mix. Put in lightly greased 2-quart casserole. Combine stuffing mix and melted butter. Place on top of spinach. Bake at 350° for 20 minutes.

Marie Johnson (Mrs. David)

SUMMER SQUASH CASSEROLE
Recipe from Aunt Fanny's Restaurant in Atlanta, Georgia

3 pounds yellow summer squash
½ cup onions, chopped
½ cup cracker meal or bread crumbs
½ teaspoon black pepper (salt and pepper may be increased to suit taste)
2 eggs
½ cup butter
1 tablespoon sugar
1 teaspoon salt (not with saltines)

Wash and cut up squash. Boil until tender, drain thoroughly, then mash. Add all ingredients except ¼ cup butter to squash. Melt remaining butter. Pour mixture in baking dish, then spread melted butter over top and sprinkle with cracker meal or bread crumbs. Bake at 375° for approximately one hour or until brown on top.

Jennifer Dolin (Mrs. Ben)
Irene McMenamin (Mrs. Hugh)

SQUASH WITH SOUR CREAM

2 pounds young summer
  squash
2 tablespoons butter
¼ cup onion, chopped
salt
paprika
1 cup sour cream
1 teaspoon flour
chopped dill

Peel and remove seeds from squash. Dice the pulp and cook in small amount of boiling water with a little salt added until it is tender. In a skillet in the 2 tablespoons of butter, saute the onions until golden. Add the cooked squash, well drained, and seasoned to taste with salt and paprika to the onions. Mix 1 cup of sour cream with one teaspoon of flour. Bring to a boil and pour over the squash. Serve hot, garnished with paprika and chopped dill.

Linda Carballido (Mrs. Jorge)

TOMATOES STUFFED WITH RICE

10 medium tomatoes
2 onions, finely chopped
2 tablespoons chopped
  parsley
1 garlic clove, chopped
2 tablespoons dill weed
1 teaspoon oregano
1 cup olive oil
1 cup rice, uncooked
½ cup pine nuts
2 tablespoons tomato paste
½ cup white wine
Salt and pepper to taste
Sugar

Cut tops off tomatoes; set aside. Scoop out pulp. Chop and reserve. Saute onions in ½ cup olive oil until golden. Add tomato pulp, parsley, garlic, dill, oregano, rice, pine nuts, salt and pepper. Stir to blend. Add tomato paste and wine. Cover and simmer 20 minutes. Arrange tomato shells in casserole. Sprinkle lightly with salt, pepper and sugar. Stuff with rice mixture and cover with tomato tops. Pour ½ cup olive oil over tomatoes and ½ cup water into pan. Sprinkle lightly with more oregano and an extra dash of wine. Bake at 350° for 35 minutes. Baste. Serve hot or cold.

Amelia Wilson (Mrs. Henry)

TOMATOES WITH HORSERADISH

8 tomatoes
1-2 tablespoons horseradish
1 cup mayonnaise
1 cup onion, grated
½ cup brown sugar
2 tablespoons white sugar
Paprika

Slice tops off tomatoes. Scrape out seeds and watery material. Place 1 tablespoon grated onion in each cavity. Let set 30 minutes. Place 1 tablespoon brown sugar in each tomato. Combine mayonnaise, horseradish, and white sugar (may add more horseradish to taste). Place some of mayonnaise mixture on each tomato. Dust with paprika. Bake at 450° for 10 minutes.

Chris Palagallo (Mrs. Gerald)

MIXED VEGETABLE CASSEROLE

2 10-ounce packages frozen mixed vegetables
1 10 ½-ounce can cream of mushroom soup
½ pound Velveeta cheese
Fresh bread cubes
¼ pound butter, melted

Cook vegetables according to package directions. Drain. Mix with soup and cheese. Completely cover with fresh bread cubes. Drizzle ¼ pound of melted margarine over all. Bake at 350° for 45 minutes.

Barbara Bordeaux (Mrs. Dean)

HOLIDAY VEGETABLES
Lovely at Christmas — good anytime!

1 medium head cauliflower (about 2 pounds)
1 bunch broccoli (about 1 ½ pounds), cut in flowerettes
1 pint cherry tomatoes (15 to 20)
Mornay Sauce:
¼ cup butter
¼ cup flour
2 cups chicken broth
¼ cup Swiss cheese, grated
¼ cup Parmesan cheese, grated
pinch each nutmeg, salt and pepper

Steam cauliflower head in covered pan until fork tender. Steam broccoli flowerettes in covered pan until fork tender. Saute cherry tomatoes in butter just until tender but not mushy. For sauce, melt butter, whisk in flour. Cook for 2 minutes. Whisk in chicken broth. Cook, stirring constantly, until thickened and smooth. Add cheeses slowly; heat until melted. Add seasonings. In 2-quart shallow casserole, spoon a layer of sauce over the bottom. Place cauliflower in the center, surround with broccoli and tomatoes. Put another layer of sauce over cauliflower only. Place under broiler to lightly brown cheese. Pass extra sauce. Serves 12.

Marilyn Bauer (Mrs. James)

SUNDAY NIGHT CASSEROLE

1 10-ounce package frozen peas, cooked and drained
1 15-ounce can bean sprouts, drained
2 4-ounce cans mushroom pieces, drained
1 8-ounce can water chestnuts, diced and drained
1 10 ½-ounce can condensed cream of mushroom soup
8 ounces cheddar cheese, grated
1 2.8-ounce can fried onion rings

Combine in 1 ½-quart casserole the peas, bean sprouts, mushrooms, and water chestnuts. Heat the can of soup and pour over the mixture. Grate the cheese and sprinkle on top. Bake at 350° for 30 minutes. Put the onion rings on top and bake 15 minutes longer, or until brown. To serve as a main course, you may add one of the following: shrimp, chicken, turkey.

Marilyn Wood (Mrs. John)

VEGETABLE SPAGHETTI SAUCE

1 large onion, chopped
8 tablespoons vegetable oil
1 pound fresh mushrooms
1 28-ounce can Italian
tomatoes
1 6-ounce can tomato paste
¾ cup red wine
2 cloves garlic, crushed
1 tablespoon oregano
1 tablespoon basil
1 tablespoon sugar
2 or 3 tablespoons cheese

Saute onions in oil until translucent (not brown), add mushrooms and stir for one or two minutes. Add tomatoes, tomato paste, wine, and spices. Add the sugar and cheese (not anymore cheese than suggested, or it will not be absorbed and stick to the pan). Simmer covered for 3 hours. Season with salt and pepper to taste.

Alice Sullivan (Mrs. E.A.)

RICE WITH MUSHROOMS

1 cup Converted Rice,
uncooked
1 10 ½-ounce can beef
consomme
1 10½-ounce can onion soup
1 4-ounce can mushrooms,
drained

Combine all ingredients and bake at 350° for 1 hour.

Mary Ann Smith (Mrs. Edward)

RICE NOODLE PILAF
Excellent with roast beef!

4 ounces raw fine noodles
½ cup butter, melted
(not margarine)
1 cup raw white rice
1 13-ounce can chicken broth
1 chicken bouillon cube
½ cup hot water

Brown noodles in melted butter. Add rice and chicken broth. Dissolve chicken bouillon cube in ½ cup hot water. Add to noodle-rice mixture. Cover and let simmer on low heat for 45 minutes or until liquid is absorbed. Serves 4.

Vivian Solomon (Mrs. Ted)

ONION RICE PILAF

1 cup raw rice
1 package onion soup mix
3 cups boiling water
¼ cup butter, melted

Mix together rice and onion soup mix. Pour into a 1 ½-quart casserole. Stir in boiling water and butter. Cover. Bake at 425° for 30-35 minutes. Fluff with fork before serving. Serves 4 to 6.

Beverly Daniels (Mrs. Roswell)

MACARONI DELUXE

1 7-ounce package (1 ¾ cups)
  macaroni, cooked
2 cups small-curd cottage
  cheese
1 cup sour cream
1 beaten egg
¾ teaspoon salt
pepper
8 ounces or more sharp
  cheddar cheese, grated
  (2 cups)

Mix all ingredients and put in buttered, 2-quart casserole. Sprinkle with paprika and bake for 45 minutes at 325°.

Joan Berney (Mrs. John)

RICE CASEROLE

½ cup margarine or butter
1 cup beef bouillon
1 cup water
1 tablespoon soy sauce
1 tablespoon Worcestershire
  sauce
½ teaspoon garlic salt
½ teaspoon celery salt
1 cup Uncle Ben's rice

Combine all ingredients in a 1-quart casserole. Bake uncovered at 375° for one hour.

Pat Callaway (Mrs. James)

MICROWAVE STEAMED RICE

1 cup long grain rice
2 cups water

Mix rice and water in a 2-quart baking dish. Microwave, uncovered, on high for 10 minutes. Cover and let stand 10 minutes. Stir rice, cover, and microwave on high 5 minutes. Stir rice, cover, and let stand 10 minutes. Serves 4.

Sandra Neu (Mrs. M. T.)

WILD RICE

1 cup onions, chopped
3 4-ounce cans mushrooms
6 tablespoons butter
½ teaspoon salt
½ teaspoon marjoram
½ teaspoon thyme
1 8-ounce can water chestnuts, sliced and drained
1 box Uncle Ben's Wild
  Rice, prepared according
  to package directions

Saute onions and mushrooms in butter for about 10 minutes. Add all the spices, water chestnuts, and cooked rice. Mix well. Bake covered, in a 300° oven, for one hour. This may be made the day before and refrigerated.

Dolores Sheen (Mrs. John)

RICE PILAF

1 onion, chopped
1 cup raw rice
2 tablespoons vegetable oil
2 cups chicken broth
2 chicken bouillon cubes
¾ tablespoon salt
¼ teaspoon pepper
¼ teaspoon thyme
½ green pepper, chopped
½ cup raisins
2 cups chicken, cooked
  and diced

Slowly cook onion and rice in oil for 5 minutes, stirring often. Add next 6 ingredients. Bring to boil; cover and simmer over low heat for 25 minutes. Add and mix chicken, cover and heat 5 minutes. Garnish with pimiento if desired.

Ann Zolin (Mrs. William)

CURRIED ORANGE RICE
Colorful side dish to dress up plain meat

¼ cup butter or margarine
1 medium onion, thinly sliced
2 teaspoons curry powder
1 cup uncooked rice
1 cup orange juice
1 cup chicken broth
1 teaspoon salt
½ cup raisins
1 bay leaf

Melt butter in a heavy saucepan. Saute onion until soft and golden, but not brown. Stir in curry and rice and cook 2 minutes longer, stirring constantly. Add remaining ingredients; stir with a fork. Bring to boiling. Lower heat, cover, and simmer 15 to 20 minutes or until rice is tender and liquid absorbed. Remove bay leaf before serving. Serves 6.

Bernadette Shekleton (Mrs. Michael)

FETTUCINI ALFREDO

Noodles:
3 cups all-purpose flour
3 eggs
2 egg yolks
1/16 teaspoon salt
Sauce:
1 stick unsalted butter
1 cup heavy cream
1 ¼ cups Parmesan cheese
Parsley

Spray the Cuisinart bowl with Pam. Put all noodle ingredients in it and work the dough, for a minute or less. Dough will be stiff. Let rest for 15 minutes. Divide dough into 4 parts and roll out each part to paper thickness. Sprinkle with flour and cut into strips. Arrange on wooden board or cookie sheet covered with a towel. Bring 4-6 quarts of water with 1 tablespoon salt to boiling. Add noodles and stir occasionally, cooking for 6-8 minutes, depending on thickness of noodles, or until noodles are al dente. Sauce: Heat butter and cream gently until butter is melted. Remove from heat and add 1 cup Parmesan cheese. Stir until the sauce is smooth. Add sauce to well-drained noodles. Toss until well coated. Cover and let stand 3-5 minutes. Toss again and sprinkle with remaining ¼ cup Parmesan cheese and some parsley. 3 Italian servings or 6 American servings.

Ines Spano (Mrs. Gregory)

GRANDMA MILLER'S NOODLES
A truly old-fashioned recipe

3 whole eggs
5 egg yolks
Cream
3 cups flour, approximately
⅛ teaspoon salt

Beat eggs and egg yolks until light. Add two half egg shells of cream. Continue beating. Add flour and salt and mix until dough is **very** stiff. Divide into 4 parts. Roll out very thin. Let dry on dish towels. Before it is brittle, cut into strips. Freeze or use immediately. To cook, drop into boiling soup or boiling, salted water and cook uncovered about 10 minutes.

Lois Ward (Mrs. Edward)

POPPY SEED LOAF DELIGHT
This is our favorite Christmas bread. Great for gifts!

Bread:
3 cups flour
2 ¼ cups sugar
1 ½ cups milk
1 ⅛ cups vegetable oil
3 eggs
1 ½ tablespoons poppy seeds
1 ½ teaspoons salt
1 ½ teaspoons baking powder
1 ½ teaspoons vanilla
1 ½ teaspoons almond extract
1 ½ teaspoons butter flavoring
Glaze:
¾ cup sugar
¼ cup orange juice
½ teaspoon vanilla
½ teaspoon almond extract
½ teaspoon butter flavoring

Combine all of the ingredients for the bread and mix 1 to 2 minutes with electric mixer. Pour into 2 greased and floured 9 x 5-inch loaf pans. Bake 350° for 1 hour. Let cool in pan about 5 minutes, then glaze. Mix all glaze ingredients well and pour over warm bread while still in pans.

Marianne Wright (Mrs. Robert)

COLUMBIAN CHEESE BREAD
Good for breakfast and for snacks.

¼ cup butter, melted
½ cup sugar
2 eggs
1 cup Bisquick
½ cup milk
¼ cup Parmesan cheese

Mix ingredients together in the order given. Bake in a greased 8 x 8 x 3-inch pan for 30 minutes at 350°.

Clara Remolina (Mrs. Rodrigo)

MOTHER'S SPOON BREAD

1 cup cornmeal
2 cups cold water
1 teaspoon salt
1 cup milk
2 eggs, well beaten
2 teaspoons melted butter

Mix cornmeal, water, and salt. Boil for five minutes, stirring constantly. Add milk, eggs, and melted butter. Mix well. Pour into a buttered, 2-quart casserole. Bake 45 minutes at 400°. Serve immediately with butter.

Margaret Norris (Mrs. Paul)

LEMON POPPY SEED BREAD
This bread freezes very well.

1 package lemon or white
  cake mix
4 eggs
1 cup hot water
¼ cup poppy seeds
1 teaspoon lemon extract
½ cup oil
1 3 ¾-ounce package lemon
  instant pudding

Mix all ingredients in a large bowl. Beat for four minutes. Bake in two 9 x 5-inch, or ten small, or one large and 5 small greased and floured bread pans at 350° for 25-30 minutes. Let cool on racks for 10 minutes, then remove from pans.

Pat Russo (Mrs. Frank)

PUMPKIN BREAD AND FROSTING

3 cups sugar
4 eggs
⅔ cup shortening
3 ⅓ cups flour
½ teaspoon baking powder
2 teaspoons baking soda
1 teaspoon salt
1 teaspoon cinnamon
½ teaspoon cloves
1 teaspoon ginger
2 cups pumpkin meat
⅔ cup water
1 cup walnuts, chopped
Frosting:
  8 ounces cream cheese
  honey

Beat sugar, eggs and shortening. Sift dry ingredients. Add to creamed mixture. Add water alternately with the flour. Then add pumpkin and nuts. Place in two greased loaf pans. Bake at 350° for one hour. Remove from pan when cool and frost. Frosting: Add enough honey to cream cheese to make it spreadable.

Mary Ellen DeBord (Mrs. Alan)

ENGLISH MUFFIN BREAD

5 ½ to 6 cups flour, spooned
   lightly into cup
2 packages active dry yeast
1 tablespoon sugar
2 teaspoons salt
¼ teaspoon baking soda
2 cups milk
½ cup water
cornmeal

Combine 3 cups flour, yeast, sugar, salt, and soda. Heat liquids until very warm (125°). Add to dry mixture. Beat well. Stir in enough more flour to make a stiff batter. Grease 2 8½ x 4½-inch bread pans and sprinkle with cornmeal. Spoon batter into pans and sprinkle cornmeal on top. Cover. Let rise in warm place 45 minutes. Bake at 400° for 25 minutes. Remove from pans at once and cool.

Berenice Consigny (Mrs. Paul)

12 GRAIN BREAD
Ingredients may be found in health food stores.

1 package (1 tablespoon)
   yeast
1 tablespoon honey
½ cup lukewarm water
4 cups stone-ground whole
   wheat flour
¼ cup wheat germ
¼ cup rolled oats
½ cup 7 Grain Cereal
1 tablespoon sunflower seed
¼ cup dark burgal
1 tablespoon millet
1 tablespoon sesame seed
1 tablespoon caraway seed
1 teaspoon salt
1 tablespoon oil
½ cup raw honey
1 ½ cups water

Proof yeast with 1 tablespoon honey and ½ cup lukewarm water (110-115 degrees). Let stand while combining the flour, grain, seeds, and salt. Then add the oil, ½ cup honey, and the yeast mixture along with 1 ½ cups water to form a soft dough. Place in oiled bread pan and let rise 30 minutes in a warm place. Bake at 350° for 35-40 minutes.

Joyce Rashid (Mrs. Ameel)

HEALTH BREAD

2 cups unbleached flour
1 cup whole wheat flour
1 tablespoon wheat germ
2 packages dry yeast
1 cup rolled oats
1 cup bran
1 cup seedless raisins
1 ½ cups low-fat cottage cheese
2 tablespoons vegetable oil
1 tablespoon salt
½ cup honey
2 ½ cups boiling water
Approximately 4 ½ cups unbleached flour

In a large mixing bowl stir together the 2 cups unbleached flour, whole wheat flour, wheat germ, and yeast. Set aside. In a separate bowl combine the rolled oats, bran, raisins, cottage cheese, oil, salt, and honey. Cover with boiling water and stir until thoroughly mixed. Cool to lukewarm and add to dry ingredients in mixing bowl. Beat ½ minute at lowest speed on electric mixer, scraping bowl constantly. Beat 3 minutes at highest speed. Stir in about 4 ½ cups of flour by hand until mixture forms a moderately stiff dough. Turn out onto floured board and knead until smooth and elastic, about 10 minutes. Place in a greased bowl, turning once to grease surface. Cover with dampened towel and let rise until double in bulk, about 1 hour. Punch down and divide into thirds. Cover and let rest 10 minutes. Shape into 3 loaves. Place in 3 greased 8 ½ x 4 ½ x 1 ½-inch loaf pans. Brush tops lightly with vegetable oil. Cover and let rise until double, about 35 to 45 minutes. Bake in a 375° oven 35-40 minutes or until golden brown. Remove from pans and let cool on rack.

Lois Berg (Mrs. Ben C.)

STRAWBERRY BREAD
"Berry" good

3 cups flour
1 ½ teaspoons cinnamon
1 teaspoon baking soda
1 teaspoon salt
2 cups sugar
2 10-ounce packages frozen
  sliced strawberries in
  syrup, thawed, undrained
4 eggs, beaten
1 ¼ cups vegetable oil
1 cup pecans, chopped

Sift flour, cinnamon, baking soda, and salt together; combine with sugar in a large bowl. Make well in center; put strawberries, eggs, oil, and pecans in well and stir until moistened. Pour batter into 2 greased and floured 9 x 5-inch loaf pans. Bake at 350° for 60 to 75 minutes or until toothpick inserted in center comes out clean. Makes 2 loaves.

Pat Russo (Mrs. Frank)
Marianne Wright (Mrs. Robert)

BANANA CHOCOLATE BREAD
Makes a special Christmas present when tied up with bright ribbons.

⅓ cup shortening
⅔ cup sugar
2 eggs
¼ cup milk
¾ teaspoon vinegar
1 cup ripe bananas, mashed
1 cup plus 2 tablespoons
  unsifted flour
1 teaspoon baking powder
½ teaspoon salt
½ teaspoon baking soda
1 6-ounce package semisweet
  chocolate pieces
1 cup raisins
½ cup nuts, finely chopped

In large bowl combine shortening, sugar, and eggs; beat until creamy. In small bowl combine milk and vinegar; stir in mashed banana. In small bowl combine flour, baking powder, salt, and baking soda. Stir flour mixture into creamed mixture alternately with banana mixture. Fold in chocolate, raisins, and nuts. Spread into four well-greased and floured 6 x 3 ½ x 2-inch loaf pans. Bake at 375° for 25-30 minutes. Wrapped tightly in foil, these freeze well. Makes 4 loaves.

Jo Dorsch (Mrs. Tom)

BROWN BREAD

2 cups milk
¼ teaspoon vinegar
1 teaspoon baking soda
2 cups whole bran
2 cups flour
1 teaspoon baking powder
1 cup brown sugar
1 cup raisins
½ teaspoon salt

Combine milk, vinegar, baking soda and whole bran in a bowl. In another bowl combine flour, baking powder, brown sugar, raisins and salt. Add to first mixture. Place in a buttered loaf pan and bake at 375° for one hour; or bake in two loaf pans for 50 minutes.

Doris Dirkse (Mrs. Paul)

BOSTON BROWN BREAD

1 cup boiling water
1 cup raisins
1 cup dates, chopped
3 tablespoons butter
1 ½ teaspoons baking soda
2 eggs
1 cup sugar
1 ¾ cups flour
½ teaspoon salt
1 teaspoon vanilla
½ cup nuts, chopped (walnuts, pecans, etc.)

Pour boiling water over raisins, dates, butter, and baking soda and let stand a few minutes. Beat well the eggs, sugar, flour, salt, and vanilla. Combine with fruit mixture and beat well. Add chopped nuts. Bake at 350° for 45 to 50 minutes in a well-greased and floured loaf pan or cans.

Ann Zolin (Mrs. William)

SPIEDINI BREAD

1 cup butter, room temperature
1 ¼ tablespoons crushed basil
garlic powder to taste
2 tablespoons capers, rinsed (optional)
salt to taste
16 ounces mozzarella cheese
2 small loaves French bread

Cream butter in basil. Blend in garlic powder, capers, and salt. Trim off top and sides of bread. Slice 1 ½-inch slices, leaving bottom intact. Cut cheese into as many slices as bread. Place cheese between cuts. Spread butter over bread top and sides. Wrap in foil. Bake at 400° degrees for 20 minutes. Open foil and brown.

Sally Gibson (Mrs. William)

ZUCCHINI BREAD

2 cups sugar
1 ½ cups whole wheat flour
1 ½ cups white flour
1 teaspoon salt
1 teaspoon cinnamon
1 teaspoon soda
¼ teaspoon baking powder
2 eggs
1 cup vegetable oil
2 teaspoons vanilla
2 cups shredded, raw
  zucchini
½ to 1 cup chopped nuts

Sift dry ingredients into a bowl. Add other ingredients. Mix well with electric mixer. Put into two regular, or four small bread pans, greased and floured. Bake at 350° for 60 minutes in regular pan, 45 minutes in small pans.

Gladys Powers (Mrs. Norman E.)

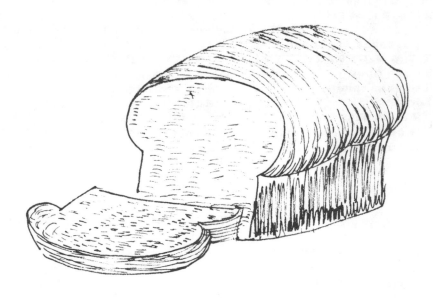

CHERRY COFFEE CAKE

1 cup butter
1 ¾ cups sugar
4 eggs
1 teaspoon vanilla
3 cups flour
1 ½ teaspoons baking powder
½ teaspoon salt
2 21-ounce cans cherry pie
  filling
powdered sugar

Beat butter, sugar, eggs, and vanilla at medium speed about two minutes until light and fluffy. Combine flour, baking powder, and salt, adding gradually to creamed mixture. Beat well. Spread in greased 11 x 15 ½-inch jelly roll pan, saving about 1 ½ cups of batter for topping. Spread cherry pie filling over dough to edges of pan. Spoon rest of dough over cherries. Bake at 350° for 45 minutes. Sprinkle with powdered sugar before serving. Cut in squares.

Marie Johnson (Mrs. David)

STREUSEL COFFEE CAKE

2 cups milk
¾ cup sugar
½ cup margarine
2 teaspoons salt
2 eggs
2 packages dry yeast
½ cup warm water
9 cups flour
8 ounces raisins
Topping:
  2 cups sugar
  ½ cup flour
  ½ cup butter

Bring milk just to a boil (Scald). Remove from heat. Add ¾ cup sugar, margarine and salt. Stir until dissolved. When cool, beat in eggs. Stir yeast into warm water (it should bubble). Add yeast mixture to milk mixture. Then add flour and raisins. Cover mixture and let rise until double in size. When doubled, punch down and knead, then let rise again. Spread evenly in a greased cookie sheet with sides. Let rise until doubled. Mix together the 2 cups sugar with ½ cup flour. Add ½ cup butter. Spread topping over dough. Bake at 375° until light brown, about 30 minutes.

Ruth Giunta (Mrs. Edward)

COFFEE CAKE EXCEPTIONALE
Easy to make and freezes well.

¾ cup butter or margarine
1 ½ cups sugar
3 eggs
1 ½ teaspoons vanilla
3 cups flour
1 ½ teaspoons baking powder
1 ½ teaspoons baking soda
¼ teaspoon salt
1 ½ cups sour cream
Cinnamon Nut Filling:
  ½ cup brown sugar
  ½ cup chopped nuts
  1 ½ teaspoons cinnamon

Preheat oven to 350°. Grease a tube pan. Cream butter and sugar thoroughly. Beat in eggs and vanilla. Stir flour, baking powder, baking soda, and salt together. Mix into creamed mixture, alternating with sour cream. Spread one-third batter into pan. Sprinkle with ⅓ cup filling. Repeat twice. Bake 50-60 minutes. Cool slightly before removing. Filling: Mix brown sugar, nuts, and cinnamon together.

Kristy Gorenz (Mrs. David)

BLITZ KUCHEN
German Coffee Cake

¼ cup shortening or butter
1 cup sugar
2 eggs, separated
¼ teaspoon salt
1 ½ cups cake flour
1 teaspoon baking powder
½ cup milk
2 tablespoons butter, melted
Cinnamon
Sugar

Cream shortening or butter and sugar. Add egg yolks and salt. Mix well. Sift cake flour and baking powder together. Add to first mixture alternately with milk. Beat egg whites until stiff; fold in. Pour into greased and floured 9 x 9-inch pan. Pour 2 tablespoons melted butter over the top. Sprinkle with cinnamon and sugar. Bake at 350° for 30 minutes.

Beth Shay (Mrs. Thanad)

CRESCENT CARAMEL SWIRL

½ cup butter or margarine
½ cup nuts, chopped
1 cup brown sugar
2 tablespoons water
2 8-ounce cans Pillsbury Refrigerated Quick Crescent Dinner Rolls

Preheat oven to 375° (350° for colored, fluted tube pan). In small saucepan, melt butter. Coat bottom and sides of a 12-cup fluted tube pan with 2 tablespoons melted butter; sprinkle pan with 3 tablespoons chopped nuts. Add remaining nuts, brown sugar and water to butter; heat to boiling, stirring occasionally. Remove crescents from cans in rolled sections; do not unroll. Cut each section into 4 slices. Arrange 8 slices in pan, separating each pinwheel slightly to allow sauce to penetrate. Spoon half of sauce over dough. Repeat with remaining dough on top of slices in pan; pour remaining caramel sauce over dough. Bake 25-30 minutes (30-35 minutes for colored fluted tube pan) until deep golden brown. Cool three minutes; turn onto serving platter.

Joan Leu (Mrs. Richard)

CHRISTMAS CRANBERRY MUFFINS

1 cup raw cranberries, chopped
½ cup sugar
2 cups flour
¼ teaspoon salt
¾ teaspoon baking soda
¼ cup sugar
1 egg, beaten
¾ cup sour milk or buttermilk
¼ cup shortening, melted

Combine cranberries and ½ cup sugar. Sift flour, salt, soda, and ¼ cup sugar. Mix together egg, milk, and shortening; add to the dry ingredients and stir just until mixed. Add cranberries, mixing slightly, just enough to distribute them through the batter. Fill greased muffin pans ⅔ full. Bake in 400° oven about 20 minutes. Makes 1 dozen muffins.

Marilyn Leyland (Mrs. John)

BRAN MUFFINS

1 cup boiling water
1 cup Nabisco 100% Bran
½ cup margarine
1 ½ cups sugar
2 eggs
2 cups buttermilk
2 ½ teaspoons soda
1 teaspoon salt
2 ½ cups flour
2 cups Kellogg All Bran

Pour ½ cup boiling water over Nabisco Bran; let cool. Cream together margarine and sugar. Add eggs, buttermilk, and remaining ½ cup hot water. Mix well. Sift together soda, salt, and flour; add to creamed mixture with both brans. Bake in greased muffin tins at 400° for 15-20 minutes. Makes a large batch. Batter keeps up to 6 weeks in the refrigerator.

Charlotte Barbour (Mrs. O. E.)

DANISH PUFFS

1 cup flour
½ cup margarine
2 tablespoons water
1 cup water
½ cup margarine
1 tablespoon almond extract
1 cup flour
3 eggs
Frosting:
  8 ounces confectioner's
    sugar
  ¼ cup margarine
  1 teaspoon vanilla
  warm milk

Put flour into a bowl. Cut in margarine thoroughly. Add 2 tablespoons water. Mix well. Press into two 12 x 3-inch strips on greased cookie sheets. Bring 1 cup water and ½ cup margarine to a boil. Take off stove. Add almond extract and flour all at once. Stir in the eggs, one at a time. Spread on crust. Bake on hour at 350°. Frost while warm. Best used the day of baking. Frosting: Combine confectioner's sugar, margarine and vanilla. Add enough warm milk to make spreading consistency.

Beverly Daniels (Mrs. Roswell)

MAYONNAISE MUFFINS

1 cup self-rising flour
2 tablespoons mayonnaise
½ cup milk

Combine ingredients and stir until smooth. Fill greased muffin tins ⅔ full. Bake at 425° for 10 to 12 minutes. Yields 6 muffins.

Berenice Consigny (Mrs. Paul)

SOUTHERN BISCUIT MUFFINS
From K-Pauls in New Orleans

2 ½ cups flour
¼ cup sugar
¼ teaspoon salt
1 ½ teaspoons baking powder
½ cup plus 2 tablespoons
  unsalted butter, softened
1 cup milk

Mix dry ingredients well. Work in the butter with your hands until it looks like cornmeal, leaving no lumps. Gradually add the milk, stirring with a spoon, being careful not to overbeat. Use enough milk so batter is wet but not runny. Spoon into greased 12-cup muffin pan. Bake in a 350° oven for 35 to 45 minutes or until golden brown. Make 12 muffins.

Berenice Consigny (Mrs. Paul)

BLUEBERRY MUFFINS

1 cup sugar
3 cups flour
3 teaspoons baking powder
3 eggs
1 cup milk
5 tablespoons margarine,
  melted
1 ½ cups blueberries

Sift sugar, flour and baking powder together. Beat eggs, milk, and margarine together. Combine the two mixtures and blend only until moistened. Add blueberries. Put in well-greased muffin tins. Bake at 400° for 20-25 minutes. Makes 24 muffins.

Ruth Giunta (Mrs. Edward)

SIX-WEEK BRAN MUFFINS

4 eggs
1 quart buttermilk
1 cup vegetable oil
1 15-ounce box raisin bran
3 cups sugar
5 cups flour
5 teaspoons baking soda
2 teaspoons salt

Mix eggs, buttermilk and oil. Add to the remaining ingredients and mix well. Fill muffin tins, greased or lined with cupcake papers, ⅔ full and bake at 400° for 15 minutes. This batter may be stored, covered, in the refrigerator for 6 weeks. Use as desired. Hot muffins every morning!

Tish Roberts (Mrs. Stuart)

SALLY LUNN
This is delicious sliced cold, toasted, and buttered.

1 package dry yeast
¼ cup lukewarm water (110°-115°)
2 cups milk
4 tablespoons sugar
1 cup shortening, melted
3 eggs
5 cups flour, sifted
1 teaspoon salt

Dissolve yeast in lukewarm water. Warm the milk to the temperature of the water, and add to yeast with sugar and shortening. Beat eggs well and add to liquid. Sift flour and salt together and stir into liquid mixture. Dough will be fairly stiff. Mix well and cover. Let rise in a warm place for 2 hours. Grease a large angel food cake pan (10-inch tube pan). Punch dough down and place in pan. Cover and let rise to within an inch of the top. Place in a cold oven and turn oven to 350°. Bake for 1 hour. Serve piping hot!

Lois Berg (Mrs. Ben C.)

MINI BISCUITS
These biscuits are good with ham or to serve for a luncheon.

1 cup self-rising flour
1 cup whipping cream, not whipped
3 tablespoons sugar (or less for less sweetness)

Mix together all ingredients and pour into greased miniature muffin cups. Bake in a preheated 450° oven for 10-15 minutes or until brown.

Vivian Solomon (Mrs. Ted)

EASY WHITE BREAD OR ROLLS
Makes delicious hamburger buns!

1 package active dry yeast
1 ¼ cup lukewarm water
2 tablespoons soft shortening
2 tablespoons sugar
1 teaspoon salt
3 cups flour

Dissolve yeast in the lukewarm water. Add remaining ingredients and mix well, forming into a ball. Let rise 30 minutes in mixing bowl covered with plastic. Knead and form into loaves or rolls; put into greased pans. Cover, and let rise 40 minutes. Bake at 375° until brown and firm.

Beverly Daniels (Mrs. Roswell)

ICE BOX ROLLS

1 cup (½ pound) lard
¾ cup sugar
1 cup boiling water
1 package dry yeast
1 cup lukewarm water
2 eggs, well beaten
6 cups sifted flour
2 teaspoons salt

Combine lard and sugar. Add boiling water. Mix well. Set aside to cool. While cooling, dissolve yeast in lukewarm water. Add to cooled first mixture. Add eggs, flour, and salt. Stir. Put in greased pie plate. May be refrigerated several weeks. Roll out cold dough on greased cookie sheet. Let rise 2 hours. Punch down and form into Parker House rolls.* Place close together so they touch. let rise 2 hours. Bake at 425° for 12 to 15 minutes.

* To make Parker House rolls, cut in small circle, indent across center, dip in melted butter and fold over.

Mary Owen (Mrs. Walter)

GRANDMA MILLER'S GREAT CORN FRITTERS
Especially good with chicken!

1 egg
¼ cup milk
1 cup pancake flour
1 cup whole kernel corn,
    drained

Blend egg and milk together. Add remaining ingredients and hand beat together lightly until fluffy. Drop by teaspoon into 1 inch of deep hot vegetable oil (375°). Cook about 4 minutes until golden brown. Drain on paper towels. Serve with syrup, jelly, or sprinkle with powdered sugar. Makes 10-12.

Pat Russo (Mrs. Frank)

EGGPLANT FRITTERS

1 large eggplant
1 egg
4 tablespoons sugar
1/16 teaspoon salt
1 cup flour
2 ½ teaspoons baking
    powder
2 teaspoons vanilla

Peel eggplant and cut into cubes. Boil in small amount of water until tender. Drain and mash eggplant. Beat egg and add other ingredients. Add eggplant and mix together. Drop teaspoon of mixture into hot grease and cook until light brown. Sprinkle with white granulated sugar and serve.

Mary Putman (Mrs. Harrison C. III)

ZUCCHINI FRITTERS

2 eggs, beaten
1 cup flour
½ teaspoon baking powder
½ teaspoon salt
½ teaspoon pepper
2 cups zucchini, coarsely
    shredded
6 drops Tabasco sauce
½ cup onions, chopped
1 cup cheddar cheese, grated

Mix together eggs, flour, baking powder, salt and pepper. Add remaining ingredients. Fry in half butter and oil until brown on both sides. May be wrapped in foil and frozen after cooking.

Mary Ward (Mrs. C.V., Jr.)

GRATED ZUCCHINI FRITTERS

1 large zucchini, coarsely grated with skin
2 teaspoons salt
1 cup chickpea flour*
1 teaspoon each turmeric, cayenne, cumin/corriander powder, and salt
1 teaspoon sugar
4 cups cooking oil in a wok or deep saucepan or Corning dish on glasstop stove
***May substitute 1 cup whole wheat flour and 1 egg**

Remove large seeds from grated zucchini, if present. Place zucchini in large bowl and mix in salt and let set 5 minutes. Drain well. Put drained zucchini in bowl and add flour, all spices, and sugar. Stir with wooden spoon or by hand. Will be thick paste. Add extra whole wheat or chickpea flour if too runny. Heat oil to medium hot. Drop spoonfuls of fritter batter into oil. Cook on one side until golden brown and turn and cook for 3 minutes. Remove from oil and drain. Repeat with remaining batter. Better fresh and hot.

Jenny Shah (Mrs. K. G.)

CELERY WALNUT STUFFING

1 large onion, chopped
½ cup margarine
2 envelopes instant chicken broth
2 teaspoons salt
¼ teaspoon pepper
8 cups (1 pound) bread cubes
2 cups celery, chopped
1 cup walnuts, chopped
2 eggs, beaten

Saute onion in margarine. Remove from heat. Stir in chicken broth packets, salt, and pepper. Combine bread cubes, celery and walnuts in large bowl. Pour in onion mixture and then beaten eggs. Toss until cubes are well coated. Makes enough to stuff a 12-pound turkey.

Carolyn Jakopin (Mrs. Robert)

MELISSA'S SASSY APPLE CAKE

¼ cup sugar
½ teaspoon cinnamon
¼ teaspoon nutmeg
2 7.5-ounce cans refriger-
    ated biscuits
1 golden delicious apple,
    peeled, cored, and sliced

Mix together sugar, cinnamon, and nutmeg. Roll biscuits in mixture. Arrange one can of biscuits in a buttered round cake pan. Place apple slices on top of biscuits. Arrange second can of biscuits on top of apples. Put a dab of butter on top of each biscuit. Bake at 450° for 10 minutes or until browned.

Pat Russo (Mrs. Frank)

APRICOT GLAZED POUND CAKE

1 cup margarine, softened
3 cups sugar
6 eggs, separated
3 cups cake flour
1 cup whipping cream
2 teaspoons vanilla
1 teaspoon almond extract
Glaze:
½ cup apricot nectar
2 cups confectioner's sugar
1 tablespoon butter

Cream margarine and sugar. Add egg yolks slowly, beating well. Add egg whites and cream well. Alternating, add flour and cream. Add flavorings. Bake in a lightly greased 10-inch tube pan or bundt pan at 325° for one hour and 15 minutes. Remove from oven and let sit 10 minutes. Remove from pan and spread glaze over warm cake. For glaze, heat nectar and add sugar, stirring until dissolved. Add butter and stir until melted.

Dottie Flores (Mrs. Richard)

APPLE CAKE

1 ¼ cups vegetable oil
2 cups sugar
2 eggs
3 cups flour
1 teaspoon baking soda
1 teaspoon cinnamon
½ teaspoon nutmeg
½ teaspoon salt
3 to 4 cups apples, diced
1 cup nuts, chopped
2 teaspoons vanilla
Glaze:
1 cup sugar
½ teaspoon baking soda
1 teaspoon vanilla
½ cup buttermilk
½ cup margarine

Mix oil, sugar, and eggs in a large bowl. Add dry ingredients and beat well. Batter will be stiff. Add nuts, apples, and vanilla. Mix well and pour into greased 9 x 13-inch pan. Bake at 350° for 45 minutes. Cake may appear to be undercooked in the center. Combine all ingredients for glaze in a medium saucepan and boil for 3 minutes. Poke holes in top of cake with a fork and spoon hot glaze over warm cake.

Linda Clementz (Mrs. Gregory)

APPLE NUT CAKE

1½ cups oil
1 ½ cups sugar
½ cup firmly packed light brown sugar
3 eggs
3 cups flour
2 teaspoons cinnamon
1 teaspoon baking soda
½ teaspoon nutmeg
½ teaspoon salt
3 ½ cups peeled tart apples (about 2 pounds), cut into large dice (Preferably Granny Smith or Newton)
1 cup very coarsely chopped English walnuts
2 teaspoons vanilla
Glaze:
3 tablespoons butter
3 tablespoons brown sugar
3 tablespoons sugar
3 tablespoons whipping cream
¼ teaspoon vanilla

Heat oven to 325°. Grease and flour a 10-inch tube pan. Combine first three ingredients, add eggs one at a time, beating well after each. Sift together dry ingredients; add. Fold in apples, nuts, vanilla. Spoon into pan; spread evenly. Bake about 1 ¾ hours until cake tests done. Let cool in pan 20 minutes. Turn out on rack. Cool and prepare glaze and pour over **warm** cake.

Glaze: Place all ingredients into medium saucepan. Boil one minute over medium heat, stirring constantly. Pour over warm cake.

Marie Adland (Mrs. Moris)

APRICOT NECTAR CAKE

Cake:
1 package yellow cake mix
  (not pudding)
1 3-ounce package lemon
  Jello
4 egg yolks
½ cup oil
1 cup apricot nectar
1 teaspoon orange extract
1 teaspoon lemon extract
4 egg whites, stiffly beaten
Glaze:
½ cup confectioner's sugar
Juice of 2 lemons
¼ cup orange juice
  (preferably fresh)

In large bowl, combine cake mix and lemon Jello. Add all remaining ingredients except egg whites. Mix well at medium speed. Fold in egg whites. Pour mixture into an angel food cake pan. Bake in a 350° oven for 55 minutes or until done. Remove from oven and while still in pan and hot, pour the glaze over cake. (Should be thin enough to soak into the cake.) Leave in pan until cool.

Liz Cram (Mrs. Richard)

APRICOT CAKE

1 18 ½-ounce box yellow
  cake mix
1 3 ¾-ounce package lemon
  instant pudding
¾ cup vegetable oil
2 teaspoons apricot or
  lemon extract
4 eggs
¾ cup apricot nectar
Glaze:
1 cup powdered supar
1 tablespoon apricot nectar
2 teaspoons Marie Brizzard
  Apricot Liqueur

Mix cake mix and pudding in a bowl. Add oil, extract, eggs, and apricot nectar. Beat 15 to 20 minutes. Put in a greased and floured 10-inch bundt or tube pan. Bake at 325° for 1 hour and 15 minutes. Cool. Remove from pan. Combine ingredients for glaze and frost cooled cake.

Mimi Adland (Mrs. Moris)

FROSTY APPLESAUCE RING

½ cup butter or margarine, softened
1 cup sugar
3 eggs
1 cup flour, sifted
2 teaspoons baking powder
½ teaspoon salt
1 teaspoon cinnamon
1 teaspoon cloves
½ teaspoon nutmeg
½ cup milk
½ cup dark raisins
½ cup golden raisins
½ cup nuts, chopped
¾ cup sweetened canned applesauce
1 cup old-fashioned oats, uncooked

Beat butter and sugar together until creamy. Add eggs one at a time, beating well after each addition. Sift together the dry ingredients and add to creamed mixture alternately with milk. Stir in remaining ingredients. Pour into well-greased and floured 1 ½-quart ring mold. Bake in preheated 350° oven for 45 to 50 minutes. Loosen edges; cool 10 minutes, then remove from pan. Cool. Frost with thin confectioners sugar frosting. Makes one cake ring.

Barbara Adams (Mrs. Philip)

FRENCH BUTTER CAKE

1 yellow cake mix
2 eggs
½ cup butter, melted
1 1-pound box confectioners sugar
2 eggs
1 8-ounce package cream cheese
powdered sugar for garnish
whipped cream
strawberries

First Layer: Beat cake mix, 2 eggs, and butter together until well blended and stiff. Pour into a 9 x 12-inch cake pan. Second Layer: Beat confectioners sugar, 2 eggs, and cream cheese together with electric mixer. Pour over first layer. Bake at 350° for 40 minutes or until well browned on top. Sprinkle with powdered sugar and cool. Very rich—serve small squares topped with whipped cream and strawberries.

Angela Kenny (Mrs. J. N.)

BUTTER BRICKLE CAKE
Good for breakfast, too!

1 package yellow cake mix
  (not pudding)
1 3 ¾-ounce package instant
  butterscotch pudding
4 eggs
¾ cup oil
¾ cup water
1 cup sugar
1 cup walnuts, chopped
½ teaspoon cinnamon

Combine first five ingredients; beat three minutes. Combine sugar, walnuts, and cinnamon. Grease and flour a 9 x 13-inch pan. Pour half of batter into pan, sprinkle with half of sugar mixture, top with remaining cake batter, then sugar mixture. Bake at 350° for 40-50 minutes.

Jo Baker (Mrs. Donald)

SHELLY'S CARROT CAKE
This recipe is an old family recipe from my sister-in-law. She is an outstanding cook.

1 ½ cups sugar
1 cup salad oil
3 eggs, beaten
2 cups flour
1 teaspoon salt
2 teaspoons soda
1 teaspoon cinnamon
1 teaspoon vanilla
1 cup crushed pineapple
  (do not drain)
2 cups carrots, shredded
1 cup pecans, chopped
1 cup flaked coconut
Frosting:
1 3-ounce package cream
  cheese, softened
¼ cup butter or margarine
  softened
2 cups powdered sugar
3 drops maple flavoring
1 teaspoon vanilla

Combine sugar, oil, and eggs, mixing well. Add flour, salt, soda, and cinnamon. Mix well. Then add rest of ingredients, mixing well. Pour in a greased and floured 9 x 13-inch pan. Bake 35-40 minutes in a 350° oven. Frost when cooled. Mix all ingredients for frosting until smooth and spread on cake. I sometimes double frosting recipe.

Marianne Wright (Mrs. Robert)

CARROT CAKE

2 cups sugar
3 cups flour
2 teaspoons baking powder
2 teaspoons baking soda
4 eggs
1 ¼ cups vegetable oil
2 cups grated raw carrots
½ cup pecans, chopped
Frosting:
1 3-ounce package cream
   cheese, softened
1 cup powdered sugar
¼ teaspoon vanilla

Sift together dry ingredients. Beat eggs and add to dry ingredients. Add oil and beat until smooth. Add carrots and nuts. Bake in a greased and floured 10-inch tube pan at 350° for 1 hour. Mix together frosting ingredients and spread on cooled cake. Serves 10 to 16.

Pat Russo (Mrs. Frank)

CHOCOLATE CAKE

1 cup Crisco oil
1 cup buttermilk (or milk
   soured with 2 teaspoons
   vinegar)
1 tablespoon baking soda
2 ¼ cups flour, unsifted
2 cups sugar
½ cup cocoa
¼ teaspoon salt
2 eggs
1 teaspoon vanilla
Frosting:
6 tablespoons margarine
1 3-ounce package cream
   cheese
1 teaspoon milk
1 teaspoon vanilla
2 ½ cups powdered sugar

Mix all cake ingredients and add one cup boiling water. Bake in a 9 x 13-inch pan at 325° for 45 minutes. Frosting: Beat all ingredients together until smooth. Frost cooled cake.

Kathleen Palmer (Mrs. Ron)

CHOCOLATE NUT CAKE
Waldorf Astoria Hotel "$100 recipe"

2 cups cake flour
2 teaspoons baking powder
½ teaspoon salt
½ cup butter
2 cups sugar
2 eggs
1 teaspoon vanilla
2 ounces unsweetened
    chocolate, melted
1 ½ cups milk
1 cup walnuts, chopped fine,
    and mixed with 2 tea-
    spoons flour
Frosting and Filling:
½ cup butter
3 cups powdered sugar
1 whole egg
2 ounces unsweetened
    chocolate, melted
1 tablespoon lemon juice
1 teaspoon vanilla
1 cup walnuts, chopped
Black coffee

Sift together flour, baking powder, and salt. Set aside. Cream butter and sugar. Add eggs, one at a time, beating well after each addition. Add vanilla. Add melted chocolate and dry ingredients alternately with milk. Fold in chopped nuts. Bake in two 8 or 9-inch greased, layer pans at 350° for 40 minutes or until done.

Frosting and filling: Cream butter and sugar. Add egg and beat well. Add melted chocolate, lemon juice, vanilla, and chopped nuts. Thin with black coffee.

This recipe dates back to the 40's and was secured for a price ($100) from the Waldorf. It is a wonderful cake for a special occasion.

Dottie Flores (Mrs. Richard)

CHOCOLATE CHIP DATE NUT CAKE

1 teaspoon baking soda
1 cup chopped dates
1 cup hot water
1 cup shortening
1 cup sugar
2 eggs
1 teaspoon vanilla
1 ¾ cups flour
½ teaspoon salt
2 tablespoons cocoa
1 6-ounce package choco-
    late chips
½ cup nuts

Add baking soda to dates and pour hot water over them. Cool. Cream shortening and sugar. Add eggs one at a time. Mix well. Add vanilla. Sift dry ingredients together and add alternately with date mixture. Mix well. Pour into a 9 x 13-inch pan. Put chocolate chips and nuts on top before baking. Bake at 375° for 40 minutes.

Kathleen Palmer (Mrs. Ron)
Sharlyn Munns (Mrs. James)

MEMERE'S DATE CAKE

½ cup margarine or butter, melted
1 cup dark brown sugar
2 eggs
1 ½ cups all-purpose flour
1 teaspoon baking soda
½ cup walnuts, chopped
1 ½ cups dates, diced
½ cup hot water
1 teaspoon vanilla
½ cup maraschino cherries, sliced
Glaze:
1 cup confectioner's sugar, sifted
2 tablespoons milk
¼ teaspoon almond extract

Place melted margarine or butter in large bowl. Add brown sugar and beat until smooth and well blended. Beat in the eggs one at a time. Combine flour, soda, nuts, and dates in another bowl. Mix with hands to separate date pieces. Beginning with the flour mixture, alternate a dry addition with the water twice. Beat well between additions. Add vanilla and cherries and blend well. Pour batter into a 9 x 5 x 3-inch loaf pan, or six-cup ring mold, or 2 one-pound coffee cans. Bake for 50 to 60 minutes depending on size of pan at 350°. Cool completely. Combine glaze ingredients and mix well until smooth. Pour over cake.

Lorraine El-Deiry (Mrs. Adel)

FRANGELICO RUM CAKE
"Heavenly"

1 cup nuts, chopped (I use pecans)
2 tablespoons sugar
1 3 ¾-ounce package instant vanilla pudding
4 eggs
½ cup water
½ cup oil
¼ cup rum
¼ cup Frangelico liqueur
1 18-ounce package yellow cake mix
Syrup:
½ cup butter or margarine
¼ cup water
1 cup sugar
¼ cup rum
¼ cup Frangelico

Mix nuts and 2 tablespoons sugar. Sprinkle bottom of a well-greased and floured bundt pan. Blend in mixer 5 minutes, the pudding, eggs, water, oil, rum, and liqueur. Add cake mix and blend well with mixer. Pour into bundt pan. Bake at 325° for 1 hour. Leave in pan. While warm, poke lots of holes in cake with fork. For syrup, combine butter, water and sugar in medium saucepan. Boil 5 minutes, stirring constantly. Add rum and Frangelico. Pour hot syrup over cake. Cool cake completely in pan before removing. 10-12 servings.

Marianne Wright (Mrs. Robert)

HUMMINGBIRD CAKE
This cake is moist and turns out perfect every time.

3 cups flour
2 cups sugar
1 teaspoon salt
1 teaspoon baking soda
1 teaspoon cinnamon
3 eggs, beaten
1 ½ cups vegetable oil
2 cups bananas, chopped
1 8-ounce can crushed pineapple, undrained
1 cup pecans, chopped
1 ½ teaspoons vanilla
Frosting:
2 8-ounce packages cream cheese, softened
1 cup butter, softened
2 1-pound boxes confectioner's sugar
2 teaspoons vanilla

Cake: Combine flour, sugar, salt, baking soda, and cinnamon. Add eggs and oil, stirring until moistened. Do not beat. Stir in bananas, pineapple, pecans, and vanilla. Pour batter into 3 greased and floured 9-inch cake pans. Bake at 350° for 25 to 30 minutes. Cool in pans for 10 minutes. Remove and cool completely. Frosting: Cream butter and cream cheese until smooth. Add confectioner's sugar, beating until light and fluffy. Stir in vanilla. Spread frosting between layers and on top and sides of cake. Decorate if desired with chopped pecans.

Marianne Wright (Mrs. Robert)

MANDARIN ORANGE CAKE

2 cups sugar
2 cups flour
2 eggs
2 teaspoons soda
2 teaspoons vanilla
1 teaspoon salt
2 11-ounce cans mandarin
  oranges, drained
Topping:
6 tablespoons milk
6 tablespoons butter
1 ½ cups brown sugar

Mix together first six ingredients. Add mandarin oranges; beat. Pour into greased 9 x 13-inch pan. Bake at 350° for 40 minutes. Topping: Combine ingredients and bring to a boil. Pour over hot cake. Serve with whipped cream.

Sharlyn Munns (Mrs. James R.)

PEACH UPSIDE DOWN CAKE

Part A:
¼ cup margarine
⅔ cup brown sugar
1 tablespoon flour
¼ cup water
1/16 teaspoon salt
3 large fresh peaches, sliced
Part B:
½ cup cake flour
1/16 teaspoon salt
½ cup sugar
½ teaspoon baking powder
2 eggs, separated
¼ cup water
¼ teaspoon cream of tartar
½ teaspoon vanilla

Part A: Melt margarine in a round glass 2-quart baking dish. Add brown sugar, flour, water, salt, and sliced peaches. Over low heat, let simmer and thicken for 5 minutes.
Part B: In a bowl, sift cake flour, salt, sugar, and baking powder together. Beat egg yolks with the ¼ cup water and add to dry ingredients. Beat egg whites with cream of tartar and fold into mixture. Add vanilla. Pour batter over hot peaches (be sure peaches are not bubbling). Bake at 350° for 30 minutes. Let cool slightly before inverting on a rimmed cake plate. Topping will run slightly but will solidify as it cools.

Liz Cram (Mrs. Richard)

PINEAPPLE CAKE DESSERT

2 cups flour
2 cups sugar
2 teaspoons baking soda
¼ teaspoon salt
20-ounce can crushed pineapple with juice
2 eggs
1 teaspoon vanilla
Icing:
8 ounces cream cheese
½ cup butter
1 ⅔ cups powdered sugar
½ cup chopped nuts

Mix or whisk all ingredients together well
and pour into a greased 9 x 13-inch pan.
Bake at 350° for 30 to 40 minutes. Frost.
Refrigerate until serving time. For icing,
mix all ingredients well in a mixer.

Charlotte M. Barbour (Mrs. O. E.)

ZUCCHINI CAKE

3 eggs, well beaten
¾ cup oil
2 cups sugar
2 cups flour
2 teaspoons baking soda
½ teaspoon baking powder
1 teaspoon salt
2 cups zucchini, grated,
  unpeeled
½ cup chopped nuts
3 teaspoons cinnamon
3 teaspoons vanilla

Beat together eggs, oil, and sugar. Add
and beat in flour, soda, baking powder,
and salt. Add and stir in zucchini, nuts,
cinnamon, and vanilla. Bake in a greased
and floured tube or bundt pan at 350° for
45 to 60 minutes.

Rita Leutkemeyer (Mrs. Richard)

ZUCCHINI CAKE

1 box Pillsbury Coconut
  Pecan Frosting Mix
2 ½ cups flour
1 ¼ cups sugar
1 tablespoon cinnamon
1 teaspoon salt
1 teaspoon baking soda
2 cups shredded zucchini,
  drained
1 cup cooking oil
3 eggs
1 tablespoon vanilla
Glaze:
1 cup powdered sugar
1 tablespoon butter
1 to 2 tablespoons milk

Mix all ingredients together at high speed until completely mixed. Pour batter into a greased bundt pan. Bake in a 350° oven for 60 to 70 minutes or until toothpick comes out clean. Cool upright, then remove from pan. Glaze: Mix all ingredients together. Pour over cooled cake.

Julie Horvath (Mrs. Frederic)

CHOCOLATE NUT ZUCCHINI CAKE

3 squares unsweetened
  chocolate
4 eggs
3 cups sugar
1 ½ cups salad oil
3 cups flour
1 ½ teaspoons baking
  powder
1 teaspoon baking soda
1 teaspoon salt
3 cups zucchini, finely grated
1 cup nuts, finely chopped

Preheat oven to 350°. Grease and flour a 10-inch tube or bundt pan. Melt chocolate and cool. Beat eggs in a large mixing bowl on high speed until thick and light. Add sugar a little at a time; beat. Add salad oil and chocolate; beat. Sift together the flour, baking powder, baking soda and salt. Add to egg mixture at low speed. With wooden spoon add zucchini and nuts. Pour into prepared pan. Bake 1 hour and 15 minutes or until tester is clean. Cool in pan. Turn out and dust with powdered sugar.

Berenice Consigny (Mrs. Paul)

POUND CAKE SQUARES

1 box Dromedary cake mix
½ cup butter, softened
4 eggs
1 8-ounce package cream cheese
1 1-pound box confectioners sugar
1 teaspoon vanilla
½ cup pecans, chopped

Combine cake mix, butter and 2 eggs. Mix until well blended. Spread mixture into a greased 9 x 13-inch pan. Combine cream cheese, confectioners sugar (reserve 3 tablespoons), 2 eggs, and vanilla. Spread over cake mix mixture. Sprinkle pecans over top. Bake at 350° for 45 minutes. While cake is still warm, sift reserved confectioners sugar over top. Serve as brownies or large squares with whipped cream.

Alice Sullivan (Mrs. E.A.)

ELEGANT WHITE FRUIT CAKE

1 cup vegetable oil
1 ½ cups sugar
4 eggs
2 cups flour
1 teaspoon baking powder
2 teaspoons salt
1 cup pineapple or apple juice
1 cup flour
1 cup citron, thinly sliced
1 cup candied lemon peel, thinly sliced
1 cup candied pineapple, cut in 1-inch pieces
1 ½ cups candied cherries, whole
3 cups seedless white raisins, 1 pound
2 cups nuts, chopped in large pieces

Mix together oil, sugar, and eggs. Beat vigorously with a spoon or mixer for 2 minutes. Sift together 2 cups flour, baking powder and salt. Stir into oil mixture alternately with the pineapple or apple juice. Mix 1 cup sifted flour with the candied fruits, raisins, and nuts. Pour batter over fruit, mixing thoroughly. Line with brown paper 2 greased loaf pans, 8 ½ x 4 ½ x 2 ½-inch. Pour batter into pans. Place a pan of water on lower oven rack. Bake cakes 2 ½ to 3 hours in a 275° oven. After baking let cakes stand 15 minutes before removing from pans. Cool thoroughly on racks without removing paper. When cool remove paper. Store by wrapping tightly in aluminum foil. Keep in a cool place to ripen.

Lois Berg (Mrs. Ben C.)

CAKE DECORATOR'S FROSTING

Recipe from a cake decorating course. Has a good flavor and excellent for cake decorating.

¾ cup Crisco shortening
⅔ cup milk or water
1 teaspoon salt
1 teaspoon vanilla and 1 teaspoon almond extract, or 2 teaspoons any flavoring
2 pounds powdered sugar

Mix first five ingredients for 5 minutes and add 2 pounds powdered sugar slowly.

Pat Russo (Mrs. Frank)

DIFFERENT CUPCAKES

4 ounces semi-sweet chocolate
1 cup margarine
1 ½ cups pecans, chopped
1 ¾ cups sugar
1 cup unsifted flour
4 large eggs
1 teaspoon vanilla
1 tablespoon cinnamon

Melt chocolate and butter. Add nuts. Stir, do not beat. Mix sugar, flour, eggs, vanilla, and cinnamon. Combine all ingredients, do not beat. Fill paper bake cups in muffin pan half full. Bake at 325° for 35 minutes. Makes 2 dozen cupcakes.

Sharon Gulley (Mrs. R. Michael)

BROWNIE CUPCAKES

4 1-ounce squares semi-sweet chocolate
1 cup margarine or butter
1 cup nuts, chopped (optional)
1 ¾ cups sugar
1 cup all-purpose flour
4 eggs, slightly beaten
1 teaspoon vanilla
1/16 teaspoon salt
6 ounces chocolate chips

Preheat oven to 325°. Melt chocolate squares and butter. Cool slightly; Stir in nuts. Combine sugar, flour, eggs, vanilla, and salt. Combine with chocolate, stirring only until blended. Stir in chocolate chips. Do not beat. Pour into paper lined cupcakes pans. Bake at 325° for 30 minutes. No frosting is needed. Makes 20 cupcakes.

Bonnie Fenton (Mrs. Craig)

APPLE PIE

Crust:
2 cups flour
1 teaspoon salt
⅔ cup plus 2 tablespoons
  shortening
¼ cup (or less) water
Filling:
3 large Granny Smith apples
1 cup sugar
2 tablespoons flour
¾ cup half and half
Cinnamon

Crust: Combine flour and salt in a bowl. Cut in shortening thoroughly. Sprinkle in water, 1 tablespoon at t time, mixing until all flour is moistened. Gather dough into a ball. Divide in half. Makes one double crust or 2 single crust 9-inch pie shells. May freeze for later use.

Filling: Peel apples and slice into prepared 9-inch pie shell. Mix flour and sugar. Add cream. Pour over apples. Sprinkle cinnamon on top. Bake 15 minutes at 450°, then 45 minutes to 1 hour at 350°. May cover edge with strip of aluminum foil last 15 minutes of baking time to prevent excessive browning. Makes one 9-inch pie.

Mari Jo Baker (Mrs. Donald)

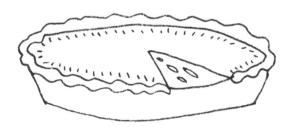

CHOCOLATE BAVARIAN PIE
Lo cal—great dessert for weight watching!

1 envelope unflavored
  gelatin
½ cup cold water
1 cup hot evaporated milk
2 envelopes Alba '66 Hot
  Cocoa Mix
1 teaspoon instant coffee
½ cup chilled evaporated
  milk
Cool Whip
Shaved chocolate

Dissolve gelatin in ½ cup cold water. Add hot milk, Alba, and coffee. Mix well and chill until thick. Beat with hand held mixer until mixture is fluffy. Add chilled milk and continue beating until smooth. Pour into an 8-inch pie plate. Refrigerate until firm. Garnish with Cool Whip and shaved chocolate if desired. Makes 8 servings, 94 calories per serving.

Carol Nelson (Mrs. John)

FROZEN CHOCOLATE PECAN PIE
A rich, melt-in-your mouth dessert that can be made months ahead.

Crust:
2 cups pecans, finely
  chopped and toasted
5 ⅓ tablespoons brown sugar, packed
5 tablespoons butter (no substitutes)
2 tablespoons dark rum
Filling:
6 ounces semisweet
  chocolate
½ teaspoon instant coffee
4 eggs at room temperature
1 tablespoon dark rum
1 teaspoon vanilla
1 cup whipping cream
Garnish, optional:
½ cup whipping cream
3 tablespoons shaved
  chocolate

For crust, chop pecans (food processor works great) and spread on a cookie sheet. Toast very carefully under broiler. Blend all crust ingredients until mixture holds together. Press into bottom and sides of a 9-inch pie plate. Freeze for at least one hour. For filling, melt chocolate with coffee in top of a double boiler over hot water. Remove from heat; whisk in eggs, rum and vanilla until mixture is smooth. Cool five minutes. Whip one cup cream until stiff. Gently fold into chocolate mixture, blending completely. Pour into crust and freeze. Transfer to refrigerator one hour before serving. Can be frozen up to three months before serving. Optional: Whip ½ cup whipping cream and pipe or dollop over pie. Sprinkle with shaved chocolate.

Marilyn Bauer (Mrs. James)

HERSHEY PIE

1 chocolate graham cracker crust (commercial)
1 large 8-ounce Hershey bar with almonds
20 large marshmallows
½ cup milk
1 8-ounce carton Cool Whip

Melt Hershey, marshmallows, and milk (microwave works well). Cool slightly and add Cool Whip. Pour into crust and refrigerate. Top with sliced almonds and dash of Cool Whip. I usually put crust in oven for a few minutes while mixing rest of ingredients. Be sure to cool crust before filling.

Joan Berney (Mrs. John)

SOUTHERN CHOCOLATE PIE

1 4-ounce package Baker's German Sweet Chocolate
¼ cup butter or margarine
1 13-ounce can evaporated milk
1 cup sugar
3 eggs
1 teaspoon vanilla
1 unbaked 9-inch pie shell with high rim
1 ⅓ cups Baker's Angel Flake Coconut
½ cup chopped pecans

Stir chocolate and butter over low heat until melted and smooth. Remove; blend in evaporated milk and sugar. Beat in eggs and vanilla. Pour into pie shell. Top with coconut and pecans. Bake at 375° 45 to 50 minutes, or until top is puffed. Filling will set slightly while cooling. Refrigerate 4 hours.

Margaret Norris (Mrs. Paul)

AMARETTO ICE CREAM PIE
Easy and delicious

1 package (about 11 large) macaroons
1 ½ ounces Amaretto
½ gallon butter almond ice cream

Crush and toast macaroons. Add Amaretto to crumbs and pat all but 3 tablespoons in bottom of a 9-inch pie pan. Cool before adding ice cream. Add ice cream and sprinkle with remaining crumbs. Freeze.

Kay Bickerman (Mrs. Ray)

CREME DE MENTHE ICE CREAM PIE
Easy, elegant!

5 ½ tablespoons butter
1 8 ½-ounce box Nabisco
   Famous Chocolate Wafers
½ gallon vanilla ice cream,
   divided
5 tablespoons green creme
   de menthe
Hershey's chocolate syrup

Melt butter and crush wafers (food processor works great). Mix butter and crumbs and press into the bottom of a 9-inch spring-form pan. Let ice cream soften to foldable stage. Take two cups of vanilla ice cream and reserve. Add creme de menthe to rest of the ½ gallon. Mix well. Pour into crumb crust and spread evenly. Return to freezer. Whip the reserved 2 cups ice cream in blender and pour over creme de menthe mixture to form a smooth white layer. Return to freezer and freeze at least 3 hours. To serve, cut in wedges and serve topped with Hershey's chocolate syrup.

Marianne Wright (Mrs. Robert)

CRUNCHY ICE CREAM PIE

½ cup butter or margarine,
   melted
1 cup brown sugar, packed
3 cups uncrushed corn-
   flakes
1 cup chopped nuts
1 cup flaked coconut
1 quart ice cream (vanilla,
   chocolate revel, or coffee)

Stir butter and sugar. Mix with cornflakes, coconut, and nuts. Line sides and bottom of 9-inch pie pan with two-thirds of the crumb mixture. Fill with ice cream. Sprinkle with remaining crumb mixture and press down. Chill in freezer for several hours. May be served with hot fudge sauce. Serves six to eight.

Pat Russo (Mrs. Frank)

ICE CREAM PIE

1 9-inch pie shell, baked
2 bananas
1 pint vanilla ice cream, softened
1 21-ounce can cherry pie filling
Whipped cream

Slice bananas on bottom of pie shell. Spread softened ice cream over bananas. Spread cherry pie filling over ice cream. Freeze. Remove from freezer 10-15 minutes before serving. Serve with whipped cream.

Rhoda Turow (Mrs. I. L.)

KEY LIME PIE

1 14-ounce can sweetened condensed milk
4 egg yolks
½ cup lime juice
1 egg white
Meringue:
3 egg whites
½ teaspoon cream of tarter
6 tablespoons sugar
1 baked pie shell

Combine first three ingredients. Beat one egg white stiff. Fold into the mixture. Put into baked pie shell. Beat 3 egg whites and cream of tartar till soft peaks form. Gradually add sugar, beating till stiff and all sugar is dissolved. Spread meringue over pie, sealing to edge of pastry. Bake at 350 degrees for 12 to 15 minutes, or till meringue is golden brown. Refrigerate before serving.

Marilyn Leyland (Mrs. John)

LEMON SOUR CREAM PIE

1 cup sugar
3 tablespoons cornstarch
¼ cup butter
¼ cup lemon juice
3 egg yolks
1 lemon rind, grated
1 cup milk
1 cup sour cream
1 9-inch pie shell, baked

Combine sugar and cornstarch in a pan. Add butter, lemon juice, egg yolks, milk, and lemon rind. Cook over medium heat, stirring constantly until thickened and smooth. Chill. Fold sour cream into chilled mixture and spoon into pie shell. Serve topped with whipped cream.

Maryann Bugaieski (Mrs. Stanley)

MISSISSIPPI MUD PIE
Love chocolate? You'll "love" this!

22 Oreo cookies
2 tablespoons butter or
   margarine, melted
1 quart dark fudge ice cream
   (Baskin & Robbins)
1 quart coffee ice cream
2 tablespoons instant coffee
   granules or powder
2 tablespoons coffee liqueur
3 tablespoons brandy or
   cognac
Whipped cream (optional)
Chocolate shavings (optional)
Hershey's chocolate sauce

Place cookies in food processor and blend until the crumbs are finely textured. Mix with melted butter and press into a 10-inch pie plate. Place crust in freezer while preparing filling. Place softened ice cream in a large bowl. Stir in the coffee, liqueur, and brandy and mix until completely blended. Pour into crust and return to freezer and allow to freeze solidly. If pie is not to be eaten within the day, cover with freezer wrap to preserve freshness. Remove pie from freezer 15 minutes before serving. Decorate with whipped cream and chocolate shavings, if desired. Place pitcher of Hershey's Chocolate Syrup on the side and let each person pour on their own syrup. Serves 8-10.

Marianne Wright (Mrs. Robert)

MARSHMALLOW CUSTARD PIE

12 large marshmallows
⅓ cup sugar
¼ teaspoon salt
2 cups milk
3 eggs
nutmeg
1 9-inch pie shell, unbaked

Dissolve marshmallows, sugar, and salt In mllk over low heat. Beat eggs lightly. Add a small amount of hot milk to the eggs and then add to the scalding milk mixture. Pour into unbaked crust and sprinkle with nutmeg. Bake for five minutes at 400° then at 325° until knife comes out clean.

Sharlyn Munns (Mrs. James)

PECAN PIE

1 cup sugar
1 cup white corn syrup
3 eggs
1 teaspoon vanilla
⅛ teaspoon salt
1 tablespoon vinegar
½ cup coconut
½ cup ground pecans
1 9-inch unbaked pie shell

Beat together lightly the sugar, corn syrup, eggs, vanilla, salt and vinegar. Add coconut and pecans. Pour into pie shell. Bake 10 minutes at 375°. Reduce heat to 350° and bake 50 minutes longer.

Sharlyn Munns (Mrs. James)

PECAN CRUNCH PIE

3 eggs
½ teaspoon baking powder
1 cup sugar
11 whole graham crackers
1 cup pecans, chopped
1 teaspoon vanilla
1 cup whipping cream

Beat eggs, baking powder and sugar very slowly. Beat until very stiff. Crush graham crackers. Add crackers and pecans to egg mixture, folding in. Add vanilla. Spread into a heavily buttered 10-inch pie pan. Bake at 350° for 30 minutes. Chill at least 4 to 5 hours. Whip cream and spread over pie. Serves 6.

Joyce Rashid (Mrs. Ameel)

PECAN PIE DELUXE ALA BLENDER

3 eggs
½ cup (less one tablespoon) heavy cream
¾ cup sugar
½ teaspoon vanilla
2 tablespoons butter
2 tablespoons sherry
½ cup dark corn syrup
⅛ teaspoon salt
1 ½ cups pecans (reserve 10 -12 for top)
1 9-inch pie shell, unbaked

Put all ingredients except pie shell in a blender in the order listed and blend for 10 seconds. Put mixture into pie shell and bake at 400° for 25 minutes. Put reserved nuts on top and bake another 10 minutes. Cool and serve with a dab of whipped cream or Cool Whip. To prevent a soggy crust, bake crust for 10 minutes in a 400° oven with pie shell covered with foil and with dried beans in it. Take out and brush with 2 egg yolks and bake 2 minutes more, then fill and bake as directed above.

Mimi Adland (Mrs. Morris)

FRESH STRAWBERRY PIE

1 9-inch pie shell, baked
2 cups fresh strawberries, whole
2 cups strawberries, mashed
3 tablespoons cornstarch
1 tablespoon lemon juice
1 cup sugar

Place fresh whole strawberries in pie shell. Set aside. Combine mashed strawberries and remaining ingredients. Boil until thick. Pour over fresh berries in shell; chill. Top with whipped cream.

Alta Myers (Mrs. Robert)

STRAWBERRY PIE

1 cup sugar
1 cup boiling water
2 tablespoons cornstarch
3 heaping tablespoons strawberry Jello
1 quart fresh strawberries, cleaned and hulled
1 9-inch pie shell, baked
Whipped cream or dessert topping

Mix first three ingredients together and cook until thick. Remove from heat. Add strawberry Jello. Place strawberries in pie shell (cut berries in half lengthwise if they are large). Pour hot mixture over berries. Chill for 3 hours. Serve topped with whipped cream or dessert topping.

Vivian Solomon (Mrs. Ted)

A B C NEVER-FAIL PIE CRUST
Recipe from the late Miss Ida Schmidt of the Bradley Home Ec. Dept.

2 cups bread flour
1 teaspoon salt
¼ teaspoon baking powder
12 tablespoons vegetable shortening
5 tablespoons milk

Sift together twice the flour, salt, and baking powder. Cut in shortening with two knives or pastry blender. Add milk by sprinkling over flour mixture while stirring lightly with a fork. Roll on a floured board or cloth with a floured rolling pin. Yields two single crusts or one double crust.

Kathleen Heinzen (Mrs. F.J.)

NEVER FAIL PIE CRUST

2 cups flour
1 rounded teaspoon salt
⅓ cup water
1 cup shortening

Mix flour and salt together. Take one-fourth of flour mixture and add to the water. Set aside. Cut shortening into remaining flour mixture until it is the size of a pea. Then mix both mixtures together. Makes 2 single or one double.

Sharon Gulley (Mrs. R. Michael)

COCOA BALLS

2 cups chocolate wafer or lady finger crumbs
2 cups confectioner's sugar
1 cup almonds or pecans, finely ground
¼ cup cocoa
1 cup almonds or pecans, chopped
½ cup rum, whiskey, or sherry
3 tablespoons white corn syrup
½ cup confectioner's sugar

Combine first five ingredients and mix with hands until well blended. Combine liquor and syrup and pour into dry ingredients. Pinch off a heaping teaspoonful and roll into a ball the size of a walnut, no bigger. Work quickly rolling balls or mixture will dry. Roll balls in sugar and place in a tight container. Store in refrigerator for a few days before serving. Makes four dozen.

Mimi Adland (Mrs. Moris)

AUNT MERKEL'S COOKIES

1 cup margarine
¾ cup sugar
1 teaspoon baking soda
1 ½ cups flour
½ cup chopped nuts

Using large beaters, beat on high for fifteen minutes the margarine, sugar, and soda. Stir in the flour and nuts. Drop by heaping teaspoonful on greased cookie sheets and bake in a 300° oven for 20 to 30 minutes. Makes about 50 cookies.

JoAnne Richardson (Mrs. Robert)

AUNT TILLY'S CHOCOLATE ORANGE CRUNCHIES

1 cup vegetable shortening
1 cup sugar
Rind of one large or two
  small oranges
Juice of one orange
1 egg
2 cups flour
¾ teaspoon salt
½ teaspoon baking soda
1 12-ounce package choco-
  late chips
1 cup walnuts, chopped

Cream shortening and sugar. Add orange rind, orange juice, and egg. Sift together flour, salt, and soda and add to mixture. Fold in chocolate chips and nuts. Drop well-rounded teaspoonfuls on lightly greased cookie sheets about 2 ½ inches apart. Flatten cookies with a damp cloth over the bottom of a 3-inch glass. Bake at 375° for 15 minutes.

Kathleen Heinzen (Mrs. F.J.)

BASIC CAKE MIX COOKIES

1 box any brand cake mix,
  not pudding
⅓ cup vegetable oil
3 tablespoons water
2 eggs
nuts or chocolate chips
  (optional)

Mix all ingredients together. Add nuts or chocolate chips if desired. Drop by teaspoon 2 inches apart on ungreased cookie sheet. Bake at 350° for 12-15 minutes.

Irene Crane (Mrs. Donald)

BUTTER BUTTER COOKIES

1 cup butter
½ cup sugar
1 egg
1 teaspoon almond extract
2 ⅓ cups all-purpose flour

Cream butter and gradually add sugar, beating until light and fluffy. Beat in eggs and almond extract. Gradually blend in flour. Fill cookie press with ¼ of the dough at a time. Form desired shapes on ungreased cookie sheets. Bake in preheated 350° oven for 8 to 10 minutes. Remove to wire racks to cool immediately. Yields about 7 dozen.

JoAnne Richardson (Mrs. Robert)

BROWNIE DROPS

2 ounces German's sweet
  chocolate
1 tablespoon butter
2 eggs
¾ cup sugar
¼ cup flour
¼ teaspoon baking powder
¼ teaspoon cinnamon
⅛ teaspoon salt
½ teaspoon vanilla
¾ cup pecans, chopped

Melt chocolate and butter over hot water; cool. Beat eggs until foamy. Add sugar 2 tablespoons at a time. Beat until thick, about 5 minutes on medium speed. Blend in chocolate. Add flour, baking powder, cinnamon, and salt. Blend. Stir in vanilla and nuts. Drop by teaspoonfuls onto greased cookie sheet. Bake at 350° for 8-10 minutes. Cool slightly on sheet. Makes about 3 dozen cookies.

Alta Myers (Mrs. Robert)

CARROT COOKIES

1 cup butter or shortening
¾ cup sugar
1 egg, beaten
1 cup cooked mashed car-
  rots (or baby food carrots)
2 cups flour, sifted
1 teaspoon baking powder
1 teaspoon salt
1 teaspoon vanilla
½ teaspoon lemon extract
Frosting:
2 cups powdered sugar
1 teaspoon orange peel
2 tablespoons orange juice

Cream shortening and sugar. Add beaten egg, mashed carrots and flour sifted with baking powder. Add salt and flavorings. Drop by teaspoonfuls on oiled cookie sheet. Bake at 350° for 10 to 15 minutes or until nicely browned. Frosting: Combine all ingredients. Frost cookies while warm.

Angela Kenny (Mrs. J.N.)

CREAM CHEESE COOKIES

½ cup butter or margarine
1 cup sugar
1 egg, well beaten
1 ½ ounces cream cheese
2 ½ cups flour, sifted
⅛ teaspoon baking soda
½ teaspoon baking powder
½ teaspoon salt
2 tablespoons sour milk
½ teaspoon vanilla
Date Filling:
1 cup chopped dates
6 tablespoons sugar
5 tablespoons boiling water
½ teaspoon lemon rind,
  grated
2 teaspoons lemon juice
2 teaspoons butter
⅛ teaspoon salt

Cream butter and sugar together. Add egg and cream cheese and blend well. Sift dry ingredients together and add to creamed mixture along with sour milk and vanilla. This dough may be used in a cookie press or rolled and used for filled cookies, using the date filling or jam. When making filled cookies, roll out dough and cut into rounds. Place ½ teaspoon filling between 2 rounds or on half of a round and fold over other half. Seal edges with fork. Prick top with fork to allow steam to escape. Bake at 350° for 10 to 15 minutes.

For Date Filling: Mix all ingredients in a saucepan. Boil and stir until thick.

Muggs Giebelhausen (Mrs. G.W.)

CREAM WAFERS
Wonderful for a special tea or light dessert

1 cup butter, softened
⅓ cup whipping cream
2 cups flour
granulated sugar
Filling:
¼ cup butter, softened
¾ cup confectioner's sugar,
  sifted
1 egg yolk
1 teaspoon vanilla

Mix thoroughly butter, cream, and flour. Cover and chill at least 1 hour. Preheat oven to 375°. Roll about ⅓ of dough at a time ⅛-inch thick on a floured cloth-covered board. Keep remaining dough refrigerated until ready to roll. Cut in 1 ½-inch circles. Transfer rounds with spatula to a piece of waxed paper that is heavily covered with granulated sugar; turn each round so that both sides are coated with sugar. Place on ungreased cookie sheet. Prick rounds with fork about 4 times. Bake 7 to 9 minutes or just until set but not brown. Put cookies together in pairs with creamy filling. Filling: Cream together butter, sugar, egg yolk, and vanilla until light and fluffy. May tint with a few drops of food color if desired. Makes 5 dozen cookies.

Eleanor Flinn (Mrs. Robert)

COCONUT MACAROONS

3 egg whites, at room
  temperature
½ cup sugar
1 teaspoon vanilla extract
⅛ teaspoon salt
2 cups flaked coconut
⅓ cup all-purpose flour

Preheat oven to 325°. Lightly grease 2 cookies sheets. In small bowl with mixer at high speed, beat egg whites until soft peaks form. Beating at high speed, gradually beat in sugar, 2 tablespoons at a time, beating well after each addition until sugar is completely dissolved. Beat in vanilla and salt. (Whites should stand in stiff, glossy peaks.) With rubber spatula, gently fold coconut and flour into egg white mixture. Drop by heaping teaspoonful about 1 inch apart onto cookie sheets. Bake 20 minutes or until lightly browned. With metal spatula, carefully remove cookies to wire racks to cool, about 30 minutes. Store macaroons in tightly covered containers. Makes about 2 ½ dozen.

Carol Nelson (Mrs. John)

DANISH NUTBALLS

1 cup butter
4 tablespoons sugar
2 teaspoons vanilla
2 cups cake flour
2 cups pecans, chopped fine
Powdered sugar

Cream butter; add sugar, vanilla, flour, and nuts. Make into small balls in palm of hand. Bake 30 minutes at 325°. Roll in powdered sugar as soon as removed from oven. Roll in powdered sugar again when cool. Makes 4-5 dozen.

Ruth Giunta (Mrs. Edward)

DATE NUT DROP COOKIES

2 cups dates, chopped
½ cup sugar
½ cup water
1 cup butter or margarine
1 cup sugar
1 cup brown sugar
3 eggs
1 teaspoon vanilla
4 cups flour
1 teaspoon baking soda
1 teaspoon salt
½ cup nuts, chopped (optional)

Cook dates, sugar, and water until thick. Mash and cool. Cream butter and sugars. Add eggs and vanilla. Sift dry ingredients and add to creamed mixture. Add cooled date mix and nuts if desired and blend well. Drop on greased cookie sheet. Bake in a 350° oven 10 to 15 minutes until light brown. Makes 5-6 dozen.

Jo Baker (Mrs. Donald)

FRUIT CAKE COOKIES

½ cup margarine
1 cup light brown sugar
4 eggs
4 cups flour, sifted
1 teaspoon cinnamon
1 teaspoon cloves
1 teaspoon allspice
1 teaspoon salt
3 scant teaspoons baking soda, dissolved in 4 tablespoons buttermilk
1 cup bourbon
1 pound candied pineapple, chopped (3 colors)
1 pound candied cherries, chopped (red and green)
1 cup white raisins
1 cup dates, chopped
¼ cup candied lemon peel, chopped
¼ cup candied orange peel, chopped
6 cups pecans, chopped

Cream margarine and sugar. Add eggs, one at a time, mixing well after each addition. Sift together dry ingredients, reserving 1 cup of flour to dredge fruit and nuts. Combine flour and liquids with creamed mixture. Add floured fruit and nuts. Drop by the teaspoonful on greased cookie sheets. Bake 20 to 25 minutes in a slow oven, 275°. Makes approximately 175 cookies. *All fruit should be chopped by hand.

Muggs Giebelhausen (Mrs. G.W.)

HAWAIIAN MACADAMIA BITES

1 ½ cups all-purpose flour
½ cup sugar
½ cup butter or margarine, softened
1 egg
1 tablespoon vanilla extract
⅛ teaspoon salt
1 5-ounce can Macadamia nuts
¼ cup chocolate chips
1 teaspoon shortening

In medium bowl, with hand, knead first six ingredients until well mixed. Mixture will be stiff. Preheat oven to 350°. With hands, shape one teaspoonful of cookie dough around a Macadamia nut; roll into a ball. Repeat with remaining dough and nuts, placing cookies on ungreased cookie sheet one inch apart. Bake 10 minutes or until lightly golden. Remove cookies to wire rack to cool. Meanwhile in a heavy 1-quart saucepan over low heat, melt chocolate pieces and shortening. With spoon, drizzle chocolate mixture over cookies. Allow chocolate to dry. (Refrigerate cookies if necessary.) Store in tightly covered container. Makes about 5 ½ dozen.

Carol Nelson (Mrs. John)

MOLASSES COOKIES

1 cup sugar
¾ cup shortening
1 egg
¼ cup molasses
1 tablespoon baking soda
1 teaspoon ginger
1 teaspoon cinnamon
1 teaspoon vanilla
1 teaspoon salt
2 cups flour

Cream first four ingredients. Add remaining ingredients and chill overnight. Roll dough into balls and then roll balls in granulated sugar. Bake on a greased cookie sheet in a 350° oven about 10 minutes.

Irene McMenamin (Mrs. Hugh)

OATMEAL-MOLASSES COOKIES
Crisp and spicy!

1 ½ cups flour
1 cup sugar
1 teaspoon baking soda
½ teaspoon salt
1 teaspoon ground ginger
¼ teaspoon ground cloves
½ cup shortening
1 egg
¼ cup molasses
¾ cup quick-cooking rolled
  oats

Stir together flour, sugar, soda, salt, ginger, and cloves. Add shortening, egg, and molasses. Beat until smooth. Stir in oatmeal. Drop from teaspoon onto ungreased cookie sheet. Bake in a 375° oven for 10 to 11 minutes. (3 dozen)

Berenice Consigny (Mrs. Paul)

ORANGE PECAN COOKIES

1 cup butter
½ cup brown sugar
½ cup granulated sugar
1 egg, well beaten
2 teaspoons orange rind,
  grated
2 tablespoons orange juice
2 ½ cups flour
1 teaspoon baking soda
¼ teaspoon salt
¾ cup pecans, chopped

Cream butter; add sugars and mix until light. Add eggs, rind, and juice. Add dry ingredients; mix. Add pecans. Shape into rolls 1 ½ inches in diameter. Wrap in waxed paper or plastic wrap. Chill several hours. Slice thin. Bake at 350° for 10-12 minutes on ungreased pan.

Sandy Rivan (Mrs. Robert)

SOUR CREAM COOKIES

1 cup butter or margarine
2 cups sugar
3 eggs
3 cups flour
1 teaspoon baking soda
¼ teaspoon salt
½ teaspoon nutmeg
4 teaspoons vanilla
1 8-ounce carton sour cream

Cream margarine and sugar together. Beat in eggs. Set aside. Mix dry ingredients together in a separate bowl and set aside. Mix vanilla and sour cream together. Add flour mixture and sour cream mixture to creamed mixture alternately, beating after each addition. Place in refrigerator 4 or 5 hours, until thoroughly chilled. Drop by teaspoon on greased cookie sheet. Sprinkle with sugar. Bake at 400° for 10 to 12 minutes.

Linda Clementz (Mrs. Gregory)

SHIRLEY'S BEST EVER COOKIES
An excellent glorified chocolate chip!

1 cup margarine
1 cup oil
1 cup light brown sugar
1 egg
3 ¼ cups flour
1 teaspoon salt
2 teaspoons vanilla
1 teaspoon cream of tartar
1 cup quick oats
1 cup coconut
1 cup Rice Krispies
2 cups chocolate chips
1 cup white sugar

Mix together margarine, oil, brown sugar, egg, flour, salt, vanilla, and cream of tartar. Set aside. In another bowl combine the oats, coconut, Rice Krispies, chocolate chips, and white sugar. Add to first mixture. Drop by teaspoonfuls onto lightly greased cookie sheet. Bake at 375° for 12 minutes.

Alice Sullivan (Mrs. E.A.)

THE WORLD'S BEST COOKIE
These cookies stay moist and keep beautifully. This recipe makes a large batch which is great for bake sales.

1 cup butter
1 cup sugar
1 cup brown sugar, firmly packed
1 egg
1 cup salad oil
1 cup rolled oats, regular
1 cup corn flakes, crushed
½ cup shredded coconut
½ cup pecans or walnuts, chopped
3 ½ cups all-purpose flour, sifted
1 teaspoon soda
1 teaspoon salt
1 teaspoon vanilla extract

Preheat oven to 325°. Cream together butter and sugars until light and fluffy. Add egg, mixing well; then add salad oil, mixing well. Add oats, cornflakes, coconut and nuts, stirring well. Then add flour, soda, salt, and vanilla. Mix well and form into balls the size of walnuts. Place on ungreased cookie sheet. Flatten with a fork dipped in water. Bake for 12 minutes. Allow to cool on sheets a few minutes before removing. For extra sweetness, sprinkle warm cookies with granulated sugar.

Marianne Wright (Mrs. Robert)

GRANDMA'S SUGAR COOKIES

½ cup shortening
1 ½ cups sugar
2 eggs
1 cup cream
4 cups plus flour (enough to make dough handle well)
¼ teaspoon baking soda or cream of tartar
3 teaspoons baking powder
¼ teaspoon salt

Combine all ingredients. Chill dough. Roll or press and bake at 350° for 10 minutes.

Alta Myers (Mrs. Robert)

BLUEBERRY CHEESECAKE BARS

½ cup butter, softened
⅓ cup brown sugar
1 cup flour
1 cup pecans, chopped
1 8-ounce package cream
  cheese
¼ cup sugar
1 egg
1 tablespoon lemon juice
2 tablespoons milk
1 teaspoon vanilla
2 21-ounce cans blueberry
  pie filling

Cream butter and brown sugar; add flour and nuts. Make crumb mixture as you mix. Press into bottom of ungreased 9 x 11-inch pan. Bake at 350° for 10-12 minutes. Blend sugar with cream cheese until smooth. Add egg, lemon juice, milk, and vanilla; beat well. Spread over crust. Bake 25 minutes at 350°. Cool. Refrigerate for at least 1 hour. When thoroughly chilled, pour cans of pie filling over crust evenly. Refrigerate. Cherry pie filling may also be used.

Irene Crane (Mrs. Donald)

BLUEBERRY BARS

1 ¾ cups sugar
1 cup margarine
4 eggs
1 teaspoon vanilla
3 cups flour
1 ½ teaspoons baking powder
½ teaspoon salt
1 21-ounce can blueberry
  pie filling
Glaze:
1 ¼ cups powdered sugar
1 tablespoon butter, melted
2 tablespoons lemon juice

Mix sugar and butter until light and fluffy. Add eggs and vanilla. Stir dry ingredients together and add to sugar mixture. Spread one-half of the dough in ungreased 10 x 15-inch pan. Spread blueberry filling over dough. Drop the rest of the dough on top of blueberries by the teaspoonful. Bake at 350° for 45 minutes. Cool. Combine last three ingredients for glaze and drizzle over bars. Cut into bars.

Rita Luetkemeyer (Mrs. Richard)

BROWNIE COOKIES

¼ cup butter or margarine
1 ounce unsweetend
    chocolate
½ cup sugar
1 egg
¼ cup unsifted flour
⅛ teaspoon salt
¼ teaspoon vanilla
⅓ cup nuts, finely chopped

Melt butter or margarine and chocolate over hot water. Remove from heat. Stir in remaining ingredients except for nuts. Spread in two greased 8-inch square pans. Sprinkle with nuts. Bake at 350° for 10 to 12 minutes. Cool slightly and cut. When cold, remove from pan.

Kathleen Heinzen (Mrs. F.J.)

MOM'S BROWNIES

1 cup hot butter or margarine
6 tablespoons cocoa
3 cups sugar
6 eggs, beaten
2 ¼ cups flour
1 ½ teaspoons salt
1 teaspoon baking powder
2 teaspoons vanilla
1 cup nuts, chopped
    (optional)

Combine hot butter, cocoa, and sugar. Add beaten eggs. Mix together the flour, salt, and baking powder. Add to the butter-egg mixture. Blend in the vanilla and nuts. Bake in a greased and floured 12 x 18-inch jelly roll pan in a 350° oven for 20 minutes.

Jo Anne Richardson (Mrs. Robert)

BROWNIES

¾ cup sifted flour
¼ teaspoon baking soda
¼ teaspoon salt
⅓ cup shortening
½ cup sugar
2 tablespoons water
1 6-ounce package
    chocolate chips
1 teaspoon vanilla
2 eggs

Sift together flour, soda, and salt and set aside. Combine shortening, sugar, and water in a saucepan and bring to a boil over moderate heat. Stir in chocolate chips and vanilla until smooth after removing from heat. Beat in eggs, one at a time. Add flour mixture and chopped nuts if desired. Bake in a greased 8-inch square pan at 325° for 25 minutes. Cool. Dust with powdered sugar.

Beth Shay (Mrs. Thanad)

APPLESAUCE BROWNIES

2 ounces unsweetened
  chocolate
½ cup butter
½ cup applesauce
2 eggs
1 cup brown sugar
1 teaspoon vanilla
1 cup flour
½ teaspoon baking powder
¼ teaspoon baking soda
¼ teaspoon salt
¾ cup chopped nuts

Melt chocolate and butter. Mix apple-sauce, eggs, sugar, and vanilla. Sift together dry ingredients and add applesauce mix-ture. Mix well. Stir in chocolate and nuts. Pour into a 9-inch square greased pan. Bake at 350° for 30 minutes.

Linda Carballido (Mrs. Jorge)

TWO-TONED BROWNIES
For your food processor

1 cup cool butter, cut in
  chunks
2 cups plus 2 tablespoons
  sugar
4 large eggs
¼ teaspoon salt
1 cup unsweetened cocoa
1 ½ to 2 cups walnuts
1 cup flour
Filling:
1 8-ounce package cream
  cheese
⅓ cup sugar
1 egg
½ teaspoon vanilla

With steel knife, blend butter, sugar, eggs, and salt until light and fluffy. Add cocoa and nuts and blend until nuts are coarsely chopped. Add flour and mix just until moistened. Pour half the batter into a greased 9 x 13-inch baking pan. Spoon out remaining batter into a bowl and rinse processor and knife. With steel knife, blend all filling ingredients until smooth. Spread mixture over batter in the pan. Spread remaining chocolate batter over filling. Swirl slightly with a spatula or spoon. Bake in preheated 350° oven for 35 to 40 minutes.

Marilyn Wood (Mrs. John)

CHERRY ALMOND BARS
Absolutely delicious

1 ¼ cups flour, sifted
½ cup brown sugar
½ cup margarine
½ cup coconut
1 8-ounce package cream cheese, softened
½ cup white sugar
1 egg
1 teaspoon vanilla
1 21-ounce can cherry pie filling
½ cup slivered almonds

Combine flour, brown sugar, and margarine and blend to fine crumbs. Add coconut and mix well. Set aside ⅓ of mixture for top. Pat remaining mixture into a 9 x 13-inch pan. Bake at 350° for 15 minutes or until lightly browned. Beat cream cheese, white sugar, egg, and vanilla until smooth; spread on hot baked bottom layer. Return to oven for 10 minutes. Remove from oven and spread cherry pie filling over cheese. Sprinkle on slivered almonds and reserved crumb mixture. Bake 15 minutes more. Keep refrigerated.

Linda McLelland (Mrs. Bruce)

CHOCOLATE CHERRY BARS

1 package Pillsbury Plus Devil's Food Cake Mix
1 21-ounce can cherry fruit filling
1 teaspoon almond extract
2 eggs, beaten
Frosting:
1 cup sugar
⅓ cup milk
5 tablespoons margarine or butter
1 cup (6 ounces) chocolate chips

Heat oven to 350°. Grease and flour jelly roll pan or 9 x 13-inch pan. Combine first four ingredients in large bowl; stir by hand until well mixed. Pour into prepared pan. Bake: jelly roll pan, 20-25 minutes; 9 x 13-inch pan, 25-30 minutes, or until toothpick comes out clean. In small saucepan combine sugar, milk, and margarine. Boil one minute, stirring constantly. Remove from heat; stir in chocolate chips until smooth. Pour over warm bars.

Pam Albers (Mrs. William)

LEMON BAR COOKIES

½ cup butter, melted
1 egg, slightly beaten
1 18.5-ounce box lemon or yellow cake mix
1 teaspoon lemon extract
1 8-ounce package cream cheese
2 eggs
1 1-pound box confectioners sugar (reserve ¼ cup for topping)

Mix together butter, egg, and cake mix until texture resembles pie dough. Pat into a 9 x 13-inch pan. Combine the lemon extract, cream cheese, eggs, and sugar until creamy. Pour over crust mixture. Bake at 325° for 45 to 60 minutes. When cool, sprinkle with reserved powder sugar. Makes 2-3 dozen.

Marianne Wright (Mrs. Robert)

PEANUT BUTTER BARS
Good! Good!

1 ¾ cups graham cracker crumbs
1 cup butter or margarine, softened
1 1-pound box powdered sugar
1 12-ounce jar peanut butter
2 12-ounce packages chocolate chips

Blend first 4 ingredients and pat in a 11 ½ x 17-inch pan. Melt chocolate chips in a double boiler or microwave. Pour over top and sprinkle with chopped nuts. Place in refrigerator for 2 hours to set. Cut in small squares to serve.

Mimi Adland (Mrs. Moris)

DORIS' PEANUT BUTTER BARS

½ cup butter or margarine
½ cup sugar
½ cup light brown sugar
1 egg
⅓ cup creamy peanut butter
½ teaspoon soda
½ teaspoon salt
½ teaspoon vanilla
1 cup flour
1 cup rolled oats
1 cup chocolate chips
½ cup powdered sugar
¼ cup creamy peanut butter
2-4 tablespoons milk

Cream butter with sugars. Blend in egg, ⅓ cup peanut butter, soda, salt, and vanilla, mixing well. Stir in flour and oats. Spread in a greased 9 x 13-inch pan. Bake in a 350° oven for 20 to 25 minutes. Remove from oven and sprinkle with 1 cup chocolate chips. Let stand 15 minutes, then spread evenly over bars. Combine powdered sugar, ¼ cup peanut butter, and milk. Drizzle or spread over chocolate.

Marianne Wright (Mrs. Robert)

PUMPKIN BARS

1 cup oil
2 cups sugar
4 eggs
2 cups pumpkin
½ teaspoon salt
½ teaspoon pumpkin pie
  spice
2 teaspoons cinnamon
2 teaspoon baking powder
1 teaspoon baking soda
2 cups flour
Frosting:
6 tablespoons margarine
2 cups powdered sugar
4 ounces cream cheese
2 teaspoons milk
1 teaspoon vanilla

Mix oil, sugar, and eggs well. Add remaining ingredients. Pour into a greased 11 x 15-inch cookie sheet. Bake in a 350° oven for 20 to 25 minutes. Mix ingredients for frosting and spread on cooled bars. Freezes well.

Jo Baker (Mrs. Donald)

TURTLE BARS

1 14-ounce package Kraft caramels
⅓ cup evaporated milk
1 package German chocolate cake mix
¾ cup margarine
⅓ cup evaporated milk
1 cup nuts, chopped
1 cup chocolate chips

Melt caramels with ⅓ cup evaporated milk. Then mix together with a beater cake mix, margarine and ⅓ cup evaporated milk. Spread half of batter in a greased 9 x 13-inch pan. Bake at 350° for 6 minutes. Remove and sprinkle on top the nuts and chocolate chips. Pour caramel mixture over this evenly. Then carefully spread rest of batter over top and bake at 350° for 20 to 25 minutes. Cool before cutting.

Berenice Consigny (Mrs. Paul)

FROZEN FRANGO BARS

1 cup vanilla or chocolate cookie crumbs
¼ cup margarine or butter, melted
1 cup margarine or butter
2 cups powdered sugar
4 squares (1 ounce each) unsweetened chocolate, melted
4 eggs
¾ teaspoon peppermint or rum flavoring
1 ½ teaspoons vanilla

Mix the cookie crumbs and ¼ cup margarine and place in the bottom of 24 cupcake liners, preferably foil. Cream 1 cup margarine and sugar until light. Add the melted chocolate and then the eggs, one at a time, beating constantly. Mix in thoroughly the peppermint (or rum) flavoring and vanilla. Pour over crumb mixture in liners and freeze. Makes 24.

Chris Palagallo (Mrs. Gerald)

ENGLISH SHORTBREAD
This is an old English recipe for a melt-in-the-mouth cookie that bakes up quickly and easily. Terrific for holiday gift giving.

4 cups all-purpose flour
2 cups butter or margarine, softened
1 ¼ cups confectioners sugar
1 teaspoon baking powder
¼ teaspoon salt

Preheat oven to 325°. Into a large bowl, measure all ingredients. With hands, knead ingredients until well blended (dough will be soft). Pat dough evenly into two 9-inch round cake pans, With fork, prick dough in many places. Bake shortbread about 45 minutes or until golden. While still warm, cut into 12 wedges. Cool in pans on wire racks. Remove from pans. Store in tightly covered container. May be frozen in same container up to 3 months. Makes 2 dozen.

Lorraine El-deiry (Mrs. Adel)

CHEESECAKE TARTS
An Elegant Finger Dessert

2 8-ounce packages cream cheese, softened
¾ cup sugar
2 eggs
1 tablespoon lemon juice
1 teaspoon vanilla
24 vanilla wafers
1 21-ounce can cherry pie filling

Beat cheese, sugar, eggs, lemon juice, and vanilla until light and fluffy. Line muffin pans with foil muffin papers. Place a wafer in the bottom of each cup. Fill cup ⅔ full with cream mixture. Bake at 375° for 15-20 minutes or until set. Top each with 1 tablespoon pie filling. Chill. Good with any flavor fruit filling. Serves 24.

Bonnie Fenton (Mrs. Craig)

CREME DE MENTHE SQUARES

1 ¼ cups butter or margarine, divided
½ cup unsweetened cocoa powder
3 ½ cups sifted powdered sugar, divided
1 egg, beaten
1 teaspoon vanilla
2 cups graham cracker crumbs
⅓ cup green creme de menthe
1 ½ cups semisweet chocolate pieces

Bottom layer: In saucepan, combine one half cup margarine and cocoa powder. Heat and stir until well blended. Remove from heat; add ½ cup powdered sugar, egg, and vanilla. Stir in graham cracker crumbs and mix well. Press into bottom of ungreased 9 x 13 x 2-inch pan. Middle Layer: Melt ½ cup of margarine. In small bowl mix melted margarine and creme de menthe. At low speed of electric mixer, beat in remaining 3 cups of powdered sugar, until smooth. Spread over bottom layer. Chill one hour. Top Layer: In small saucepan, combine remaining margarine and chocolate pieces. Cook and stir over low heat until melted. Spread over mint layer. Chill one to two hours. Cut into small squares and store in refrigerator. Makes about 96 squares.

Joan Leu (Mrs. Richard)

TOFFEE COOKIES

1 cup butter
1 cup brown sugar
1 cup nuts, chopped
whole graham crackers
6 to 8 small Hershey bars

Combine butter, brown sugar, and nuts. Cook 2 minutes over low heat. Line a 10 x 15-inch pan with whole graham crackers. Pour hot mixture over crackers and bake 10 minutes at 350°. Remove from oven and while hot put Hershey bars on top. Spread when melted. Cut into bars while warm.

Berenice Consigny (Mrs. Paul)

JAN HAGELS

1 cup butter
1 cup sugar
2 cups flour, sifted
1 teaspoon cinnamon
1 egg yolk
1 egg white
slivered almonds

Cream butter and sugar together. Add flour, cinnamon and egg yolk. Press mixture into a buttered 10 x 15-inch cookie sheet. Brush top with egg white and sprinkle with slivered almonds. Bake at 375° for 30 minutes. Cut into bars.

Shirley Bennett (Mrs. Gaylord)

KEY LIME DESSERT
Easy! Makes a refreshing summertime dessert!

1 ¼ cups graham cracker crumbs
¼ cup granulated sugar
¼ cup margarine, melted
1 14-ounce can Eagle Brand Milk
2 6-ounce cans frozen limeade, thawed
1 13-ounce container Cool Whip, thawed
few drops green food coloring

In a medium bowl, combine graham cracker crumbs, sugar, and butter. Blend well with a fork. Reserve ¼ cup crumbs for topping and press rest in a 9 x 13inch pan. Beat together Eagle Brand Milk and limeade. Add Cool Whip and beat again. Stir in a few drops green food coloring. Pour over crust. Top with remaining crumbs. Chill and serve.

Marianne Wright (Mrs. Robert)

MAUREEN'S FABULOUS CHEESE CAKE

Crust:
6 ounces Zwieback
4 tablespoons sugar
1 teaspoon cinnamon
½ cup butter or margarine, melted
Filling:
3 tablespoons flour
¼ teaspoon salt
1 ½ cups sugar
18 ounces cream cheese, softened
6 eggs, separated, room temperature
1 ½ cups sour cream
1 teaspoon vanilla
2 tablespoons sugar

Crush Zwieback and combine with sugar, cinnamon, and melted butter. Mix and set aside ¼ of mixture. Use the rest to cover the bottom and 1 or 2 inches up the side of a 10-inch springform pan. Sift together flour, salt and 1 ½ cups sugar. Cream thoroughly with cream cheese. Beat 6 egg yolks and add to cheese mixture. Add sour cream and vanilla. Set aside. Beat 6 egg whites until stiff, gradually adding 2 tablespoons sugar. Fold whites into cheese mixture. Pour into prepared pan and sprinkle top with remaining crust crumbs. Bake at 300-325° for 1 hour. Turn off oven and let set inside for 2 hours. **Do not peek!** Refrigerate before serving.

Marianne Wright (Mrs. Robert)

LEMON APRICOT TORTE
A very special cake with a lovely flavor!

1 ½ cups sugar
¾ cup butter
3 egg yolks
1 tablespoon lemon peel,
  finely shredded
½ teaspoon lemon extract
2 ½ cups cake flour
1 tablespoon baking powder
¼ teaspoon salt
1 cup milk
3 egg whites
1 12-ounce jar apricot preserves (about 1 cup)
Lemon Butter Frosting:
6 tablespoons butter
2 cups powdered sugar
1 egg yolk
½ teaspoon lemon extract
1 teaspoon lemon peel
2 cups powdered sugar
Few drops yellow food
  coloring
3 tablespoons milk,
  approximately

Beat sugar and butter together until light. Add egg yolks, lemon peel, and extract. Beat well. Sift dry ingredients. Add alternately with milk, beating well after each addition. In small bowl, beat egg whites until stiff peaks form. Fold into batter. Bake in two greased and floured round 9-inch cake pans at 350° for 30 minutes. Cool 10 minutes. Heat preserves. Split each cake layer. Spread one fourth of preserves on each layer. Frost sides of cake with lemon butter frosting and spread preserves on top of cake. Pipe lattice topping with frosting on cake.

Lemon Butter Frosting: Beat butter; gradually beat in 2 cups powdered sugar. Beat in egg yolk, lemon extract, and lemon peel. Gradually blend in another 2 cups powdered sugar, food coloring, and milk.

Dottie Flores (Mrs. Richard)

STRAWBERRY DELIGHT

½ cup butter
¼ cup brown sugar
1 cup flour
½ cup nuts, chopped
1 10-ounce package frozen
 strawberries, partially
 thawed
2 egg whites
1 cup sugar
1 tablespoon lemon juice
1 teaspoon vanilla
1 cup whipping cream

Mix butter, brown sugar, flour, and nuts together lightly. Spread in a pan and bake at 400°, stirring frequently, until golden brown, about 15 minutes. Sprinkle half in the bottom of a 9 x 13-inch cake pan. Reserve other half for topping. Place all remaining ingredients except whipping cream in a large mixing bowl. Cover mixer with a large brown paper bag and whip at high speed, approximately 15 minutes. Volume will increase until you have a bowl full. Whip cream separately in a small bowl. Fold into strawberry mixture. Spoon filling onto crumbs in pan. Sprinkle reserved crumbs on top. Freeze. Remove from freezer when ready to serve. Cut in pieces. Garnish with whipped cream. Serves 15.

Eleanor Pflederer (Mrs. Robert)

TOFFEE MERINGUE TORTE

3 egg whites
1 teaspoon vanilla
1 cup sugar
Dash salt
¼ teaspoon cream of tartar
Filling:
2 cups heavy cream, whipped
1 6½-ounce package brickle
 bits
1 6-ounce package semi-
 sweet chocolate chips,
 crushed

Beat egg whites slowly. Add rest of ingredients and whip until stiff. Make 2 9-inch circles out of brown paper. Spread ½ of the mixture on each circle on a cookie sheet. Bake at 275° for one hour. Turn off oven and leave in oven for at least 2 hours. DO NOT PEEK! Cool. Filling: Fold brickle bits and crushed chocolate chips into whipped cream. Fill and frost meringue layers like layer cake (sides and top). Chill at least 8 hours. Makes 10 or more servings.

Debbie Coon (Mrs. John)

CHOCOLATE MOUSSE CAKE

**7 ounces semisweet choco-
late**
½ cup unsalted butter
7 eggs, separated
1 cup sugar
1 teaspoon vanilla
⅛ teaspoon cream of tartar
Whipped Cream Frosting:
1 cup whipping cream
⅓ cup powdered sugar
1 teaspoon vanilla

Preheat oven to 325°. In a small saucepan, melt chocolate and butter over low
heat. In a large bowl, beat egg yolks and
¾ cup sugar until very light and fluffy,
about 5 minutes. Gradually beat in warm
chocolate mixture and vanilla. In another
large bowl, beat egg whites with cream of
tartar until soft peaks form. Add remaining ¼ cup sugar, one tablespoon at a
time. Continue beating until stiff. Fold
egg whites carefully into chocolate mixture. Pour ¾ of the batter into an ungreased 9 x 3-inch springform pan. Cover
remaining batter and refrigerate. Bake
cake 35 minutes. Prepare Whipped Cream
Frosting; set aside. Remove cake from
oven and cool. Cake will drop as it cools.
Remove outside ring of springform pan.
Stir refrigerated batter to soften slightly.
Spread on top of cake. Refrigerate until
firm. Spread Whipped Cream Frosting
over top and sides. Garnish with chocolate leaves if desired. Refrigerate several
hours or overnight.

Whipped Cream Frosting: In a small
bowl, beat whipping cream until soft peaks
form. Add powdered sugar and vanilla.
Beat until stiff.

Marie Adland (Mrs. Moris)

CHOCOLATE MOUSSE CAKE

¾ cup unsalted butter,
   cut in pieces
6 1-ounce squares unsweetened chocolate, broken in
   half
4 eggs separated plus 2 egg
   yolks
¾ cup sugar
1 teaspoon vanilla
4 tablespoons chocolate
   sprinkles

In a small saucepan over low heat, stir butter and unsweetened chocolate until melted and smooth; set aside. In a medium bowl beat all 6 egg yolks slightly. Add sugar gradually, beating until thick and pale in color. Gradually stir in chocolate mixture and vanilla. In a clean bowl with clean beaters, beat 4 egg whites until stiff but not dry. Stir half the egg whites into chocolate mixture, then fold in remaining whites. Measure and reserve ¾ cup mousse mixture. Pour remaining mousse mixture into a greased 8-inch springform pan. Bake in a preheated 350° oven 35 to 40 minutes until pick in center comes out clean. Top will look cracked. Cool in pan 5 minutes. Run knife around edges to loosen; remove sides of pan. Cool completely on rack. (Cake falls as it cools.) Spread top with reserved mousse mixture and sprinkle with chocolate sprinkles. Serve immediately or refrigerate. Bring to room temperature before serving in very thin wedges. Serves 12-16. If 12 servings — 270 calories per serving.

Bonnie Fenton (Mrs. Craig)

FROZEN CHOCOLATE MOUSSE
(Food processor) Very good with fresh strawberries

¼ cup sugar
⅓ cup water
1 ½ cups heavy cream
1 6-ounce package semi-
  sweet chocolate pieces
3 tablespoons dark rum
3 egg yolks
½ cup toasted almonds
  (optional)

Combine sugar and water in a small saucepan and boil 3 minutes. With metal blade of food processor, process cream uninterrupted until thick, about 1 minute. Transfer to a large bowl. Without washing beaker, reinsert metal blade and add chocolate pieces. Process, turning on and off, 15 to 20 seconds. Continue processing and gradually pour in **hot** syrup, rum, and egg yolks. Add almonds. Process, turning on and off, until almonds are coarsely chopped. Using a spatula, scrape chocolate mixture over whipped cream and fold together. Freeze in decorative mold at least 6 hours. Serves 6.

Jo Dorsch (Mrs. Tom)

BUSTER BAR DESSERT
A real kid pleaser!

42 Oreo cookies
¼ cup melted butter
½ gallon vanilla ice cream
1 jar chocolate fudge topping
1 cup Spanish peanuts
1 (8 ounce container) Cool
  Whip

Crush cookies and mix with butter. (I use food processor to crush cookies.) Spread evenly in bottom of a 9 x 13-inch pan, reserving ½ cup of crumbs for topping. Soften ice cream and spread over crumbs. Place in freezer until firm. Spread fudge topping on ice cream. Sprinkle peanuts over fudge topping. Spread Cool Whip on top and sprinkle with reserved cookie crumbs. Cover with foil and keep in freezer; cut in squares to serve. (Also good with caramel topping.)

Marianne Wright (Mrs. Robert)

BRANDY ICE

½ gallon best vanilla ice
cream softened
⅓ cup Cointreau
⅓ cup apricot brandy
⅓ cup Kahlua

Stir liqueur into softened ice cream. An electric mixer may be used at low speed but never a blender. Pour into tightly covered plastic container and freeze at least a day ahead of serving. This will be softer than ordinary ice cream, so serve immediately after scooping into sherbet or parfait glasses.

Dottie Flores (Mrs. Richard)

COFFEE ICE CREAM DESSERT

Coffee Ice Cream
1 tablespoon creme de
cacao per serving
⅛ teaspoon ground coffee
per serving

Place scoops of ice cream in individual serving dishes. Pour over liqueur and sprinkle with coffee.

Tish Roberts (Mrs. Stuart)

SUNSETS—MY DESSERT

2 quarts coffee or vanilla ice
cream, softened
½ cup rum or brandy

Place in blender and blend well. Pour in pretty glass cups, or rounded or stem glasses. Also, try chocolate ice cream with Grand Marnier or Triple Sec.

Mimi Adland (Mrs. Moris)

PEACHES AND CREAM DESSERT

¾ cup flour
1 3 ½-ounce package regular vanilla pudding mix
1 teaspoon baking powder
1 egg, beaten
½ cup milk
3 tablespoons margarine, melted
1 16-ounce can peach slices
1 8-ounce package cream cheese
½ cup sugar
1 tablespoon sugar
½ teaspoon cinnamon

Stir together flour, pudding mix, and baking powder. Combine egg, milk, and melted margarine. Add to dry ingredients; mix well. Spread in a greased 8 x 8 x 2-inch pan. Drain peaches, reserving ⅓ cup liquid. Chop peaches and sprinkle atop batter. Beat together the cream cheese, ½ cup sugar, and reserved peach liquid. Pour atop peaches. Combine 1 tablespoon sugar and the cinnamon. Sprinkle over all. Bake in a 350° oven for 45 minutes. Cool.

Jane Myrna (Mrs. Ted)

BRADFORD'S RASPBERRY DELIGHT

40 vanilla wafers
¾ cup soft butter
2 cups powdered sugar
2 eggs
1 teaspoon lemon juice
chopped nuts
1 3-ounce package raspberry jello
2 10-ounce packages frozen red raspberries
1 cup whipping cream
3 tablespoons sugar

Crush vanilla wafers. Line bottom of a 9 x 13-inch pan with half of crumbs, reserving remaining half. Combine butter and powdered sugar. Beat eggs with lemon juice. Add butter mixture to eggs and beat well. Spread mixture over crumbs carefully, using back of a wet tablespoon. Sprinkle with a layer of chopped nuts. Dissolve jello in one cup boiling water. Add frozen raspberries. Chill until quite thick. Spread this mixture over the layers already in pan. Whip the cream and sweeten with the 3 tablespoons sugar. Spread over jello. Top with reserved crumbs. Refrigerate overnight.

Kacky Heinzen, (Mrs. F. J.)

WALLY'S FROZEN LEMON DESSERT

1 can Eagle Brand Sweetened
  Condensed Milk
⅓ cup lemon juice, fresh
2 tablespoons lemon
  rind, grated
½ pint cream, whipped
vanilla wafer crumbs

Combine milk, lemon juice and rind. Fold in whipped cream. Cover bottom of a 9 x 13-inch pan with crumbs, reserving some for top. Add filling. Cover top with crumbs. Freeze. Serve frozen. May also be made in cupcake papers.

Rita Luetkemeyer (Mrs. Richard)

LAYERED ICE CREAM DESSERT

1 8 ½-ounce package Salerno
  Coconut Bar Cookies
1 16-ounce can Hershey's
  chocolate syrup
1 quart chocolate ice cream
1 quart strawberry ice cream
2 Heath Bar candy bars

Oil a 9-inch springform pan, bottom and sides. Crush about 26 cookies. Soften ice cream at room temperature so it is spreadable, but do not let it melt. Crush Heath Bars (put in plastic bag and use a hammer). Put half of crushed cookies in bottom of pan. Spread one quart of chocolate ice cream on top of cookies, working quickly. Put remaining crushed cookies on top of chocolate ice cream. Drizzle some chocolate syrup over crushed cookie layer. At this point, put pan in freezer for 10 minutes if chocolate is beginning to melt. Spread one quart of strawberry ice cream on top of last cookie layer. Sprinkle with crushed Heath bar pieces; cover with heavy foil and freeze. To serve, remove from spring-form pan. Slice like cake. Top each slice with additional chocolate syrup. Can be made a couple of weeks in advance.

Vivian Solomon (Mrs. Ted)

QUICK CHERRY CREAM PARFAITS

1 cup milk
1 cup dairy sour cream
¼ teaspoon almond extract
1 3 ½-ounce package vanilla instant pudding
1 21-ounce can cherry pie filling

Combine milk, sour cream, and almond extract in a small mixing bowl. Add vanilla pudding mix and beat with electric mixer until creamy and well blended, about 2 minutes. Fill parfait glasses with alternate layers of pudding mix and cherry pie filling. Chill. Makes 6 parfaits. Slivered almonds may be used as a garnish.

Pat Russo (Mrs. Frank)

MARY KAE'S CHERRY JUBILEE

2 ½ cups graham cracker crumbs
1 cup brown sugar
¾ cup margarine, melted
1 8-ounce package cream cheese, softened
1 cup powdered sugar
1 teaspoon vanilla
2 packages Dream Whip, prepared as directed
½ cup nuts, chopped
2 21-ounce cans cherry pie filling

Mix graham cracker crumbs, brown sugar, and margarine. Press into a 9 x 13-inch pan. Combine cream cheese, powdered sugar, vanilla, Dream Whip, and nuts. Spread on graham cracker crust. Chill for 12 hours. Cover with cherry pie filling.

Pat Russo (Mrs. Frank)

AMARETTO MOCHA CREME

1 teaspoon instant coffee
1 cup whipping cream
1 cup Kraft Marshmallow Creme
1 tablespoon Amaretto liqueur
¼ cup toasted almonds, chopped
chocolate curls (garnish)

Dissolve instant coffee in whipping cream. Combine the marshmallow creme, 2 tablespoons of the whipping cream mixture, and the Amaretto. Mix with electric mixer or whisk until blended. Whip remaining whipping cream mixture; fold with the chopped almonds into the marshmallow creme mixture. Spoon into wine glasses. Freeze one to two hours. Garnish with chocolate curls. Serves 4. To make ahead, prepare as directed. Freeze several hours or overnight. Place in refrigerator ½ hour before serving.

Dottie Flores (Mrs. Richard)

MINOR MOUSSE

**6 ounces semisweet
  chocolate morsels
2 tablespoons sherry
4 egg whites
¼ teaspoon salt**

In top of double boiler, melt chocolate pieces with sherry. While they melt, beat egg whites with salt until stiff. Take chocolate-sherry mixture off the stove and fold the beaten egg whites into it. Pile it all into 8 small dishes or demitasse cups. Refrigerate for at least 3 hours before serving.

Carol Nelson (Mrs. John)

CHOCOLATE MOUSSE

**3 eggs
¼ cup sugar, rounded
2 ounces semisweet choco-
  late, grated
½ pint whipping cream,
  whipped**

Beat with electric mixer eggs and sugar in top of double boiler over water. Stir in chocolate. Let cool slightly. Fold in whipped cream. Pour into 4 to 6 ramkins. Freeze. Thaw before serving. Sprinkle shaved semi-sweet chocolate lightly on top.

Mary Owen (Mrs. Walter)

BREAD PUDDING WITH RUM SAUCE

6 slices stale bread
Butter
½ cup golden raisins
3 cups milk
2 eggs
½ cup sugar
¼ teaspoon salt
1 teaspoon vanilla
½ cup flaked coconut
Rum Sauce:
1 cup butter, room
  temperature
1 ½ cups sugar
2 eggs, beaten
½ cup dark rum

Butter one side of bread slices. Place slices, buttered side down, in a 1 ½-quart greased casserole dish. Distribute raisins between slices as you layer. In another bowl whisk milk, eggs, sugar, salt, vanilla, and coconut together. Pour over bread. Let stand **one hour**. Bake at 350° for one hour. Serve with Rum Sauce.

Sauce: Cream butter and sugar until light and fluffy. Transfer to top of double boiler set over gently simmering water and cook, stirring frequently, until mixture is very hot, about 30 minutes. Whisk 4 tablespoons of hot butter mixture into beaten eggs 2 tablespoons at a time. Stir mixture back into top of double boiler and whisk until thickened, 4 to 5 minutes; do not let water boil. Remove from heat. Cool, whisking occasionally. Blend in rum. Makes 2 cups. Recipe may be halved.

Joan Leu (Mrs. Richard)

BAKED BANANAS

6 very ripe bananas
¼ cup butter, melted
¼ cup sugar
¼ cup rum or milk

Peel bananas and place in a baking dish. Pour butter over bananas and sprinkle with sugar. Pour on rum or milk. Bake at 350° for 15 to 20 minutes.

Clara Remolina (Mrs. Rodrigo)

MEXICAN FLAN

1 ¾ cups sugar
8 whole eggs
2 13-ounce cans evaporated
milk
2 teaspoons vanilla

Preheat oven to 375°. Place 1 cup sugar in a 2-quart heavy pan or skillet. (Corningware works well.) Cook over medium heat, stirring constantly with a wooden spoon until sugar melts and becomes a deep golden color. (This will take a while; but don't burn the sugar!) Then either pour carmelized sugar into a casserole and tip dish around, or if cooking with a casserole, merely tip dish and swirl until caramel almost completely coats dish. Invert and set aside to cool.

In a large bowl combine eggs, ¾ cup sugar, evaporated milk, and vanilla. Beat well with a whisk. Strain into caramel coated dish. Place in a larger pan, set on middle rack of oven and add enough hot water to outer pan so that water comes half way up sides of casserole. Bake for about 1 hour, or until a dinner knife inserted half way between the center and edge comes out clean. (Be careful not to let knife touch caramel coating.) A lid may be put on casserole at least for the first ½ hour. When done, remove from oven, cool and refrigerate until serving time. To serve run knife around rim of custard, immerse most of dish in hot water briefly and invert onto a rimmed platter or serving dish.

Joyce Rashid (Mrs. Ameel)

FROZEN CREME COGNAC

1 cup sugar
¾ cup water
8 egg yolks
⅓ cup good cognac (Cour-
voisier or Hennessy)
1 cup whipping cream

Combine sugar and water in pan. Bring to a boil over high heat. Stir until sugar dissolves. Continue boiling, without stirring, for 5 minutes. Meanwhile, beat egg yolks in a large bowl at high speed. Reduce speed to medium. With mixer running, add hot syrup to yolks in a thin stream, beating constantly until mixture is thick and completely cool (increasing speed to high when mixture begins to thicken), about 20 to 25 minutes. Gradually fold in cognac. Whip cream in a chilled bowl with chilled beaters until stiff peaks form. Carefully fold in half of yolk mixture. Fold mixture back into remaining yolks. Divide among 8 wine glasses. Cover with Saran Wrap. Freeze until almost firm, about 8 hours.

Julie Horvath (Mrs. Frederic)

SCHAUM TORTE

10 to 11 egg whites, room
temperature
1 teaspoon vanilla
1 teaspoon cream of tartar
⅛ teaspoon salt
2 cups sugar

Preheat oven to 450°. Beat egg whites just until frothy. Add vanilla, cream of tartar and salt. Beat until stiff (3 to 5 minutes). Gradually add sugar and beat until glossy and very stiff. Be sure sugar is well absorbed into whites. Pour into an ungreased spring-form pan. Remove 6 or 7 teaspoons of whites to make little dollops on top. Put dollops on top of whites. Run a spatula along sides of pan to get rid of bubbles. Put in hot oven and immediately turn oven off. Do not open until completely cool (5 to 6 hours). Before serving, remove dollops and sides of spring-form pan. Top meringue with your favorite fruit and with whipped cream. Decorate top with reserved dollops. Fresh or frozen raspberries are super. Serves 10 to 12.

Dr. Sara Rusch (Mrs. Tom Cusack)

TAFFY APPLES
"An apple a day"

30 medium apples, plus
   sticks
1 ⅓ cups sweetened
   condensed milk
½ cup butter or margarine
2 cups dark brown sugar
¾ cup white corn syrup
pinch of salt
ground nuts, optional

Wash apples and put a stick in each. Mix other ingredients together and heat to boiling, stirring constantly. Boil 5 minutes and remove from heat. Dip each apple in caramel and then into nuts, if desired. Set apples in paper muffin cups or on waxed paper.

Marilyn Leyland (Mrs. John)

APPLE CRISP
This is so easy and so good!

7-8 medium apples
sugar
¾ cup margarine
1 cup sugar
1 cup flour

Peel, core, and slice apples and fill an 8-inch square pan, sugaring slightly between layers. Melt margarine. Mix sugar and flour and add to melted margarine mixing well. Pat over apples. Bake at 350° until apples are tender and crust is golden. Can be served with whipped cream, but it isn't necessary.

Gene Belsley (Mrs. J. P.)

BAKED APPLES

¼ cup flour
¼ cup sugar
¼ cup butter
¼ teaspoon cinnamon
⅛ teaspoon mace
pinch salt
4 large firm apples, peeled
   and cored (Granny Smith
   recommended)
4 tablespoons rum
⅓ cup orange juice
1 tablespoon lemon juice
¼ cup water

Mix flour, sugar, butter, cinnamon, mace and salt and blend with fingers until crumbly. Fill the apples with the mixture, reserving a little to be sprinkled over the top. Add 1 tablespoon rum to each apple. Put apples in a buttered baking dish. Mix orange juice, lemon juice, and water and add to the dish. Bake at 375° for about 45 minutes or until apples are cooked. If desired, serve hot apples with whipped cream or ice cream.

Clara Remolina (Mrs. Rodrigo)

BROILED BANANAS

6 bananas
½ cup sugar
½ cup butter, melted
½ cup hot rum

Peel the bananas and put on a baking dish; then brush them with melted butter and broil under medium heat for about 6 to 10 minutes until they look golden brown. Sprinkle with sugar 2 minutes before they are done. Remove from broiler and pour the hot rum over the bananas and ignite. Serve immediately. Good with ice cream or Cool Whip.

Clara Remolina (Mrs. Rodgrigo)

DIPPING STRAWBERRIES
Very pretty, very good!

½ cup sour cream
¼ cup heavy cream, whipped
4 tablespoons brown sugar
2 tablespoons Grand
** Marnier liqueur**
2 tablespoons light rum
crushed ice
2 quarts fresh strawberries
** cleaned, stems on**

In a small bowl combine first five ingredients. Transfer to a small serving dish. Mound crushed ice on a large glass platter. Make an indentation in the center of the ice for the dish of sauce. Set berries around the sauce on the ice.

Mimi Adland (Mrs. Moris)

FRUIT PIZZA

1 8-ounce package Pills-
** bury's refrigerated sugar**
** cookies**
1 8-ounce package cream
** cheese**
⅓ cup sugar
½ teaspoon vanilla
Assorted fresh or canned
** fruits**
½ cup orange marmalade
2 tablespoons water

Slice dough into ¼-inch slices. Line a 14-inch pizza pan with cookie slices overlapping slightly. Bake at 375° for 12 minutes. Cool. Combine softened cream cheese, sugar, and vanilla. Spread mixture over crust. Arrange fruit over cream cheese. Glaze with marmalade mixed with water. Chill and cut into wedges to serve 10-12.

Kathleen Palmer (Mrs. Ron)

MICROWAVE CARAMEL CORN

1 cup brown sugar
½ cup margarine
¼ cup white corn syrup
½ teaspoon salt
½ teaspoon baking soda
3-4 quarts popped corn (or
16 cups popped corn)

Combine all ingredients except baking soda and popcorn in a 1 ½-2 quart dish. Bring to a boil; cook on full power (high) for 2 minutes. Remove from microwave and stir in baking soda. Put popped corn in a large brown grocery bag. Pour syrup over corn. Close bag and shake. Cook in bag on high in microwave for 1 ½ minutes. Shake and cook another 1 ½ minutes. May need to shake and cook for 1 ½ minutes more. Pour onto cookie sheet and allow to cool.

Marianne Wright (Mrs. Robert)

MICROWAVE RICE KRISPIE SQUARES
An easy twist for an old favorite!

4 tablespoons margarine
5 cups miniature
marshmallows
5 cups rice krispies

In a large mixing bowl, melt margarine in microwave on high for 45 seconds. Add marshmallows. Microwave on medium-high for 2 minutes or until melted. (I use power level 7.) Stir after each minute. Stir in Rice Krispies. Press into a buttered baking dish (9 x 13). Cool and cut into squares.

Marianne Wright (Mrs. Robert)

ALMOND ROCHA
This candy is so good it's a sin! Must use an electric skillet to prepare.

1 cup broken almonds
1 cup granulated sugar
¼ cup butter
¼ cup margarine
2 cups ground almonds

Melt butter and margarine at a low temperature, 250°, in electric skillet. Add sugar and stir until well blended. Add broken almonds. Heat at 325° for 7 minutes. Sugar mixture will take on a creamy color and will not cling to nuts. Oil may separate from the mixture. Toward the end of 7 minutes the mixture will turn slightly tan. Heat to 350° and stir constantly until more tan in color, almonds will crack. Mix until nuts cling to mixture. This means the candy is ready. Total time 10-15 minutes. Spread the ground almonds ¼-inch deep on a lipped cookie sheet. Pour candy ⅛ inch thick over this. Allow to cool and break into small pieces.

Alice Sullivan (Mrs. Gene)

CARAMELS

1 cup butter or margarine
1 pound brown sugar
1/16 teaspoon salt
1 cup light corn syrup
1 15-ounce can Eagle Brand milk
1 teaspoon vanilla

Melt butter in heavy three-quart saucepan. Add brown sugar and salt, stirring until thoroughly combined. Stir in light corn syrup and mix well. Gradually add milk, stirring constantly. Cook and stir over medium heat until candy reaches firm ball stage (245°). Remove from heat and stir in vanilla. Pour into a 9 x 13-inch buttered cake pan. Cool and cut into squares. Yields 2 ½ pounds.

Margaret Norris (Mrs. Paul)

CHOCOLATE COVERED PEANUTS

12 ounces chocolate chips
2 pounds almond bark or
white chocolate
1 ounce unsweetened
chocolate
24 ounces Planters Dry
Roasted Peanuts or 2
pounds Spanish peanuts

Combine chocolate chips, almond bark, and chocolate in a stainless steel bowl and place in a 225° oven for 30 minutes, stirring occasionally to insure melting. Shake dry roasted peanuts in a colander, then add to chocolate mixture. Drop by spoonful onto waxed paper. May add Rice Krispies to chocolate if desired.

Microwave method: Melt chocolate chips, almond bark, and chocolate in a large microwave-safe bowl on medium power in the microwave. Stir every two minutes until melted. Add peanuts and drop by teaspoonfuls on waxed paper. Cool. Chocolate and almond bark may also be melted in a crockpot or double boiler.

Rita Luetkemeyer (Mrs. Richard)
Marianne Wright (Mrs. Robert)

CREOLE PRALINES

½ cup butter or margarine
¼ cup water
1 cup white sugar
1 ¾ cups light brown sugar
2 cups pecans
1 teaspoon vanilla extract

Melt butter in water on medium heat. Add rest of ingredients and cook on high heat until it bubbles well. Reduce heat and cook about 10 minutes, stirring occasionally. Remove from heat, add vanilla, and beat by hand about 15 times. Drop by spoonfuls on waxed paper for pralines to harden. (Place a few sheets of newspaper underneath the waxed paper to keep wax from coating countertops.) Makes about 28 pralines.

Mary Putman (Mrs. Harrison C. III)

COLONEL MURRAY'S BOURBON BALLS

½ cup butter
1 package (16 ounce) confectioner's sugar
4 tablespoons bourbon
1 cup finely chopped pecans
½ of a quarter pound block of paraffin
12-ounce package Nestle's Semi-sweet Chocolate Chips

Mix butter and confectioner's sugar, add bourbon, then the pecans. Mix well and form into small balls. Refrigerate a few hours until cold and firm. Melt the paraffin over hot water in double boiler. Slowly add the chocolate chips. Do not let water boil. Using a toothpick, dip each ball into chocolate and then place onto waxed paper. (If chocolate thickens during the dipping process, add a small amount of vegetable oil.) When hard, place into tins with waxed paper between the layers. Keep refrigerated. These candies look elegant in individual paper candy cups.

Linda McLelland (Mrs. Bruce)

"GRANDPA'S MICRO FUDGE"

¼ cup milk
1 16-ounce box powdered
  sugar
½ cup cocoa
¼ cup margarine
1 ½ teaspoons vanilla
½ cup nuts, raisins, coconut,
  liqueur (any flavor)

"Dump" first 4 ingredients in a micro-safe bowl. Do not stir. Cook on high for two minutes. Remove (it will look uncooked) and stir well. Add vanilla and nuts, or other suggested ingredients. Immediately pour onto waxed paper and push or pat to desired thickness. Let cool. Wrap in foil so it will not become too hard.

Joan Berney (Mrs. John)

FRUIT NUT BALLS

1 cup raisins
1 cup pitted dates
1 cup pitted prunes
1 cup dried figs
1 cup walnut meats
½ cup dried apricots
12 ounces semisweet
  chocolate

Force first six ingredients through food chopper, using coarse blade. Mix well. Form in small balls. Refrigerate until chilled. Melt semisweet chocolate. Dip fruit balls in melted chocolate. Dry on foil overnight.

Doris Dirkse (Mrs. Paul)

MUDDY PUTTY

1 ½ cups sugar
½ cup margarine
2 envelopes Choco-Bake or
  6 tablespoons cocoa
4 tablespoons corn syrup
1/16 teaspoon salt
½ cup milk
2 tablespoons vanilla

Combine first 5 ingredients in a saucepan. Cook over medium heat, stirring until blended. Add milk and bring to a boil, stirring constantly until thickened. Remove from heat; stir in vanilla. Serve warm over ice cream or anything your chocolate lover's heart desires. Refrigerate, then reheat leftovers.

Pam Albers (Mrs. William)

CARAMEL SAUCE

½ cup margarine
½ cup brown sugar
½ cup white sugar
1 to 2 tablespoons flour
⅓ cup half and half

Combine ingredients. Bring to a boil and simmer until thick. Serve warm over ice cream or desserts.

Dottie Flores (Mrs. Richard)

CARAMEL SAUCE
Microwave

½ cup sugar
¼ cup dark brown sugar
½ cup light corn syrup
½ cup cream (half and half)
3 tablespoons butter

Mix all ingredients in a 4-cup glass dish. Microwave for 5 minutes on full power. Cool and serve over ice cream.

Barbara Corley (Mrs. Richard)

FUDGE SAUCE

2 cups sugar
⅔ cup cocoa
¼ cup flour
2 cups water
¼ teaspoon salt
2 tablespoons butter
1 teaspoon vanilla

Mix sugar, cocoa, flour, and salt in a heavy saucepan. Add water and butter. Cook to boiling. Reduce heat and cook about 8 minutes longer, stirring constantly. Cool. Stir in vanilla. Store in refrigerator. Serve warm or cold over ice cream. Makes about 2 ½ cups.

Muggs Giebelhausen (Mrs. G. W.)

FUDGE SAUCE FOR HOT FUDGE SUNDAES

5 ounces unsweetened
  cocolate
½ cup butter
3 cups powdered sugar
1 ⅔ cups evaporated milk
1 ¼ teaspoons vanilla
2 teaspoons frozen orange
  juice concentrate

Melt chocolate and butter in saucepan over low heat. Stir in powdered sugar alternately with evaporated milk, blending well. Bring to a boil over medium heat, stirring constantly. Cook and stir until sauce becomes thick and creamy, about 8 minutes. Stir in vanilla and orange juice concentrate. Serve warm. Makes 3 cups. May be reheated in the microwave. Refrigerate unused portion.

Dottie Flores (Mrs. Richard)

PEACH PARFAIT OR SUNDAE SAUCE

2 cups crushed fresh
  peaches (about 4 large)
½ cup sugar
½ cup orange juice
2 teaspoons lemon juice
1 teaspoon vanilla extract
Vanilla ice cream
Chopped nuts, if desired

Peel, pit, and crush peaches. Mix crushed peaches, sugar, orange juice in 1 ½-quart pan. Cook and stir over high heat until it boils. Turn heat low. Simmer uncovered about 15 minutes or until thick. Take from heat. Stir in lemon juice and vanilla. Serve warm or chill. Makes 1 pint.

To make parfait, arrange alternating layers of ice cream and sauce in parfait glasses, beginning with ice cream and ending with sauce. For peach sundae, put one scoop vanilla ice cream into sherbet glass. Spoon sauce, warm or cold, over ice cream. Top with chopped nuts, if desired.

Barbara Grawey (Mrs. Gerald)

SARA SLOAN'S YUM BALLS

1 cup creamy peanut butter
1/4 cup honey
2 cups unsweetened
  shredded coconut
1/2 cup chopped dates
1/2 cup raw sunflower seeds
1/4 cup walnuts or cashews,
  chopped
1 tablespoon orange juice
  frozen concentrate,
  undiluted

Combine all ingredients. Mix well and form into 1-inch balls. Place on ungreased cookie sheet and refrigerate until firm. May roll in unsweetened coconut as an attractive holiday treat. Store in the refrigerator in an airtight container.

Janet Shipley (Mrs. William)

BRANDIED CRANBERRIES

3 cups (12-ounce package)
   fresh cranberries
1 ½ cups sugar
⅓ cup brandy

Combine cranberries, sugar, and brandy. Mix well. Place in a 9 x 13-inch baking dish. Cover with foil. Bake in preheated 300° oven for one hour. Refrigerate until cool. Reheat if desired and serve as an accompaniment with ham, poultry, or pork. Also delicious served over ice cream.

Ann Miller (Mrs. William)

HERBED BUTTER

1 cup soft margarine
1 tablespoon chives
¼ teaspoon oregano
1 tablespoon Parmesan
   cheese
Italian dressing to taste

Combine above ingredients and use as a spread for French or Italian bread.

Liz Cram (Mrs. Richard)

TOMATO MARMALADE

2 ½ cups tomatoes, skinned,
   diced, and seeded
2 ½ cups sugar
1 3-ounce package red
   raspberry jello
2 drops lemon juice

Combine tomatoes and sugar and boil 17 minutes. Add raspberry jello and lemon juice. Put in containers and freeze.

Berenice Consigny (Mrs. Paul)

SPICED NUTS

½ cup brown sugar
½ cup white sugar
1 teaspoon cinnamon
¼ teaspoon nutmeg
Dash salt
1 egg white
1 tablespoon cold water
1 pound pecan halves

Mix sugars, spices, and salt in separate bowl. Combine egg white and water in large mixing bowl. Add nuts and stir until nuts are coated well. Add sugar mixture. Stir until coated well. Bake on a greased cookie sheet in a 250° oven for 1 hour, stirring occasionally.

Ruth Giunta (Mrs. Edward)

ENGLISH PASTRY

2 cups flour
2 teaspoons baking powder
1 teaspoon salt
⅔ cup shortening
½ cup hot water
1 tablespoon lemon juice
1 egg yolk, unbeaten

Sift first three ingredients together and set aside. Mix remaining ingredients together well and stir into flour mixture. Chill. Pat out ¾ of pastry and line a 2-quart (8 inch) casserole. Fill with your favorite stew or pot pie ingredients. Cover with remaining pastry. Bake at 425° for 25 minutes.

Marilyn Leyland (Mrs. John)

RHUBARB STRAWBERRY JAM
A delicious jam—like spread

5 cups rhubarb, cut into
  small pieces
4 cups sugar
1 3-ounce package
  strawberry jello

Combine rhubarb and sugar in saucepan. Boil for 10 minutes. Remove from heat and crush with potato masher. Add package of strawberry jello. Pour into pint fruit jars and keep refrigerated.

Doris Dirkse (Mrs. Paul)

SPICED PEACHES

½ cup sugar
½ cup peach juice
¼ cup vinegar
8 to 10 whole cloves
1 stick cinnamon
1 29-ounce can peach
   halves, drained

Combine sugar, juice, vinegar and spices (tied in cheesecloth). Bring to a boil and simmer 10 minutes. Add fruit and heat thoroughly. Remove to a flat refrigerator dish. Be sure all fruit is covered with syrup. Allow to stand in refrigerator overnight.

Ann Miller (Mrs. William)

QUICK PICKLED PEACHES
Good with ham or fowl

1 29-ounce can peach halves
1 tablespoon mixed
   pickling spices
1 teaspoon whole cloves
1 tablespoon vinegar

Combine and simmer 5 minutes. Drain and cool.

Rhoda Turow (Mrs. I.L.)

TOM'S TRAIL MIX
Great to serve for card parties, pool parties, or to take camping

1 7-ounce jar sunflower seeds
1 7-ounce jar wheat nuts
1 16-ounce jar dry roasted
   peanuts
1 1-pound package M & M's
1 9-ounce box raisins

Mix all ingredients together and serve. Can be made and stored in closed container for months!

Pat Russo (Mrs. Frank)

FOOLPROOF HOLLANDAISE SAUCE

2 egg yolks
1 ½ tablespoons lemon juice
1 ½ tablespoons cold water
½ stick butter, hard

Combine all ingredients **cold** in saucepan and stir constantly over low heat until desired consistency. If too thick, add 1 tablespoon cream. If too thin, add 1 tablespoon mayonnaise.

Berenice Consigny (Mrs. Paul)

PIZZA SAUCE

1 clove garlic, sliced
2 tablespoons olive oil
2 10 ¾-ounce cans tomato
  puree
½ cup water
1 teaspoon sugar
½ teaspoon salt
1 teaspoon basil
1 teaspoon French's pizza
  seasoning

Lightly brown garlic slices in oil over medium heat — do not burn. Discard the garlic. Add remaining ingredients to the oil. Simmer over low heat for 45 minutes, stirring occasionally. Extra sauce may be frozen.

Barbara Corley (Mrs. Richard)

CHERRY SAUCE
For cornish hens or roast chicken

1 ½ tablespoons cornstarch
4 tablespoons sugar
¼ tablespoon salt
¼ tablespoon dry mustard
¼ tablespoon ginger
1 tablespoon slivered
  orange rind
½ cup orange juice
1 1-pound can water-packed,
  pitted, sour cherries
¼ cup currant jelly
2 tablespoons dry sherry

In saucepan, combine cornstarch, sugar, salt, dry mustard, and ginger. Drain cherries and add the liquid to the cornstarch mixture; add orange rind, orange juice, and currant jelly. Cook, stirring constantly, until mixture thickens. Add drained cherries and sherry just before serving.

Jo Dorsch (Mrs. Tom)

UNCOOKED TOMATO SAUCE

3 pounds tomatoes,
  peeled and cored
1 medium onion, peeled
  and diced
2 cloves garlic, peeled
  and quartered
⅓ cup fresh basil, or 1 ½
  tablespoons dried
⅓ cup olive or salad oil
1 teaspoon salt
Pepper to taste

Chop tomatoes, onion, garlic, and basil finely. Add oil, salt, and pepper. Let stand one hour to use sauce fresh, or pack into containers and freeze. Before serving, heat; adjust seasonings. Makes about 5 cups.

Joan Leu (Mrs. Richard)

LEON STYLE BARBECUE SAUCE

1 cup catsup
2 tablespoons cornstarch
9 tablespoons cider vinegar
⅓ cup packed brown sugar
2 teaspoons steak sauce
½ teaspoon each: seasoned
  salt, hickory smoked salt,
  hot pepper sauce to taste
8 teaspoons Worcestershire
  sauce

Mix ingredients in medium saucepan. Heat to boiling. Simmer uncovered, 30 minutes. Use when barbecuing ribs. Makes enough for four pounds of ribs.

Rita Luetkemeyer (Mrs. Richard)

NOTES

TABBULI (WHEAT GARDEN SALAD)

1 cup burghul (cracked wheat)
1 bundle parsley, chopped
   fine
1 bunch green onions,
   chopped or 1 medium
   onion, chopped fine
3 fresh tomatoes, chopped
   small
salt and pepper to taste
Mazola oil

Wash and soak burghul for ½ hour; drain well. Mix parsley, onions, and tomatoes. Add wheat and seasonings. Add enough oil to make mixture moist.

Isabelle Couri (Mrs. Peter)

LEBANESE GREEN BEANS

1 pound beef (ground round
   or chuck, or uncut round
   or chuck)
1 onion, chopped
2 pounds green beans
1 15-ounce can tomato sauce
Salt, pepper, and cinnamon
   to taste

If meat is uncut, chop in small pieces. Brown meat and onion in small amount of butter. Add green beans, tomato sauce, and ½ tomato sauce can of water. Add seasonings. Cover kettle and cook slowly, about 1 ½ hours, or until done. Serve with rice. Serves 6.

Isabelle Couri (Mrs. Peter)

ROLLED CABBAGE

1 large head cabbage
1 cup rice, uncooked
1 pound ground beef
Salt, pepper, and
   cinnamon to taste
1 6-ounce can tomato puree
2 to 3 garlic buds

Cut core from cabbage. Put in boiling water and blanch. Remove from water. Cut large leaves in half. Wash rice, add meat, and season with salt, pepper, and cinnamon. Mix well. Fill each cabbage leaf with meat mixture and roll tightly (like a cigar). Put in layers; cover with tomato puree thinned with water to tomato juice consistency. Add garlic buds. Cook slowly for approximately one hour.

Isabelle Couri (Mrs. Peter)

TURKEY ON TOP OF THE STOVE
This is the way turkey is prepared in South America since they sometimes have no ovens.

1 8-pound turkey, cut
  into pieces
1 tablespoon paprika
2 large cloves garlic, crushed
Salt and pepper to taste
1 teaspoon dijon mustard
2 tablespoons lemon juice
½ cup wine vinegar or ½ to
  1 cup white wine
2 bay leaves
4 tablespoons olive oil
4 tablespoons margarine
1 cup onion, chopped
1 or 2 tablespoons tomato
  paste
2 green peppers, sliced
¼ cup pimiento
12 large pitted green olives,
  sliced
1 tablespoon capers,
  optional

Place the turkey pieces in a bowl. Blend paprika, garlic, salt, pepper, mustard, and lemon juice and rub this mixture into the turkey pieces. Add wine or vinegar and bay leaves. Mix again and let stand for 2 hours or overnight. Drain the turkey and saute in oil and margarine until golden brown. Add onions, cook 3 more minutes, add tomato paste, green peppers, pimiento, and olives. Cook for 2 hours on very low heat until meat is tender.

Clara Remolina (Mrs. Rodrigo)

STUFFED CHICKEN

1 stewing chicken
1 cup rice, uncooked
1 pound ground beef
¼ cup butter, melted
Salt, pepper, cinnamon to
  taste

Prepare chicken for stuffing. Wash rice and mix together with meat, butter, and seasonings. Stuff chicken. Sew with thread or use skewers. Place in a large pan filled with salted water to cover chicken; remove scum which may form. Cook until tender. Remove chicken from pan. Take off skin and remove meat from bones. Mix with rice stuffing. Add broth as needed if stuffing is dry. Serves 6.

Isabelle Couri (Mrs. Peter)

RELISH COLUMBIAN STYLE
Good with hamburgers.

1 cup vegetable oil
6 medium onions, sliced in rings
4 medium green peppers, cut in julienne strips
4 medium red peppers, cut in julienne strips
1 or 2 hot banana peppers
1 teaspoon salt
½ teaspoon pepper
1 cup white vinegar
3 large cloves garlic, chopped
1 teaspoon thyme
3 bay leaves
3 carrots, crisp cooked and cut in julienne strips
1 cup green beans, cooked
1 cup cauliflower, cooked

Heat oil in a large heavy pan and cook onions until transparent. Add green, red, and hot peppers. Add salt and pepper to taste. Add garlic cloves, thyme, bay leaves, white vinegar, and all vegetables. Cook for 10 minutes. Let cool and put into glass jars. Refrigerate.

Clara Remolina (Mrs. Rodrigo)

CABBAGE SALAD

1 cup cabbage, finely chopped
2 cherry tomatoes, cut in fourths
½ cup carrots, finely grated
1 teaspoon garlic salt
1 teaspoon lime peel
1 teaspoon sugar
2 tablespoons lime juice
1 tablespoon dry shrimp, pounded
2-3 hot chili peppers, pounded

Mix all chopped vegetables together. Season with garlic salt, lime peel, lime juice, and sugar. Top with pounded dry shrimp and chili peppers. Serve with roasted chicken.

Sooksawat Radee (Mrs. Apichart)

ROASTED CHICKEN

3 cloves garlic
1 slice ginger root
1 teaspoon corriander root,
  minced
½ teaspoon pepper
1 teaspoon salt
1 tablespoon vegetable oil
1 young chicken, cut in
  four pieces

Pound together garlic, ginger root, corri-ander root, salt, and pepper. Mix with chicken. Add oil and marinate for 1-2 hours. Bake in a 375° oven for 30-40 minutes. Serve with cabbage salad.

Sooksawat Radee (Mrs. Apichart)

SPICY BEEF WITH MINT LEAVES

1 ½ cups ground beef
3 cloves garlic
1 tablespoon red onion,
  chopped
1 teaspoon corriander
  powder
1 teaspoon chili powder
1 tablespoon rice powder
  (browned)
1 tablespoon chopped green
  onion
2 tablespoons lemon or lime
  juice
1 teaspoon salt
1 tablespoon nampla
  (fish sauce)
10 mint leaves
Lettuce, long green beans,
  celery stalk

Brown ground beef, without oil, until the pink is gone. Place in a mixing bowl, let cool for 5 minutes. Using aluminum foil, wrap the chopped red onion and garlic. Put it on the heat, cook until it's almost burned. Unwrap and pound it. Add to the beef. Season beef with corriander, chili powder, rice powder, green onion, lemon juice, salt, and nampla. Pour mixture onto a serving plate. Top with mint leaves. Serve with lettuce, green beans, and celery.

Sooksawat Radee (Mrs. Apichart)

TUNA SALAD, THAI STYLE

1 cup ground pork
1 8-ounce can chunk tuna
½ teaspoon garlic powder
1 teaspoon salt
2 tablespoons lime juice
2 tablespoons ginger root,
   finely chopped
2 tablespoons red onion,
   chopped
½ tablespoon lime peel
2 tablespoons coconut,
   roasted and ground
½ cup peanuts
coriander leaves
1 teaspoon chili powder
lettuce

Brown pork in frying pan for 3 minutes, drain. Place in bowl. Drain tuna, add to pork. Mix well. Add garlic powder, salt, and lime juice. Blend together. Add chopped ginger root, red onion, and lime peel. Decorate plate with lettuce leaves. Spoon tuna mixture on individual leaf, top with roasted coconut, peanuts, coriander leaves, and chili powder. Serve as finger food.

Siri Ratan (Mrs. Rangson)

CHILI BEEF WITH RICE

1 cup sliced beef (round or
   flank steak)
1 slice ginger, crushed
1 tablespoon brown sugar
dash MSG
1 tablespoon soy sauce
½ teaspoon garlic powder
1 tablespoon flour
½ cup vegetable oil
½ cup baby corn
½ cup bell pepper, sliced
½ cup mushrooms
1 medium onion, sliced
1 tablespoon hot pepper,
   chopped
½ cup water or beef broth
1 tablespoon fish sauce, may
   substitute with salt
2 tablespoons oyster sauce
3 cups cooked rice

Combine meat, ginger, brown sugar, MSG, soy sauce, garlic powder, and flour. Marinate at least 1 hour. Heat oil in wok or sauce pan over medium-high heat and brown beef for 2 minutes. Add vegetables and stir fry 2 minutes. Add water or broth, cover and simmer for 3 minutes. Add fish sauce (or salt) and oyster sauce. Toss lightly. Serve over rice. Makes 2-3 servings.

Siri Ratan (Mrs. Rangson)

SWEET AND SOUR PORK

1 ¼ pounds pork fillet
1 teaspoon salt
1 tablespoon sherry
1 egg
2 tablespoons flour
6 cups vegetable oil
2 tablespoons ketchup
1 tablespoon sherry
¼ cup pineapple juice
2 tablespoons vinegar
2 tablespoons sugar
½ teaspoon salt
1 teaspoon cornstarch
3 tablespoons vegetable oil

Cut pork into 1 ½-inch square pieces. Marinate in 1 teaspoon salt, 1 tablespoon sherry, 1 egg, and 2 tablespoons flour. Heat 6 cups oil to 350° and deep fry the meat pieces until golden brown. Remove and drain. Mix ketchup, 1 tablespoon sherry, pineapple juice, vinegar, sugar, ½ teaspoon salt and cornstarch in a saucepan. Mix well. Add 3 tablespoons oil and bring to a boil. Drop meat pieces in, mix evenly, remove from sauce, and serve.

Lillian Tin (Mrs. George)

SAUTEED BEEF WITH GREEN ONION

12 ounces beef flank steak
1 teaspoon salt
2 tablespoons soy sauce
1 teaspoon cornstarch
½ egg
9 ounces green onion
1 small piece ginger
4 cups oil
½ teaspoon MSG
½ tablespoon sherry wine
1 tablespoon sesame oil

Cut beef against the grain into thin shreds. Marinate with ¼ teaspoon salt, 1 tablespoon soy sauce, 1 teaspoon cornstarch, ½ egg; stir and mix evenly. Cut green onion slantwise into small sections. Shred ginger. Heat 4 cups oil to 375° in a pan. Add beef shreds, fry for 10 seconds and remove. Fry ginger in 3 tablespoons hot oil, stir, add green onion, ¾ teaspoon salt, ½ teaspoon MSG, beef, 1 tablespoon soy sauce, ½ tablespoon sherry wine. Stir fry quickly over high heat, then add sesame oil, remove and serve.

Lillian Tin (Mrs. George)

DOLMADES

**50 grape leaves, purchased
in a jar
1 pound ground lamb or chuck
1 large onion, sliced
½ cup converted white rice
½ cup parsley with mint,
chopped
1 teaspoon salt
1/16 teaspoon pepper
3 tablespoons butter
Sauce:
3 eggs
Juice of 2 lemons
Juice from dolmades
2-3 tablespoons flour**

Wash and scald leaves in a large pan. Mix all remaining ingredients except 1 table-spoon butter. Wrap leaves with filling, shiny side out. They will look like cigars. Line bottom of 4-quart pan with extra grape leaves and put in 2 cups water and 1 tablespoon butter. Stack the dolmades on top of each other. Set plate on top and cover with lid. Cook on medium heat for 15 minutes. Then reduce to low heat for 30-35 minutes.

For sauce, beat eggs until creamy. Add lemon juice slowly while beating. Add dolmades juice 1 tablespoon at a time slowly. Whip in flour and cook on medium heat until it starts to thicken. Stir constantly. Pour on dolmades and serve.

Londa Vlachos (Mrs. Nick A.)

BAKED KIBBA

**2 cups No. 2 burghul
(cracked wheat)
2 pounds lamb, ground 3
times or beef round
ground 3 times
1 large onion, grated
1 teaspoon salt
1 teaspoon black pepper
2 teaspoons cinnamon
1 tablespoon dry peppermint
1 teaspoon cumin powder**

Wash and soak burghul for ½ hour; drain. Take meat, add onion and spices and mix well. Add burghul and work with hands until well blended. Add water gradually to keep kibba medium soft. Grease a 9 x 12-inch pan lightly with Mazola oil. Spread meat mixture in pan. Score through with knife into 2-inch diamond shapes. Cover completely with oil. Bake in a 350° oven approximately one hour or until deep brown or done.

Isabelle Couri (Mrs. Peter)

BAQLAVA (LAYERED PASTRY)

2 cups walnuts, chopped
½ cup sugar
1 tablespoon rose water
1 pound phyllo dough
1 pound butter, clarified
Basic Sugar Syrup:
2 cups sugar
1 cup water
Few drops lemon juice
1 teaspoon rose water

Combine nuts, sugar, and rose water. Take one sheet of phyllo dough and brush lightly with clarified melted butter. Place 3 to 5 tablespoons of nut mixture along wide edge. Roll as in a jelly roll, buttering as you roll, and place close together on a buttered 10 x 14-inch pan. Brush tops with butter. Bake at 300° until golden brown. Remove from oven. Spoon cold syrup over rolls until saturated (this takes about 3 applications). Cut diagonally into 2 to 3-inch lengths.

Syrup: Combine sugar, water, and lemon juice in saucepan. Boil over medium heat about 10 to 15 minutes or until slightly viscous (225°). Add rose water and let come to a boil. Remove from heat and cool. Tip: Place damp towel over phyllo sheets to keep from drying out while handling.

Isabelle Couri (Mrs. Peter)

SESAME SEED COOKIES
Miscotti (Italian)

12 cups flour
5 cups sugar
7 teaspoons baking powder
2 teaspoon salt
4 cups Crisco
¾ cup toasted sesame seeds
5 eggs
2 cups milk
2 teaspoons vanilla

Mix together flour, sugar, baking powder, salt, and Crisco. Add sesame seeds and mix well. Mix together eggs, milk, and vanilla. Add to flour mixture. Roll into shapes about 4 inches long and ½ inch thick making letters or numbers. Bake at 450° until brown about 8 to 10 minutes. Makes a large amount of cookies. This is an old family recipe. Mix like pie crust. the longer it sits the better the cookie. Store in Tupperware for aging.

Ruth Giunta (Mrs. Edward)

KAKH
A delicate Egyptian sweet dough cookie with a caramel and sesame seed center. Traditionally made around Christmas and Easter. All the women in the family congregate in the kitchen to prepare the cookies. This recipe has been adapted for the North American woman who has less time to spend in the kitchen and not as many relatives around to help!

Stuffing:
¼ cup butter
1 tablespoon flour
½ cup honey
1 teaspoon sesame seed
Dough:
1 package active dry yeast
1 teaspoon sugar
1 cup warm water (100° to 115°)
1 pound sweet butter
6 cups all-purpose flour

1. Prepare the stuffing first in order to give it sufficient time to cool. Melt butter in a small saucepan. Blend in the flour and cook over low heat until the mixture becomes thick and yellow. Slowly add the honey in a stream, stirring constantly until well blended. Cook at medium high heat until a candy thermometer registers 244° to 248°. Remove from heat. Add the sesame seeds and mix into caramel. Cool.

2. Mix together the yeast, sugar, and warm water. Let sit in a warm place until bubbly, about 10 minutes.

3. Clarify butter by boiling over medium heat for 10 minutes. Pour off the clear part and discard the sediment. Cool.

4. Measure 6 cups flour into a large bowl. Pour the cooled clarified butter onto the flour and mix with a spoon and then with the hands until a soft dough forms. Add the yeast mixture to the soft dough and lightly knead to form a smooth dough. Place dough in a large bowl and cover loosely with plastic wrap. Allow to rise for 1 hour in a warm, draft-free place.

5. After dough has risen, take a piece, roll it into a 1 to 1 ½-inch ball. Do not work dough too long. Indent the ball with your finger. Take a piece of caramel the size of a large pea, insert it into the ball, and seal the hole well. Flatten gently between the

palms of the hands and place on a cookie sheet. Repeat this procedure until all the dough is used. Allow cookies to rise in a warm place again, about one hour.

6. Print each cookie with a fork and bake in a 350° oven for 15 to 20 minutes.

7. Cool cookies completely. Roll in powdered sugar and serve. To store: Place in a tightly covered can. Roll in powdered sugar just before serving. Keeps about one month. Makes about 100 cookies.

Lorraine El-Deiry (Mrs. Adel)

Index

269

270

Reorder Additional Copies

COOKBOOK
Peoria Medical Society
Auxiliary, Inc.
P. O. Box 9094
Peoria, IL 61614

Please send me: _____
copies of **JUST WHAT THE DOCTOR ORDERED**
@ $15.50 $_____

(Postage and handling included)

(Make check payable to P.M.S. Charitable & Ed. Found.)

TOTAL ENCLOSED $ _____

Name _____
Street _____
City _____ State _____
Zip _____

All proceeds from the sale of this cookbook will be used by The Peoria Medical Society Charitable and Educational Foundation for scholarships.

COOKBOOK
Peoria Medical Society
Auxiliary, Inc.
P. O. Box 9094
Peoria, IL 61614

Please send me: _____
copies of **JUST WHAT THE DOCTOR ORDERED**
@ $15.50 $_____

(Postage and handling included)

(Make check payable to P.M.S. Charitable & Ed. Found.)

TOTAL ENCLOSED $ _____

Name _____
Street _____
City _____ State _____
Zip _____

All proceeds from the sale of this cookbook will be used by The Peoria Medical Society Charitable and Educational Foundation for scholarships.

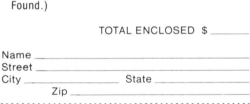

COOKBOOK
Peoria Medical Society
Auxiliary, Inc.
P. O. Box 9094
Peoria, IL 61614

Please send me: _____
copies of **JUST WHAT THE DOCTOR ORDERED**
@ $15.50 $_____

(Postage and handling included)

(Make check payable to P.M.S. Charitable & Ed. Found.)

TOTAL ENCLOSED $ _____

Name _____
Street _____
City _____ State _____
Zip _____

All proceeds from the sale of this cookbook will be used by The Peoria Medical Society Charitable and Educational Foundation for scholarships.